I0762892

Happiness Included

HAPPINESS INCLUDED

JAN BRADY AND BEYOND

EVE PLUMB WITH MARCIA WILKIE

CITADEL PRESS
Kensington Publishing Corp.
kensingtonbooks.com

CITADEL PRESS BOOKS are published by

Kensington Publishing Corp.
900 Third Avenue
New York, NY 10022

All Kensington titles, imprints, and distributed lines are available at special quantity discounts for bulk purchases for sales promotions, premiums, fund-raising, educational, or institutional use. Special book excerpts or customized printings can also be created to fit specific needs. For details, write or phone the office of the Kensington sales manager: Kensington Publishing Corp., 900 Third Avenue, New York, NY 10022, attn Sales Department; phone 1-800-221-2647.

CITADEL PRESS and the Citadel logo are Reg. U.S. Pat. & TM Off.

10 9 8 7 6 5 4 3 2 1

First Citadel hardcover printing: May 2026

Printed in the United States of America

ISBN: 978-0-8065-4503-5

ISBN: 978-0-8065-4505-9 (e-book)

The authorized representative in the EU for product safety and compliance
is eucomply OU, Parnu mnt 139b-14, Apt 123,
Tallinn, Berlin 11317; hello@eucompliancepartner.com

For my parents,
Flora and Neely Plumb

Foreword

By Christopher Knight

It was a very long time ago that Eve and I met. No doubt you saw it. Our introduction has been rerunning for over half a century. We were ten-year-old kids in 1968 when we met in the middle, and our lives would be forever altered by *The Brady Bunch*. Little did we know then that we'd be lifelong friends.

Staying friends for nearly six decades isn't something that happens automatically. We grew up, found our own paths, and grew apart. When life brought our orbits close again, we returned to each other's life with an ease and familiarity reserved for people who share a special bond—a family bond. How pleased I am that this is so, and how honored I am now that Eve has asked me to write this foreword.

The Brady Bunch was canceled over fifty years ago. Yet it still lives. For those of us in the cast, it still influences our lives. *Happiness Included* is Eve's story, the telling of her experiences and reflections, voiced personally and perceptively and shared honestly. I'm very proud of my courageous cohort and happy that she uses this opportunity to allow us to know her more clearly. I'm grateful not only for the past we share but for the future still ahead. Our friendship has been one of the great constants in my life and a reminder that regardless of our individual adult evolutions, we are, and will always be, bound to each other's immutable inner child.

Here's to the journey behind us—and all the ones still to come.

Introduction

Contrary to the long-lived rumors that I resent what *The Brady Bunch* means in my life, I actually embrace it. Many good things came from my five seasons as Jan Brady. I don't even mind when people I meet now accidentally call me Jan instead of Eve.

Life as an actress, even a child actress, before the internet and social media, was very different than it is today. It was a singular world that could only be experienced from the inside. What others might have assumed was a glamour-filled and pampered young career was actually a lot of time spent inside sunless studio stages, alleyway dressing rooms, and tiny windowless classrooms, where I received my education in twenty-minute segments.

At one time I thought about creating a T-shirt to wear to certain events with the answers to my most asked questions about *The Brady Bunch*, just for laughs. The front would read:

1. Was it fun to be on *The Brady Bunch*?
2. Do people really call you Jan?
3. What happened to Tiger the dog?
4. Did you keep that black curly-haired wig?

5. Do you still talk to (name your Brady kid)?
6. Do people always ask you to say "Marcia, Marcia, Marcia"?
7. Do you still make money from *The Brady Bunch*?
8. Why didn't you do the variety show?
9. What part of your life would you do over?

And the back of the T-shirt would have the answers:

1. Yes.
2. Daily.
3. Dogs don't live fifty-three years.
4. It was dyed red and repurposed for an *Annie* tour.
5. No one talks anymore. We all text.
6. They say it *to* me.
7. If I had a dime for every rerun episode, I'd pay off the national deficit. I don't. So I can't. You have to continue paying taxes. Sorry.
8. I thought the world needed Fake Jan.
9. I'd happily add some more years right now, postmenopause and pre-osteoporosis—after Tampax and before Fosamax.

I have no child actress horror stories to tell in this book. I had good parents and, for the most part, good directors, producers, co-stars, and teachers. What I can tell is of a time in television that will never come again: of expansive studios, no-frills rehearsals and filming, recycled costuming, Western-town backlots, tricks of the trade, what I learned from the pros, and all of the experiences that were part of my everyday life—ones that replaced normal-kid stuff, like being a Campfire Girl, grade school birthday parties, sleepovers, and schedule-free summer days. The way I spent my adolescence was not the reality of other children. If asked, "What did you do today?" my peers weren't answering, "Oh, I showed Secretary of State Henry Kissinger around Stage 5 on the Paramount lot," or "I spent the morning recording a single about the end of the world, or shooting a national commercial introducing Barbie's best friend."

These are also my memories of growing up in Hollywood, setting a career course at age six and never questioning what career I wanted as an adult. There were bumps and some bad decisions, a cross-country flight to personal freedom, a casting-off of a long-held belief system, decisions to do a *Brady* spin-off or not, films and funny guest star roles, getting married once, and then again, being mocked and impersonated, taking to the stage in a worldwide debut, and the transition from being cast as a little girl to a teenager to a young adult to playing a mom and beyond.

Oh, and question number 10 is always: "Would you let your own child go into show business?"

My answer: I had a happy childhood, with a lot of positive attention. I learned how to discipline myself, respect professionals in every field, navigate a variety of personalities, travel, tell stories on screen, and show up for commitments. Although I never asked to be in show business, I never asked to be out of it after my first commercial at age six.

Why would I advise any parents of a child who really, really wanted to be in show business to keep them away? I'm still here, still acting on TV, in an occasional film, and on stage, living in New York, creating art, traveling, and fully enjoying a lifestyle curated by my wise and reasonable parents, enough natural talent, and a long and varied career.

Chapter One

"Well, she looks like our girl."

I was in a small room with adults who created television shows. I was comfortable being there, the only child in the room, because I had been in similar situations for four years already, starting at age six. These two adults were looking at me, but talking to each other. I could almost always tell when I made television producers feel like they found the right child actress for the role, whether it was a commercial, a TV pilot, or a made-for-TV movie. Eager to please, I learned early in my career how to read the room, follow suggestions, and "imagine" myself into being the little girl described in the audition breakdowns.

On this Los Angeles afternoon, I was sitting on a couch across from Sherwood Schwartz, *The Brady Bunch* creator, and veteran TV show director John Rich in a small studio office bungalow. Their "girl" whom they thought I resembled was Florence Henderson, the actress who would play my TV mom. My own mother was elated and also surprised that my agent had called to report that I was being requested for a callback interview. My first audition for this TV pilot, weeks before, had seemed to go nowhere fast.

During a hot summer morning, I had been sent for a rare "cattle call" audition. My auditions usually involved signing into a small waiting room, with stackable utility chairs and four or five other little girls around my age, sitting with their tense or talkative moms. One at a time, we would be called into the casting office alone to read for the role or commercial for any number of adults, sometimes two, sometimes up to ten people. There was never a camera in the room and no one recorded the audition. It was all decided on through this one in-person meeting.

This cattle call audition was a first for me, but my agent thought it was worthwhile. There was a new family sitcom called *The Brady Brood* being cast that required six children: three girls and three boys. The premise was similar to a popular 1968 movie, *Yours, Mine and Ours*, starring Lucille Ball and Henry Fonda, playing a widow and widower who marry and blend their offspring to become one very large family.

Every Southern California kid with show business aspirations, or whose mom wanted them to be a little star, was at the cattle call: boys in button-down shirts and polished shoes; girls in freshly ironed dresses, clean white knee socks, and styled hair. Gathered in the studio parking lot and under the noon sun, casting assistants with clipboards divided us into groups according to gender, age, size, and hair color. The mothers stood around the periphery trying to keep an eye on their child. I was shuffled between two groups of blond-haired girls, one group taller and older than me, and the other smaller and younger. A while later I was released with the explanation that I was too young to be the oldest daughter and too old to be the youngest girl. No one had tried me out in the middle. Who knows why. My mom and I left, along with a number of other blond-haired girls, walking past three standby groups of brunette girls and boys grouped by age and size. This was mirrored by groups of redheaded boys and girls.

Sherwood Schwartz has said that he personally interviewed over 460 individual children for the six roles. Once he had cast the roles of the parents, he knew he needed three brunet boys who could pass for Robert Reed's sons and three blond girls who could be Florence Henderson's daughters. He hoped to find kids who would bring their real personalities to their character. To make sure a child had the discipline to be in a TV show, he set up a way to test their concentration skills. In front of the couch where the child sat was a coffee table holding appealing toys. If they picked up, focused on, or played with a toy during the interview, Sherwood decided the child probably wouldn't have the focus needed to learn lines and take direction on the set. Even though he was looking to cast "real" kids, he ended up choosing six young actors, all of us experienced. Not one of us had picked up a toy. We knew better. Child actors learn early on, "Don't touch or move the props."

My interview was over in ten minutes. I never read a single line. There were no additional callbacks to make sure I had chemistry with other potential cast members. All I knew was that I looked like their "girl." A phone call came from my agent a few hours after we returned home. My beaming mother gave me the news that I had been cast as the middle child of the three daughters. My name would be Jan.

I'm sure my father was also really happy about the news. I don't remember jumping up and down with excitement, like kids do when something they really want becomes reality. I had learned to temper my expectations by age nine, after doing two previous TV pilots, one playing Barbara Rush's daughter and the other playing little Bonnie Braids in a pilot for a Dick Tracy TV series. Neither show was picked up by a network.

Booking a role for a TV show, movie, or a national commercial was part of my routine life, starting in first grade. My parents were delighted in how often I was cast, chosen over other children who were auditioning. They would reaffirm to me, "You can do anything." Their belief in me gave me self-confidence. When I didn't book the role, I was more concerned about my parents' disappointment than my own.

At age nine I auditioned for the TV movie remake of *Heidi* (NBC, 1968), to play the lead. It appeared very hopeful that the role would be mine. According to my mother's datebook, after auditioning countless little girls, the field was narrowed and I remained in the running after numerous callbacks. The film was American-made, but was cast with mostly British actors, led by Michael Redgrave as Grandfather. In the end the Heidi role went to Jennifer Edwards, the stepdaughter of Julie Andrews through her marriage to Blake Edwards.

My dad wrote in a letter to my brother, Ben, who was attending Harvard for graduate school, describing the whole audition process as the "Heidi trauma."

I barely remember the audition process and don't seem to have suffered long-term effects of the "trauma" caused by the outcome. From my dad's words to my brother, my parents were obviously invested in me playing Heidi:

Little Eve did not get the Heidi role. They chose an English child with an authentic British accent, because all of the principals have that accent. Mom and I were destroyed because of it. Eve probably took it better than any of us.

I only understood that rejection was unexpected and apparently painful through my parents' reactions, not because of my own desire as a child to be on television. I thought of acting as something I *did*, not something I *wanted*.

I wouldn't be playing Heidi, but I was kept pretty busy guest starring in a number of popular TV series of the mid-1960s—playing little girls who were named Laurie, Kathy, Bonnie, Terry, Pony Alice, Sue, Marian, and Maritsa, and even an Eve. For this new sitcom pilot, I would be Jan. Other roles had come and gone. I had moved on to the next name. Little did I know that I'd be identified for decades to come by the name Jan Brady, and that my ten- to fifteen-year-old self would be introduced to new young viewers still today on small screens around the world.

My husband, Ken, and I were getting ready to meet a friend for dinner at Joe Allen restaurant in New York's Theater District one evening, when one of those "If you're over this age, you need to get this vaccine" commercials came on TV. I wasn't really paying attention to it, thinking it was specifically not applicable to me, when it suddenly occurred to me that I was now part of that age group. I don't think about my age often and I certainly don't experience it as being what I thought life must be like at my age when I was a child. Maybe forever young is the bonus of being perpetually a kid or teenager on a TV series that is in constant syndication.

I've heard countless times, since the first season of *The Brady Bunch*, that viewers related to me as the middle child because they also landed smack in the middle of the birth order in their own household. It was the baby boomer generation, after all, so two or more siblings was not uncommon. I could play a middle child, but I didn't live it. I was the baby in my real-life family, but since my brother and sister, Ben and June, were already ages fifteen and fourteen when I was born, it was more like growing up as an only child.

My mother, Flora, was thirty-eight years old when she gave birth to me, and my father, Neely, was forty-six. I arrived full-term, but so tiny my mom told me that the nurse at Providence Saint Joseph Hospital, adjacent to the Disney Studios, measured my wrist to see if I was born with dwarfism, the medical term. I was healthy and strong for my tiny size. In the late 1950s, no one thought that a pregnant woman having daily cocktails and smoking cigarettes was an issue for the growing fetus. Certainly, many babies were born to women who smoked and drank. After all, the surgeon general's report on smoking being a health issue didn't happen until 1964, and a cocktail hour before dinner was a matter-of-course for many American households.

My parents gave me the name Eve, not in deference to the very first female who apparently arrived fully formed from Adam's rib, according to the first book of the Bible, or because actress Eve Arden had her own TV show in 1957 and '58, but because a female ancestor on my father's side was named Carmichael Eve. The name Eve appeared nowhere in the top one hundred popular names for girls in 1958.

At some point in the 1980s, I attended an Academy event at the Ambassador Hotel, in what was the final years of the Cocoanut Grove, the famous ballroom where my parents first met. Actress Eve Arden, then in her seventies, was seated at a nearby table. I had always been a big fan of her decades of wide-ranging talent, from an early Marx Brothers film to her Best Supporting Actress nomination in the film noir *Mildred Pierce*, to major roles in sitcoms like *Our Miss Brooks*, up to her appearances as the high school principal in the movie *Grease*. I thought her smarty-pants sidekick roles would be so fun to play and preferred those types of character roles over any of the female leads. I wanted to role model her career, or Joan Blondell's, or any of the opinionated, mouthy broads who commanded attention on whatever screen they were on.

I decided to introduce myself and express how much I appreciated her work in television. When I said, "I'm Eve, too," she took my hand and said: "Oh, it's such a difficult name, but wonderful, too. It's a name no one forgets."

I could appreciate Eve Arden's views on our shared name in my mid-twenties; however, as a small child and a loyal *Romper Room* viewer, I was frustrated by it. Miss Nancy would never look through her magic mirror at the "children out in television land" and say, "I see Eve." And Sheriff John, the LA local host of children's programming, might sing his birthday polka song to a hundred different names, but there was never a mention of an Eve. There would be no nicknames for me, as much as I wished for one. Nicknames seemed so inclusive. No one even used my middle name, Aline. It would only be Eve. I could write my name early on—backward even. Like the names Asa and Nan, it would have been tricky to diagnose dyslexia, until a kid named Eve could write something other than her first name.

Actually, the subject of dyslexia was never talked about in the late 1950s or even the 1960s, and no one discussed postpartum depression, either. I never had dyslexia, but my mother certainly had postpartum depression, and it most likely went on for a couple of years, and lingered as she self-medicated with alcohol in the evenings. One of my earliest memories is going with my dad to the famous Bob's Big Boy restaurant on Riverside Drive in Toluca Lake for breakfast on the weekends while my mother slept in. It was my dad's way to give my mom a parenting break. When my father was at work during the weekdays, my mother would sometimes take a brief respite, which my sister later termed "mama's vacation." As a toddler I had probably pushed her to a limit of her patience in some manner. She'd tell me, "I'll be outside in the driveway." She would sit in the car for ten minutes, smoke a cigarette, and stare blankly ahead. Knowing I had upset her, I would want to follow her out to the car, but there was a deterrent. I wasn't old enough to tie my shoes, and going outside in my socks was forbidden, a rule I probably learned shortly after taking my first steps. Still today it feels like a huge trespass to step outside without shoes on. I understand why, in the commonsense way, but since I do my own laundry now, I say "the hell with it" and walk out to the mailbox.

Despite her lingering depression, my mother was never harsh to me. She even rejected the pediatrician's advice to throw a glass of cold water in my face if I was having a toddler tantrum. "That will make her stop," he promised. My mother's adaptation was to pat my sobbing face with a cold wash cloth and say, "All right now. Settle down." Her firmest solution, when she had topped out on my mood, would be to get closer to my face and say, "Listen, sister. You straighten up right now." My father, who had noted in a few of his archived letters that I was a "stubborn child," would clap his hands together close to my face to bring me back from a dramatic meltdown. It worked. I was never spanked, which was accepted parenting in the 1960s, not even once.

I think all small children have big emotions that they don't know how to regulate. I'm sure I was no different. A friend of mine, raising her toddler son, termed it "the civilization of Mikey," with the thought that it's the parents' responsibility to civilize the little beings they created. That might be one of a couple of reasons why I chose to never have children myself. It's a really tough job. My mom only went as far as the driveway for her "mama's vacation." I might have said, "I'll be in Bermuda," and headed out to the airport. I think my mom and dad did a pretty damn good job of parenting, considering I "surprised" them later in life, just when they probably thought they could start going out to dinner without looking at a kids' menu.

The approach to parenting supposedly changes by the time the third child comes along and concerns for your progeny's safety relaxes. The opposite was true with my mom and dad. Perhaps it was my tiny size that had my parents treating me like a precious and fragile being that needed overseeing, even though I was healthy and very strong for my petite frame. They were going to make sure nothing happened to me and kept me inside the guardrails of what they thought would keep me protected.

When I was two and a half, a glossy blue tricycle appeared near the Christmas tree from Santa. I loved it. Two years later, when I had outgrown it, it was still in pristine condition because it never left the house. I rode it in a loop from the living room, into the kitchen, out the dining-room doorway, and through the living room again. Around and around. The tires never saw a turn on a sidewalk or even the driveway because an occasional vehicle passed on our street. I can only imagine my parents pictured me losing control and veering in front of an oncoming mail truck.

My dad, Benjamin Neely Plumb, was born in Augusta, Georgia, but always went by Neely, which was his mother's maiden name. His father passed away when my dad was only four, leaving his mother to raise Neely and his siblings by herself. She ran a boardinghouse and a tea parlor in her home to keep them all afloat. Neely had a pitch-perfect ear for music and at a young age began playing the flute and the saxophone. Dreadfully shy as a kid, he would sit in a wagon in a cardboard box, playing his horn, as his brother towed him up and down the streets. Following high school graduation, he somehow scored a full education at Georgia Tech and earned a degree in engineering. He never left the music behind, and due to his natural and exceptional talent, he was offered chairs playing in the most popular big bands of the 1930s and '40s: Artie Shaw, Paul Whiteman, and Ray Noble and His Orchestra.

Elk City, Oklahoma, was my mom's hometown. Her dad owned the local flour mill, so they never felt the squeeze of financial hardship even throughout the Depression years. Flora June Dobry was the firstborn of three and enjoyed her father's treatment as a cherished princess. She dreamed of becoming a ballerina and her indulgent daddy provided the best in ballet training that could be found in this small southern city threaded onto the historic Route 66, like a bead on an abacus rod. With a pretty face and a dancer's body to complement her self-esteem and confidence, she became a hot catch for the local boys during her high school years. At age seventeen, she was tapped to continue ballet training in Russia. Her dad wasn't going to let his firstborn leave the country, let alone go to one under Soviet dictator Joseph Stalin. As a compromise he sent her to New York to study at Marymount School on the Upper East Side of Manhattan. From the letters my mom saved, it seems she left a small trail of lovelorn boys behind in Oklahoma. I came across a handwritten letter my mother kept with her personal mementos. It was sent to her during her first year in New York, and reads, *Flora June, if you're not going to come back to Elk City and be my girlfriend, would you please return my school ring?* She never did. I found it in the bottom of the box. Maybe one day I'll track down his family members and return the ring my mom kept for fifty-seven years. I'm sure the boy gave up on it by age twenty.

In the mid 1930s, Marymount was a boarding high school for girls that was run by nuns. Since young Flora June was going alone from Elk City to Manhattan, her father sent her off with a six-shooter for protection. She already knew how to use it. Her father afforded her a solo room at Marymount, but that didn't stop the nuns from entering without knocking whenever they felt the urge. As my mom described it, "The nuns were the bosses of every student's whole world." One evening Mom was cleaning her gun when a nun barged in, her eyes growing wide at the sight of the pistol.

My mother would laugh during the retelling, "Once she saw that I had a gun, none of the nuns entered without knocking ever again."

My mother only stayed in New York until her high school graduation. Now that she had left Elk City, Oklahoma, and been introduced to the energy of New York City, she was intrigued with further adventures. One of her teachers suggested that she and a few other girls would fare much better as a small dancing troupe in Los Angeles, with a wider variety of opportunities, including film.

She crossed the country by train in 1939, with a few other young women and took up residence in an impressive multi-floor apartment building in Hollywood, relatively new in 1929. It's now a historic structure, one that she would often point out to me as we drove from Van Nuys to the Paramount Studios lot, where *The Brady Bunch* was filmed. She described to me how she would walk down Vine Street to a big open-air market and get her vegetables and fruit. I always liked to imagine how it was for her, in search of a new adventurous life at age eighteen, living on her own in a small apartment with glamorous Hollywood Boulevard only a few short blocks away.

One evening a girl she had traveled west with told her, "We are going to the Cocoanut Grove and I'm going to set you up with the saxophonist in the big band playing there." Cocoanut Grove was in the famous Ambassador Hotel on Wilshire Boulevard in the Miracle Mile. It was an exotic nightclub that seated a thousand people on tiers among fake palm trees from a Hollywood movie set, each with a mechanical monkey with glowing eyes. The ceiling was studded with stars that lit up and the customers almost always included a Hollywood star or two or ten. There was a stage for the band and a large dance floor. As my mother would tell the story of meeting my dad for the first time, "I didn't know a saxophone from my elbow, but there I was, on the dance floor, dancing with the heir to the Dr Pepper fortune, but making eyes with the cute saxophone player in the band."

I never asked who the young Dr Pepper heir might have been, but he didn't impress my mother enough to keep her attention on him.

Somehow my mother and her friend made their way backstage where she met my father face-to-face. I'm sure she was all fluttery and talking to my dad a mile a minute. He was charmed by this young beauty and asked her out. He was eight years her senior, seemed far more worldly wise, and was dressed as dapper as Hollywood royalty.

When my mom went home to Elk City for the Christmas holidays, a past high school beau, Teb, asked her to marry him. Her high school peers were getting married and it seemed to be the expected thing to do. Good girls from her Elk City community didn't have premarital sex, which fueled the impetus to get married young. It wasn't a good reason for a lifelong commitment, but being in the "old maid" category if not married by age twenty-five was far worse. She suggested to Teb that they get married right away. Wisely, he told her, "No, Flora June, I'm going to get a good job and be able to support us."

My mother decided that his timeline didn't work for her, which meant she was free to jump feet first into her next plan, the one held secret in her heart. She would return to Los Angeles to the exciting prospect of marrying Neely Plumb. He was far more sophisticated than Teb, had a full-time job playing with popular big bands in ballrooms across the country. It seemed like a life of adventure and great fun, way beyond hanging wet laundry on a clothesline attached to some dusty little house in Elk City. My mother broke off her Oklahoma engagement to meet up with my dad and the two of them drove into Arizona and eloped. She sent a telegram to her father, announcing that she was now Mrs. Neely Plumb. A message came back immediately from her upset traditional father: *Flora June, you get to a church right now and get married for real. A justice of the peace is not the same.*

An article was published in the local Elk City newspaper stating that Flora June Dobry had "made a marriage," and the *Los Angeles Herald* and *Express* printed that Neely Plumb a "widely known musician" with the Anson Weeks Orchestra at the Cocoanut Grove had married "a belle from Oklahoma City."

By that time Flora and Neely were off on their new marital adventure. My father had secured a "sit-down" job, playing with a big band with a long-running gig in Honolulu and Hilo, Hawaii.

On their honeymoon my parents took the famed ocean liner the SS *Lurline* from San Francisco to Hawaii, a five-day trip across the Pacific on what was one of the original luxury cruise ships, with its deck chairs and shuffleboard. There was even a driving range on the upper deck, where passengers could practice their golf swing and hit balls into the ocean. No one thought about ecology in the 1940s, either. For the next four or five months, my mother happily became a young homemaker in Honolulu, while my dad played in the band as tourists danced the evening away in the big ballrooms.

Less than a year after they married, my parents returned to LA, where my father went to work at RKO Studios as a saxophone and clarinet player for films. They rented while they had a small tract house built in the Valley. After my mother gave birth to Ben and then June, and had two children under age three when she was twenty-four, my father ordered a larger, three-bedroom tract house to be built in a new development in Van Nuys. Once it was finished, the four of them moved in. My mother decorated with very cool modern furniture and wallpaper of the late 1940s, a tuxedo couch and two matching armchairs, two blond-wood step-style end tables, and a white leather chair. A rack of TV trays that were used every dinner time was nearby, as well as "the clicker," a long-wired remote my father invented to be able to turn the TV channel and lower the volume on commercials from his seat. Under all of the furnishings was wall-to-wall carpeting, a luxury at that time.

* * *

By the time I came along, a midlife baby for my parents, my father's days as a big-band musician were definitely over. He had suffered a long bout of Bell's palsy, which immobilized one side of his face. For some reason the doctors put him through a form of electroshock therapy, which only made the situation worse and he was never able to regain his embouchure. He had lost his lip, as they say. My parents' "let's go" attitudes, which had originally taken them both from their small-town upbringings to seeking adventure and change, had shifted.

When I was six, my father took my mother and me to the World's Fair in Queens, New York. He combined it with a business trip, so during the daytime hours my mother took me to the museums. At the Metropolitan Museum of Art, she found Goya's *Red Boy*, a painting of a toddler from the late 1700s, dressed in a one-piece red jumper. The child is holding a string attached to the leg of his pet magpie. In its beak the magpie holds Goya's calling card and signature, with two wide-eyed cats crouched nearby. We stood before it for quite a long time, and when I asked her about the "little girl's" pet bird, she made sure to tell me that it was a painting of a boy, even with his dark hair cut in a shoulder-length pageboy. There was a reproduction of the Goya painting in the gift shop and my mother had it shipped to our house. It was framed and hung in a place of honor over the fireplace mantel. As a child I never questioned her art acquisition, but as an adult I realized that the tiny Goya boy looked very similar to my mother as a little girl.

Our art deco living room never changed in five decades, only going through a variety of slipcovers, or fringed spreads that covered the couch, and eventually gold-colored blackout curtains and new wall-to-wall carpeting. The wallpaper in the bedrooms, appropriately modern in the 1940s—cowboys and running horses for Ben's bedroom, and ribboned bouquets of flowers and jewelry boxes with strings of pearls for June's bedroom—also were never updated.

After June left for college, I was moved into her bedroom. One evening, I heard a pounding noise coming from my room and walked in to find my mother on a stepstool with a hammer. She had decided to display my dolls and stuffed animals by hanging them on the wall from nails, usually by a rubber band around their necks. It must have been an idea she saw in a magazine or catalogue. I expressed my concern that they would all choke. Since I didn't have much time to play with them, I guess she didn't want to have to dust around them, either. By the time the house was sold in 2001, the dolls and animals were gone. Only little chips in the plaster wall, where the nails were removed, remained. For the rest of the furnishings, the vintage style was very hip once again. Full circle.

My parents remained forever curious about a variety of things, but once my mother had her secure homebase, she never wanted to move again. She was content within her modest palace, and her social life narrowed to my father's associates and whomever she interacted with on the set of my acting jobs. She wasn't a joiner, didn't want to belong to any clubs or even the PTA. She didn't even have a hairdresser, instead choosing to color and cut her own hair at home and eventually wore wigs to solve any hair needs. I never saw her place a phone call to a friend.

My father had to be more social, as his job at RCA included interacting with many musicians, bands, singers, manufacturers, and distributors. He seemed to enjoy being with my mother most of all. Because my father snored, once my brother, Ben, left for college, my parents slept in separate bedrooms, but every morning he would carry two cups of coffee into my mother's bedroom and I would hear them laugh and tell jokes and play word games to start their day. Despite the adventurous launch to their relationship, their marriage became typical of the Baby Boom years: my father going out to work, my mother raising the children and keeping house. She made it clear to me that the "man is the head of the household" and, in essence, "has the final word." Ironic, then, that I knew my mother to be very vocal to my father about what should happen next and when that should be.

Later, in my adult years, my mother told me she believed that she paid way more attention to my brother than she did my sister. I'm sure she wanted to raise her son to become an efficient leader and man who could handle life. I was only four when the family drove north of San Jose to deliver my brother to Stanford University for his freshman year of college. In between his undergraduate years at Stanford and his business degree from Harvard, Ben dated a young woman from Connecticut, where they were married. My parents and I flew to the East Coast, and I preceded the bride down the aisle in my powder-blue eyelet flower girl dress. Months later Ben left for Vietnam to serve as an officer in the army. I distinctly recall the reel-to-reel audiotapes he would ship home of him telling my parents his experiences as an officer, though my parents shielded me from hearing about the details of the war on the front lines.

My sister flourished into a buoyant personality, despite what my mother claims was a lack of attention. To me, when I was a toddler, June was the goddess of all space and time.

She was a true beauty, with a movie star smile displaying her perfectly aligned white teeth, long blond hair, and brilliant blue eyes that matched her sharp intelligence. She would head out to high school in her crinoline dress with petticoats and kitten heels. One morning, as she went to the front door, I ran after her saying, "June!! June! Say bye to me!" She extended her hand so I could kiss her lotion-soft knuckles. I did it, too, because that's how one honors a goddess. She began acting on stage in high school and fell in love with the more classic form of theater, her favorite being Shakespeare. I would sit in the audience in awe, though I probably was too young to follow the story. She won awards for Best Actress and Best Thespian, then scored a scholarship to study drama at UCLA.

As fearless as she was in her own life, my older sister made sure that I was protected. She took me around for trick-or-treating in our neighborhood when I was four. She would boost my Tweety Bird self up on the porch and ring the doorbell; then she would step down onto the sidewalk. At one house a woman dressed as a witch opened the door with a bowl of candy. June noticed and called up from the sidewalk, "Don't you scare my little sister!"It made me feel very safe to have her defend me.

Dressing up was not reserved for Halloween. My parents were both fashion-conscious people and took great care about their appearances when they would go out anywhere, even a local store. Going out to dinner meant a suit and a tie for my father, and hat and gloves for my mother. I was like her little living fashion doll. She kept me dressed up in cute little girl clothes that we would shop for at the Robinson's store in the Valley, or even a discount store, being that she was budget-conscious as well as fashion-conscious. There were white lace anklets, shiny patent leather shoes, smocked dresses, hats, and even white gloves, depending on the outing. Let's just say that no one ever looked at me and said, "Hey, kiddo, let's get on the ground and roll down that grass hill. It's fun!" My parents never encouraged a rough-and-tumble childhood for me. I overheard my mom complain to my dad, after I had a three-year-old's impulse that had ruined my total fashion look for the day: "I put Eve's white gloves on her and the first thing she does is run her hand along a dirty banister."

One of my father's favorite hobbies was photography and, before the invention of the digital camera and smartphone, I might place a bet that I was the most home-photographed child in the twentieth century. His favorite camera was a small metal-cased Minox. It was notoriously known for being a German spy camera, with its pinhole opening through which the film was exposed. He would send the film off to be developed and it would return, hundreds of two-by-three–inch black-and-white photos, each roll filed in a colorful Pop Art box. From birth, my developmental years, being natural in front of a camera seemed to be a part of life. I guess I thought posing was something every kid had to do. I didn't seem to mind it.

For most of my childhood years, I was ensconced in an adult world, going with my parents to restaurants, clubs, Las Vegas shows, and into recording studios or industry events, like a party at Tippi Hedren's home and multi-acre animal reserve in Santa Clarita. One of my father's early talent acquisitions for the RCA label was to sign Jefferson Airplane, an up-and-coming band he found in San Francisco. When he would travel for business, Mom and I, dressed as if being presented to the queen, would catch a flight with him. Travel by air was always an event that called for dressing up, which was not uncommon on commercial flights in the early 1960s. Women wore dresses, stockings, hats, and gloves; the men flew in suits. I can still feel that distinct stickiness of the vinyl airline seats on the backs of my bare legs and the seat belt over my petticoated dress. We would stay in a hotel and entertain ourselves by looking around downtown San Francisco while my father worked. There's a famous bar in Nob Hill on the penthouse level of the Mark Hopkins Hotel, overlooking the bay and also downtown with 360-degree views. Apparently, by age three I was so used to rubbing shoulders with adults that my mother recalled that I would say, "Let's go to the Top of the Mark for a grink!"

In another carbon copy of a letter my father had sent off to my brother, it seems I was pretty observant and vocal about my surroundings, hoping to entertain any adult nearby. I was five when he wrote about a work trip to Vegas: *The flight to Las Vegas was uneventful, and we went to the Hacienda in a cab. As we walked in the door, we could see the gambling tables and slot machines. Eve took one look and said, "This is a swingin' place." Our cabdriver fell over laughing.*

I was great at being around adults. It was other kids my age who were a mystery to me.

Although I had attended a small nursery school a couple of mornings a week for two hours a day, the idea of beginning kindergarten and spending a full day with twenty-four other five-year-olds, as well as the scores of older children filling the school hallways, was a shock to my system. On the first day of kindergarten, my mother dressed me up and walked me over to the school. I was fine until I comprehended that the plan was to leave me there, not only this day, but five days a week. I began to cry and cling onto her. The teacher somehow coaxed me in the door, but my mother stayed and sat on a bench outside to make sure I calmed down. I finally did. It was an eye-opening new world in which kids actually ran around, scraped up their shoes, wiped their noses on their sleeves, and sat on the asphalt playground with nothing between their clothing and the ground. I learned to adapt by deciding on my very first boyfriend. During story time, we were directed to sit in organized rows on small hooked rugs. In the row behind mine was a darling sandy-haired boy named Paul. I smiled shyly at him and he smiled back at me. I'm not sure if five-year-old children can identify flirting, but obviously our "preferences" show up early in life. While the teacher was distracted by answering another child's question about the traffic being stopped in the page-turner *Make Way for Ducklings*, I slowly scooted back one row to sit next to Paul, having the boy next to him make room for me. It didn't go unnoticed, and I was called out by the teacher on my first day of school as she strongly suggested that I return to the space in my original row.

It may have been my ability to communicate fearlessly with adults that set the scene for our new next-door neighbor, Helen, to stop to chat with me over our backyard fence shortly after my sixth birthday. As it turns out, she was a children's agent for the film and television industry. After conversing with me, Helen suggested to my mother that I'd be perfect for commercial work, considering my personality and looks. In fact, Helen was sending girl clients to a national fabric softener commercial audition the very next day. She asked my mother if she would be open to taking me to give it a try. I'm sure my mother talked it over with my dad.

My mother selected my audition outfit and we showed up to what was my first experience in a casting office. I've been told that I walked in the room by myself and said, "My name is Eve. I'm six and my mom is forty-four." I'm sure she was appreciative of that. I didn't know what would be expected of me, but I wasn't nervous. I already knew how to smile and pose for a camera. I knew how to read. I knew how to follow directions. So, when they told me to "Walk in. Stop on that piece of tape on the floor," then gave me a line to repeat, that's what I did.

Helen called later to tell my mom that the commercial was mine. I was cast.

From that day on, I became a working actress.

Chapter Two

I became my mother's full-time job, with overtime. If I wasn't in school, I was almost always with my mother. The casting offices would send the "breakdowns" (synopsis of the commercial, pilot, or episode) around to the agents at about three o'clock, and by six or seven that evening, my mother would start prepping me for the audition my agent, Helen, had lined up.

For commercials there might be a few lines to memorize, which my mother would rehearse with me, but often it was a voice-over announcer and I only had action. In one early commercial, when I was six, Baby Secret had all of the lines. She was the "must-have" doll of that year because you could pull the ripcord at her neck and she whispered with her mouth moving. I don't remember how many recorded sayings she had, but some of them would now be considered borderline creepy, like: "Is anyone else awake?" "I like to whisper in the dark." According to one of my father's memos, the producers gifted me the doll at the end of the day, but after a four-hour commercial shoot, I lost interest in whatever secrets this baby doll had left. Whatever happened to my Baby Secret has remained a secret. The doll may be forgotten, but I can still remember the worrisome feeling I had because my hair bow headband didn't stay in my baby-fine shoulder-length hair and required readjustments between takes. I couldn't say *why* I felt responsible for a hair accessory, but I did.

Over the next two years, my hair grew down to my waist, only to be trimmed, never significantly cut again until I was an adult. Maybe my agent suggested letting it grow long, but my mother took on overseeing my hair as if it was part of her job description, an asset to be monitored and protected. There would be no chlorine-glossy green-tinted "swimmer's hair" for me, even though our Van Nuys home had a backyard pool. Anytime I was in a swimming pool, my mother would make me wear a rubber bathing cap held in place with a chin strap. It was always uncomfortable, and nearly impossible to shove eighteen inches of thick hair into a rubberized cap. If water seeped in, she would wash my hair with some purple toning shampoo, to neutralize any green tint. I tolerated it all because I was drawn to any body of water like a released circus seal, straight in, never looking back.

My parents told me that I ran headlong into the Pacific surf without a care at age three, my father chasing me down before a wave crashed over my head.

Starting at age five, I was taken for lessons at the John Josephson Swim School in the Valley. While other kids trembled on the tiles surrounding the pool, I jumped right in. During one of the early sessions, all of the students were directed to put our faces into the water and listen while the instructor counted, to see how long we could each hold our breath. When I ran out of air, I lifted my mouth slightly out of the water to catch a quick breath while the counting went on. I remember getting caught, because the teacher figured it out when everyone else quit before fifteen and I was still face down at thirty.

Ocean water didn't change my hair color, so every August my scalp was set free during our beach vacations. A friend that my father knew through his RCA job had a beautiful, but simple, three-story rustic-looking apartment house right on the beach in Laguna and my parents would rent the tiny apartment on the ground floor, starting when I was a toddler until I was ten years old. It wasn't much more than a small kitchen, a bathroom, and one bedroom, but no one hung out inside for long anyway. My brother would sometimes arrive to spend the day and I would be impressed by the way he could float over the foamy sand at the edge of the tide on his polished plywood skimboard. Being a college student, he would hang out for the afternoon and be gone, back to LA, by sunset. My sister, June, would often come for a day trip, but usually with whatever handsome young man she was dating at the time. Happily for me, the family who rented the second floor had three daughters, close to my age, and we spent all day together, trading comic books, making drip castles, bobbing in the water on large blue blow-up rafts, and catching sand crabs and putting them in our buckets with wet sand to watch them dig under the surface, over and over. Our parents would set up their lawn chairs on the beach to keep an eye on us, chatted with each other, read magazines, and took turns bringing snacks and cocktails down from the house. No adults would get into the water to play with the kids, and rarely did they get in on their own. I never saw my father take a dip in the Pacific. He would laugh and claim he was "like the tuna . . . Chicken of the Sea."

In the early morning, my father would let my mother sleep an extra hour and walk me down the beach to the public swings suspended from an iron cross bar, fifteen feet up, between two vertical poles somehow anchored deep in the sand. The swings had bucket seats and ten-foot-long link chains, and he would push me so high my back would be parallel to the ground.

Despite it being our vacation weeks, my mother never turned down an offer for me to audition for a commercial or a TV show. She would collect me off the beach; I'd have to shower, wash and dry my hair, and put on a dress; then she'd drive the ninety minutes back to Los Angeles for a ten-minute audition and then drive back to Laguna. At least once or twice, I would book a commercial or guest star spot that was scheduled to be filmed the next day, so there would be no returning to Laguna Beach until it was completed.

One late afternoon, following a morning Los Angeles audition and three-and-a-half round-trip hours in the car, it became obvious that I had missed a prime sand crab catching day in Laguna. My bucket only contained wet sand, no little critters. The youngest sister of the girls who were my playmates was showing off her prize, a sand crab that was at least two inches in length, the biggest one I had ever seen. My seven-year-old self decided it should be in my bucket, as she had already kept it to herself for hours. I scooped it out of her bucket and into mine. After a verbal tussle between us, she announced she was going to report the incident to her parents and mine, making me feel angry. She trudged up the beach toward the parental circle of lawn chairs, sobbing loudly. I knew I'd soon be in trouble over my crustacean heist. My solution was to flee. Leaving the bucket and the sand crab behind, I climbed the four flights of wooden steps lining the cliff to the garage-level dead-end road, then cut up the steep alleyway to the Pacific Coast Highway. I knew I couldn't cross the busy street, so I took a left and walked down a block to a nearby hotel. Once in the parking lot, I needed a new plan. Should I go in the lobby with my bare feet and sandy swimsuit? And once I was inside, then what? I couldn't rent a room. The thought of continuing my great escape was more frightening than returning to face my parents' disapproval. I was probably only gone for fifteen minutes, but it seemed like a full day of being a fugitive. When I got back down to the beach, my parents were far more upset about me disappearing than the original crime. It was a short-duration scolding without much consequence because the phone call had come that I had booked a guest star spot on Tommy and Dick Smothers's sitcom, *My Brother the Angel*, playing a little girl who could see the angel when others couldn't. We had to go back to Los Angeles. It's not easy to ground an employed child. My mother noted in her datebook following the wrap up of the episode filming: *Everyone, even Dick and Tommy, liked Eve and gave her a hug and kiss goodbye when she finished.*

In the mid-1960s there were commercials for Mattel's talking dolls: Chatty Cathy, Chatty Baby, and Charmin' Chatty. In one of their doll commercials, my future *Brady Bunch* sister Maureen McCormick and I are at an outside doll tea party with our dolls. The next year I graduated to the Barbie doll collection and a commercial where I reveal Talking Barbie's new British best friend, Stacey, from behind a window curtain. She spoke with an accent. I guess Barbie got tired of her former best friend, Midge, who never spoke a word, and replaced her with exciting Stacey. Midge never showed up again, until the 1990s, married to

Allan, and pregnant, so radical for its time that she is now a hard-to-find relic.

In a Glad sandwich bag commercial, I was directed to run to the actress playing my mother and declare that I hated school because my sandwich was dry. I winced watching it on YouTube recently. I was usually cast as the obedient, courteous, and kind little girl. Not this time. I'm flamethrowing at my distressed mother, like Rhoda in *The Bad Seed*. Out of the sky descends the Man from Glad, wearing a pure white suit to match his pure white hair, riding in what appears to be a lawn chair with a propeller on it. In a monotone voice, he describes the new fold-over plastic baggie to the "flunking" mother (which could easily be misheard), obviously saving the day, as well as the future of my education. Another career milestone!

The more commercials or guest star spots I booked, the more my parents would give me the message that I was capable of anything and that I was exceptional at acting. I don't know how having a meltdown about stale bread on national TV was a sign of being remarkable, but I believed them. They imbued me with steady self-confidence that didn't waver.

In retrospect, part of my growing-up years were unknowingly being my mother's little Science of Mind experiment. She became enamored with the teachings of Ernest Holmes, the founder of a New Thought spiritual movement called Religious Science. Part of his teaching was that by controlling your thoughts and only focusing on the good, a person can create the desired outcome. But one must stay steady in positive thoughts and refute any negative appearances. It was quite a tall order for a small girl, but I did my best.

At first, my parents attended church services that were held in a movie theater. My acting career seemed almost preordained, considering that I was born in a hospital directly across from the Disney Studios, baptized in front of a cinema screen, and lived next door to a children's theatrical agent. Like the movie *Norma Rae*, where generations of family members before her worked away their lives in the textile mill because that's the only game in town, I was born into the show business factory.

Later on, my parents and a few other couples, along with Reverend Fletcher Harding, who had been friends with Ernest Holmes, began a small branch church called Encino Community Church, which grew rapidly in the early 1960s. Every Sunday I would be all dressed up for Sunday school or to attend the church service, sitting in the pews and listening to the sermons with its messages of staying positive by speaking affirmations.

The Science of Mind philosophy my parents followed wasn't about controlling the physical world. It's similar to Mary Baker Eddy's Christian Science . . . but with aspirin. If a doctor was needed, a visit to one happened. Actual science was not ignored. Broken arms were set in a cast, ear infections were prescribed antibiotics, and no one tried to ignore the outcome of a bout of food poisoning. There was no reason to not benefit from science, to seek out the people who know how to make things better. Science of Mind was more about controlling your personal mental world; your thoughts had great power. My mother never wanted me to tell anyone, outside of family, that I felt ill. She believed that having people think I was sick would have a big influence on my health.

My mother would apply affirmation techniques on me, saying things like, "You know what's great about you,

Eve? You love to eat vegetables!" or "We don't get allergies." On the way to an audition, she'd remind me, "People just like you. Everyone likes you."

Also intrigued by the renowned clairvoyant Edgar Cayce, who could reportedly sleep with his head resting on a book and wake up with the pages memorized, my father would have me do my times tables for him, right after we had said the "Now I lay me down to sleep" prayer together. I guess there was something about that sleepy, drowsy state that was supposed to lock information in your brain. I have a vague memory of sleeping with math flash cards under my pillow. I can certainly say I tried it with various scripts until I was in my twenties and had a "wait a minute" awakening to the absurdity of it.

Despite their determination not to acknowledge "bad stuff," to keep it from manifesting into reality, I think they were frightened about what might happen to me. Child kidnapping, beginning with the Lindbergh baby, had always been front-page and fear-filled news when my parents were younger. My mother, being the oldest child in her family, was left to babysit her little brother and sister and had a deep fear that they would be taken, since their family was one of the wealthiest in their Oklahoma town. I'm sure that fear always stayed with her. In the national news, there was a handful of children of wealthy bankers or businessmen who were held for ransom over the years, including Frank Sinatra Jr. in 1963. I didn't know about any of these crimes as a kid, and I now could never blame them for their worry. The problem was, they never admitted their worry. Instead, it was channeled into being helicopter parents. If I wasn't under a trusted adult's supervision, I was under my mother's watchful eye. My parents told me it was their responsibility to me, and mine to them, that they should know exactly where I was at every given moment.

I envied the neighborhood kids who went "out to play" and didn't have to go home until dinner. Wandering around was not an option for me.

Often, on weekends, we would go camping in the Los Angeles Forest. It was a way for my dad to get away after a high-pressure week at RCA Records and far from ringing telephones. He had a corner office overlooking Sunset Boulevard, a show of status with RCA, and a position that came with monumental stress.

A tent would be set up yards from the firepit and a Coleman cooler would be placed on the picnic table. I don't have a memory of being concerned about wild animals visiting our site. Since my father started calling us "the three bears"—Papa, Mama, and Baby Bear—I didn't think of animals as being any danger at all. Until I was almost six, I was on a long leash attached to a child harness that I had to wear while my parents sat in lawn chairs and read books and magazines, though I insisted that I didn't need it. We didn't go hiking or fishing, row a boat, or any particular outdoor activity, so I'm sure they wanted to make sure I didn't get out of their sight lines while they read. When it would start to get dark, we would eat cheese sandwiches and potato chips, or Dad would light a fire and we would roast hot dogs on straightened wire hangers.

There might be cookies for dessert and the beverage was often a Diet Rite soda, which came in kid-happy flavors like grape, raspberry, and green apple. My mother thought they were the healthy alternative to sugary drinks like Kool-Aid, and was upset when they discontinued the sweetener cyclamate, verbalizing her annoyance, saying, "For heaven's sake, you'd have to drink a bathtub full of it every day for it to hurt you."

I had been reading books in kindergarten, advanced beyond my grade level quickly, and soon joined my parents, turning pages of a chapter book in a nearby lawn chair. Instead of going out to play, my mother would often take me to a used bookstore in the Valley and let me pick out books to read while camping and on weekends. I went through most of the Nancy Drew series before third grade and moved on to ghost story and horror books. It was my way to experience the feelings of living an independent adventure or the thrill of unexpected frights or lurid danger, at least in my imagination.

Once in a while, I would be allowed to play at a friend's house if my mother trusted the child's mom. There was a girl who lived about three short blocks away in the section of larger, more elaborate homes. Her bedroom was extremely fancy and she had a swanky playhouse that was set up in the backyard. Her mother treated her like a little princess, dressing her in crinoline skirts and gold birthstone necklaces. One Sunday my parents allowed me to attend a Mormon church with her family. The hallway was expansive, straight and long like a hotel hallway, so I challenged my friend to run with me to the other end. She let me know, in her most sanctimonious seven-year-old voice, that "we don't run in the house of the Lord." After that chastisement I decided I'd never join a church where you can't happily skip down a long, open hallway.

It may have been the expectations put on her to be a dainty little lady with a sweet disposition, but I became a witness when she acted out her buried rage about it all. One afternoon we were in her playhouse and she began tossing her little china tea party set out the window to smash on the driveway, piece by piece. At first, I wanted to say, "Hey, if you don't want your tea set, I'll take it," but then I was stunned into silence by her daring to be so fearlessly reckless. I couldn't imagine doing anything close to that. I didn't know what to do about her anger, because in my Science of Mind world, there was no place for being in a bad mood or for things to be that negative. Everything was "good." There was no place or time to have a crap day or to let yourself be pissed off at life.

That afternoon I decided to walk back to my house alone, instead of waiting for my mother to pick me up. I guess her mother phoned to say I had left, and before I had walked a block, my mother pulled up next to me in the car. She wasn't exactly going to start shattering dinnerware, but she was pretty unhappy with me. As punishment she took away some anticipated activity I would have enjoyed doing. She'd say, "I was going to let you go swimming this afternoon, but clearly you're not responsible, so you won't have that privilege."

While other kids in my neighborhood walked to school, my mother dropped me off and picked me up every day. The other girls in my grammar school classes gathered for Bluebird meetings and then eventually graduated into being full-on Campfire Girls. I liked their "girls can do or be anything" messaging and envied their uniforms with their colorful wood beads sewn to their vests representing their levels of achievement. I told my mother that I wanted to be a Bluebird troop member and she reminded me, "I'm sorry, hon, but we don't really have time for that."

The troop meetings took place after school. I'm sure my mother didn't want the time conflict or, in her shyness, to have to show up with a plate of homemade cookies for a

Bluebird bake sale and chat with other mothers. It was clear that what I did was TV shows and commercials, and to do those you had to audition or interview sometimes during the school day, but most often as soon as school let out for the day. A couple of days every week, there would be a dress hanging on a hook in the backseat when my mother picked me up. The dress was my number one clue that I had an audition or interview scheduled for the next hour. I would have to get in the backseat of the car and scramble out of my school clothes and into my audition dress on the way to the Hollywood casting office as my mother drove and filled me in on whatever I was auditioning for and what lines I might need to say on camera. The message was clear: "This is what we're doing. You're going to change clothes while I drive to the audition. Then after you audition, we'll go home, eat dinner, and you can do your homework."

It wasn't something that could be argued. An audition or interview was part of my day and to be expected. Only one time did I raise an objection. I was probably nine or ten, hoping to go home and play outside. I got in the backseat and told my mother, "I don't want to audition today."

Her response was calm but direct, "All right. That's fine. We'll go home and then you have to call Helen and tell her that you don't want to go to the audition."

I changed my mind. I was raised not to let other people down. Good little soldiers know what's expected of them and do what's being asked. You show up. You try your best at every audition because you never know what might come of it. I was a good little soldier who would never break formation.

As it turned out, a whole lot came of it. From ages six to eleven, my career was like a boulevard of green lights. Perhaps it was my approach in auditioning: "Tell me what you need and I'll do it." Or maybe my small size? At age eight I could still play five or six (it's easier to get a kid in the two-shot with an adult if she's small enough to carry). It could've been my ability to converse easily with most adults, or maybe my detachment to the outcome of the audition came across as natural acting, but I would end up booking about 85 percent of the commercials and roles for which I interviewed. I really can't explain it because I could never have described to anyone the how-to of my acting method, and I certainly didn't know a single thing about technique.

Considering the Science of Mind Church philosophy about how our intentions and ideas create our reality, it seemed paradoxical that it was completely fine for me to play unfortunate children on TV. I was almost always cast as a little girl in great peril: falling down a well, the daughter of a ruthless alcoholic, kidnapped, orphaned, or terminally ill.

I innocently played a seven-year-old named Margaret in a situation that traumatized child-aged viewers of the made-for-TV movie *House on Green Apple Road*. I'm sure my parents knew the storyline of the movie, since it was originally titled *Red Kitchen Murders*, but never told me. Wearing a super-short little puffy-sleeved dress, in which I felt uncomfortably exposed getting out of a car and climbing steps, Margaret is dropped off after school by a mom and other kids in a station wagon. I enthusiastically wave goodbye and enter my house, saying "Mommy, I'm home."

I think I said it with a British accent, more of a "mummy" than a "mommy," because the director was British and was giving me line readings.

As the director explained the scene to me, "There's no

response from Mummy, so you get your little stuffed toy dog from the front room and walk down the hallway to the kitchen door." It seems the prop person fell down on their job, as my mother got a call early that morning to ask if I could bring a stuffed animal with me. I chose my little roughed-up yellow-and-white dog. "You try to open the door, but it seems to be blocked. The kitchen looks messy and not like it usually does. So, since Mummy isn't there, you decide to go next door to your aunt's house. Okay?"

I followed his directions. I found my stuffed dog and walked pensively to the kitchen door, which is closed. On the actual set, I peered around the door into the empty soundstage, and a film camera, nothing else.

In the edited movie, the TV viewer sees me looking into a blood-spattered kitchen, broken dishes, turned-over chairs, and pots and pans littering the floor and bloody handprints on the fridge. As a child actress, I didn't see any of that. I then deliver the line to my stuffed dog that we should "go see Aunt Lee," and I let the door close as a cat runs through the pools of blood on the kitchen floor and leaps out the open window.

Unlike the story of the director on the movie *Skippy* who made nine-year-old Jackie Cooper sob realistically by taking his dog off the set and having a gunshot fired, suggesting that the dog had been killed, I never had any director traumatize me for the sake of acting.

Grown men and women, who reviewed *House on Green Apple Road* on IMDb, wrote that seeing the movie as a kid was like their worst traumatic nightmare of coming home from school to a bloody murder scene. I had no idea of the plotline when I was eight, and I never watched the movie. My parents probably did after they had put me to bed.

It was an early morning when my mother drove me to Pacific Palisades for the scene in front of the house. She explained that I would be working with Julie Harris, who was playing "Aunt Lee," a really good actress, a multi–Tony and Emmy winner, a very big star, and that I was lucky to be in a movie with her. My murderous on-screen mother was played by another famous actress, Janet Leigh, but I never got to be in a scene with her. Though my mother was over the moon about my sharing the screen with Julie Harris, I was personally smitten with the handsome leading man, Christopher George (star of *The Rat Patrol*), who played the investigating officer. In the still-shot photograph to promote the movie, it's obvious that I have no idea what the movie is about. I'm standing on the front porch between Julie Harris, looking very concerned about the crime scene, and Christopher George, in professional lieutenant mode. I am beaming up at the incredibly handsome Christopher George with a lovestruck grin on my face, quite the disconnect considering I was a second grader whose mother is missing from a blood-soaked kitchen.

As a guest star on *Family Affair*, I played a classmate of Buffy and Jody's who can only attend classes by speaker-phone because I'm bedridden and terminally ill. When Buffy brings over school work for me, we strike up a friendship and play games on my bed. There are many wistful and sad looks from my TV mom and Buffy picks up on it all. Buffy believes Uncle Bill can do anything and tells him to find a doctor to cure her classmate. Uncle Bill tries, but the results are the same. No one can save little Eve. I could tell it bothered my mother tremendously to see me in jaundiced makeup to make me look ill and being pushed around in a wheelchair, every scene another confirmation that I wasn't long for the world. Still, the show went on.

Uncle Bill decides to have an early Christmas celebration for Eve, as it seems she won't make it past November. As much as he tries to spare Buffy and Jody knowing the truth, the last scene is Buffy sobbing in her bed and Uncle Bill coming in to hold her. It's one of the saddest episodes of the five seasons of *Family Affair*.

I'm surprised my mother made it through the shooting schedule. She wouldn't allow me to learn to ride a two-wheel bike for fear of a fall and injury in my real life, but on TV I could fade away from disease before age nine.

I rarely worked with other child actors, like Johnny Whitaker and Anissa Jones. There was an unspoken link among us, knowing that other children didn't have lives like ours. I had most likely auditioned with Anissa for shows and commercials in the past, as we were the same age; but as a guest star, I was well aware that I was on *her* show. The kids who were regular cast members on a series had taken the first-place prize in television acting. It was never expressed to me that way, but there was an energy of competition that I could feel starting at age six as I was trying to figure out my place in the world.

I attended on-set school with Anissa and Johnny during the filming week of *Family Affair*. I watched them closely. I didn't yet know what it was like to be on a series, to work almost all year on twenty-three episodes, but I would soon find out. To this day, when I see Mindy Cohn from *The Facts of Life*, Mary McDonough from *The Waltons*, or cross paths with Shaun Cassidy and give him a hug, it feels more like a reunion with a sibling, a tribe member of a very select group of people who were working actors as children. Our common link to one another is that we never got to do the things that most children do. The only slumber party I ever attended was the one in an episode of *The Brady Bunch*.

Anissa and I were both small for our age. At age eight Anissa was playing a six-year-old on the show. *Family Affair* went on for five full seasons, so even heading into puberty, she had to play a fourth grader at age thirteen. Like me as Jan Brady, Anissa was so identified with her Buffy character, she was often called Buffy in public. I didn't know her personally, but I understand what it must have felt like for her to no longer be sought after for being the cute, little pigtailed blond girl who knew how to take direction and deliver lines, who could merchandise a doll, and whose image was on a lunch box.

When Anissa was found dead of an overdose at eighteen, I was sad, but not shocked. When you're on a set for most of your childhood, you are socialized in a different way. Your friends are your co-stars. It's a challenge to talk to your schoolmates when you return to regular school because they've had lives that you never shared. In many ways being on a TV show is a great life in a make-believe world where you have attention from adults in an adult world. You have lots of one-on-one time in your little schoolroom and people bring you what you need. But if you don't have parents who help you process it all when it ends with your childhood, you're left to figure out where you fit in and how you matter anymore.

My parents may have been overprotective of me in real life as a child, but I'm grateful that they were protective in every single way. My father wrote in a ledger every penny I made and put it all in an account for me. They never spent my money on anything for themselves. I know quite a few child actors who ended up with very little when they needed it most, either through poor management or loopholes in the Coogan Law meant to protect child actors' incomes.

None of that was true for me. My parents may have been intrigued and fascinated by my career as a child, but I was treasured for being me, their little daughter, and I knew it. For that, I was fortunate.

Chapter Three

I've lived by myself only a few times in my life. More often than not, my home setup included another person or two, a canine or two, and me. A feline would sometimes be in the mix of the household head count. The human roommates switched in and out, depending on the year or the house I was in. A friend of a friend would need a place to live; a girlfriend would stay with me post-breakup; a fellow actor or artist would bunk at my house; I'd have a boyfriend move in for a while; and I was married . . . the first time . . . for a few years. I've now lived with my husband, Ken, for thirty-one years. Neither one of us anticipates switching out roomies for someone else.

Often my past housemates would arrive with a pet and then leave with a pet. Some came with a pet and left me with their pet. I would adopt a dog, raise a family of mice, and take in a stray cat that appeared hungry.

I bought a puppy from a breeder only once and would never do it again. There are far too many pound puppies needing a home. My Dalmatian dog, Topper, was the first dog I got all on my own. She was my constant pal, never finding fault with me even on my worst decision-making days.

Months before finding Topper, I had gone to New York with my live-in boyfriend to see the Broadway musical *Sunday in the Park with George*, which gave us the idea that we should get a Dalmatian dog and name it Dot. After I broke it off with the boyfriend, knowing that it wasn't what I wanted for my future, I still wanted a Dalmatian.

The breeder gave me a discount because the puppy was only "pet grade" due to some missing back teeth and she would never be "show grade." Pet grade was absolutely fine by me. I had no intention of making her audition to be considered hot property in the show ring. She was invaluable to me. I named her Topper, taken from the old black-and-white movie starring Cary Grant.

She learned to "count" her own barks, "do three," with the prize being a toss of her ball. She grinned, showing teeth, when really excited, and had a great nonthreatening lip curl when I softly tugged on one of her ears. She was forever patient with me. I drew multicolored additional dots on her with a nontoxic set of markers and took her with me to a big Equal Rights Amendment march that was happening downtown. She intrigued many of the marchers, with a concerning amount of people asking if that was her true fur coloring. I thought purple, red, and green spots would make it quite clear that it was only a costume.

During the down days of coming to terms with the ended relationship and spending my days alone, Topper would manage to make me laugh. One morning I looked out of the kitchen window to see Topper in the backyard, wildly tossing a piece of colored cloth up in the air over and over again. She acted as if it was the best toy she had ever been given. I couldn't figure out what she had found and went into the backyard to see what she was so happy about. Wagging her tail rapidly, she brought me the underwear I must have left on the floor of my closet before I went to sleep. I grabbed them, hoping to make my personal lingerie private once more, but Topper reckoned I was suggesting a fun game of tug-of-war. I lost.

On my worst days of post-breakup blues, and wishing I had an acting-job offer to distract me, I had no appetite and spent the day on my bed spiraling into the self-pity realm of wondering if there was anyone who would miss me if I were gone. Topper would rest her head near me, her eyes alert to my condition. She was so attentive that at one point I thought about how long it would be before Topper ate me if I died and no one realized it. It was that dark thought and a long look at my hollow-eyed reflection in a mirror that finally motivated me to get up, take a shower, go outside, and greet the day. Topper seemed delighted that my week of wallowing was over and there was a ball in the backyard ready to be thrown and chased. Topper stayed with me, as my closest companion, until I met Ken, fell in love, and seemed to be on the path to a happier life.

It was hard to let Topper go. In my reluctance to be without her, I tried every geriatric treatment available for dogs. But it eventually became clear that her last day had arrived. Ken was at work, so my neighbor and friend went with me to the vet, insisting that I would need support. He was right. Because of his kindness, I have helped a number of friends go through the same with their own dogs and cats. I may not be having a great day myself, but I still go because I know their day is worse.

Now, for the first time in over thirty-five years, I have no pets. No one *needs* to go out for a walk. I no longer have the universal conversation starter when I'm in Central Park as two leashed dogs meet across a sidewalk, causing their owners to have human interaction above them. When Ken and I go for a park walk now, people we pass may smile and nod, but no one asks questions about our breed mix or where we got each other. It's not easy to acclimate to a pet-free life. I don't know how long we will last before we bring home another housemate, because in the over-three decades we've been together, we've always had a four-legged companion walking around our house with their knee-level perspective on life. Ken occasionally tells me that if I should exit the planet first, he will move to a bit of land in upstate New York and rescue six or seven dogs. It sounds like a lot of fun. I think I'll stick around and go with him, perhaps rescue a horse or two for variety, ones that come with a barn cat.

Maggie, our rescue dog, lived with us for sixteen years in four different homes, from Southern California to New York City, but it didn't seem that long. Maggie entered our lives close to my fiftieth birthday. Ken and I were living in Laguna Beach, California, along with our eleven-year-old dog, Woody, in a bungalow-style house, which we had renovated, surrounded by a low white picket fence. We previously lived in the San Fernando Valley right after we had married, and one weekend day our neighbors had shown up on our doorstep with a box of puppies. We were "just looking," when Ken gave me a wistful expression and said, "I've never had a puppy."

"All right," I said. "Go ahead. Pick out a puppy. Whichever one you want."

He chose a brown-and-black fuzz ball, no bigger than a shoe. We were told that the puppy was a small Labrador mix, but within two months it was obvious he would soon be mostly one hundred pounds of German Shepherd. Luckily for us, Woody was the most loyal and well-behaved dog possible, even with cats. Ken's cat, Coltrane, would reach out from his perch on a chair, extend a claw, and hook Woody as he was meandering past. Instead of showing Coltrane who had the bigger set of teeth, Woody would stand perfectly still until Coltrane retracted his paw. He wasn't quite as patient with skunks and bounded into their business more than once, resulting in ketchup baths in the front yard. But he was always great with a long road trip and would sleep in the back of our Ford Explorer, only sitting up occasionally where his Yoda ears could be seen in the rearview mirror. After we relocated to Laguna Beach, we trained him to stay inside our front yard, despite the picket fence only coming to his chin. When people strolled past the house, he would drop a toy over the fence onto the sidewalk and give them a look like, "Hi! Do you mind tossing that toy back over the fence for me? I'll chase it and drop it over the fence for the next guy coming down the walk."

Although we trained Woody not to jump up on people, anyone who came inside the fence got Woody's enthusiastic nose-to-crotch greeting. Some of our guests, especially men, couldn't make it to our front door without a wince.

Woody's health began to fade at age ten, which seems to be the norm for large dogs. I was determined to search for an "overlap" dog, not wanting to face the hard reality of an ending with Woody. I scoured the photos of shelter dogs posted online. I chose a kind of wild, untrained year-old baby, a feisty-looking black-and-white terrier mutt. The caption read: *Hi, I'm Maggie. I'm looking really hard for my forever family.*

"That's the one!" I said with eureka-moment enthusiasm above the screen of my laptop.

Ken peered at the photo and caption over my shoulder. "That dog only has one eye."

"Yes. I know. It's okay," I answered. "It's why she's looking really hard. Good thing she found me and I want her."

Ken paused to glance in my direction, probably to make sure I wasn't kidding. Then he said, "Get your birthday dog," and headed to the kitchen to make dinner.

Maybe it was something about Maggie the Terrier's permanent wink that drew me to her, like she was saying, "You and I are in on the same secret."

A couple of days later, Ken, Woody, and I drove the ninety miles toward the high desert and the Santa Clarita animal shelter to meet her. Woody seemed fine with her and I could tell Maggie was winning Ken over, in spite of his initial resistance to her charms.

About a week later, I was at an art show in Santa Monica when Ken called to tell me that Woody was critically sick. He had taken him to the emergency vet, who confirmed that Woody's spleen had ruptured and there was little they could do to help him at his advanced age. Ken and I were incredibly sad, but we didn't want Woody to suffer.

The next afternoon, after a morning of tears, I asked Ken, "Listen, we are in the middle of adopting this other dog. Do you want me to stop the process? We can. I'm fine with it."

Ken shook his head. "No. No, don't stop. Go ahead and get your scruffy little dog."

We filled out adoption papers and a week later two young representatives from the rescue brought Maggie to our house to make sure it was suitable living conditions.

Maggie came through the front door, put her nose to the floor, and took a dump. I guess the road trip down to Laguna was taken without a pit stop. After the shelter reps did a quick tour of our house to make sure it was okay for a dog, they gave Maggie a pat on the head and went out the front door. As they started to get into their car, which was parked down the block, Maggie tore across the front yard and jumped over the picket fence and bounded down the sidewalk. I'm sure she thought her meal ticket was leaving without her. I ran to catch up. I thought the shelter might change their minds and think that this was an unsafe environment for Maggie. I assured them both that we would fix the fence situation. They didn't seem to have a moment of concern. They waved goodbye and drove off. Perhaps that's how it happens with "hard-to-place" dogs. Maggie's life with us, or maybe I should say our lives with Maggie, began that day. And the pet that was supposed to be *my* "scruffy little dog" became devoted to Ken, who enthusiastically took her for walks, spoiled her with treats, and never walked by her without scratching her head or patting her belly. It's not that she wasn't affectionate to me, but if Ken were in the room, her one eye would be attentive to his every move.

At age nine I had an acting job alongside the most well-behaved dog in North America. I had been cast in an episode of *Lassie* and that was a big deal to me. *Lassie* was regular Sunday-night TV viewing in my house, along with *The Ed Sullivan Show*. My parents would make homemade spaghetti sauce in the late afternoon and at seven o'clock the TV trays would be set up in the living room along the couch and the *Lassie* theme song would play as the three of us twirled pasta on our forks and watched.

My parents topped their spaghetti with parmesan cheese from the green shaker canister, but I would tear up a slice of American cheese and let that melt on top. Spaghetti is still my favorite comfort food and I never outgrew the American cheese slice as the topper.

My episode was in season 14 of *Lassie*, known as "the ranger years." As *Lassie* history had unfolded, Timmy and his parents had left the farm due to a job relocation to Australia and Lassie couldn't go. She is taken in by Forest Ranger Corey. I played a little girl whose parents gave her a Yorkie terrier puppy named Whiskers for an early Christmas present. Almost prophetic to what the real-life Maggie the Terrier did decades later, Whiskers escapes out of the white picket fence and runs away. Lassie to the rescue.

As my father wrote in a letter to the people with whom we shared the Laguna house every August as to why we would be a week late in getting to our vacation: *Eve has been selected now for the Christmas program on Lassie. She'll have a big part all the way through the show, and she will have top billing next to Lassie. We know the story, but it'll be better if we don't tell you. It's such a tear jerker that Eve and Flora even cried when they read the script.*

About a week before the filming of the episode, on a hot August morning, my parents took me to Rudd Weatherwax's large property in Van Nuys, where he trained dogs for TV and film. I wanted to meet the Lassie who would share the top billing with me. Rudd's most famous animal actors were the *Lassie* dogs. I soon found out that Lassie was a boy dog and was played by two or more trained collies, depending on what was needed in the scene. There was an "action" Lassie for running through the woods and swimming. There was the Lassie used for close-ups and photos. And a Lassie who could do all of the small tricks.

Rudd had invited us because he wanted to see how I would interact with the little Yorkie dog and get the puppy used to being around me. I'm sure he also wanted to make sure I wasn't a kid who poked dogs in the eyes.

Rudd had been up most of the night before with a new litter of Collie puppies. I really wanted to see them, but we took photos with the Yorkie and Lassie, instead.

All of my scenes for the episode were filmed on the CBS backlot, where they had a few houses set up, and various pine trees on wheeled platforms, bushes, fences, and fake landscaping could be moved around whatever direction was needed for the setting. My dressing room was a small, windowless cabin, also on wheels, that had been moved close to the backlot. It had a small couch and a makeup chair, a tall table with a lit mirror. The climate control was vented slats on the bottom half of the door. As my mother was running a brush down the length of my now–waist-long hair, I saw Lassie's legs walking past my dressing room through the vent.

"I really want to see Lassie," I told my mom, shifting from one foot to the other in anticipation of petting this magnificent Collie. My mother explained that my hair wasn't finished yet and I would see Lassie soon enough. I'm not sure who was groomed more that week, Lassie or me.

I filmed with the Lassie who could do all of the tricks: bark and whine on command, point and look attentively in whatever direction, and pick up small objects with his mouth. For this episode he had been taught to pick up a Christmas ornament (with no sharp hook) by the loop, bring it over to me, and nudge my hand so I could take it from him. In another scene, Ranger Corey allows Lassie to spend the night at our house to comfort me as I worry about my puppy out there in the vast wilderness, all alone.

Lassie is lying on top of my bedspread as I sleep. The collie was so well trained that he would move mere inches up or back or to the side at Rudd's verbal command so the director could get the shot he wanted.

A couple of days into filming the show, I came down with a sore throat and fever. As it was supposed to be cold weather in the episode, I was dressed in sweaters and tights, flannel nightgowns with a quilted robe over it, wool coats buttoned up to my neck, a hat, and gloves, despite it actually being super-warm California weather when we filmed. Then there was the additional blast of heat from the lighting equipment and reflectors that were needed even in outdoor scenes. Current-day cameras are so fast you could film in candlelight and still get sharp focus, but that wasn't true in the late 1960s, so floodlights were needed.

At three points during the episode, I was directed to cry over my lost puppy. Being bundled up head to toe, and having a sore throat and fever, the tears came easily. I didn't even have to use the trick my mother had taught me of how to bring tears to your eyes by yawning with your mouth closed. I guess she had learned that during her New York acting training.

Almost every guest star spot I did on any TV series, I needed to produce some tears for a scene or two. Usually, after the third take, my tears would no longer come naturally. When it was needed, a person from the makeup crew would use a test tube–shaped container that contained menthol crystals and blow it toward my open eyes to make them water. If that didn't work, an eyedropper with glycerin placed shiny tears on my cheeks. I didn't need any of that for this *Lassie* episode. When the cameras rolled, I really cried. And then I really cried for the second take.

Even after the director yelled "Cut," the tears still spilled out. "I can't stop crying. I can't stop!" I told my mom, feeling embarrassed and unprofessional. She took my hand and led me behind the cameras, out of sight of the director, and said, "It's okay. It's okay. You're fine now." Her voice was calm, but firm. There was no time for any meltdown. Like a good little soldier, I managed to collect myself and move on without disrupting the schedule for the day.

It was never said out loud to me on any show, but in the same way child actors know to not touch or move the props, we also understood that there aren't sick days when you're shooting an episode. Everything is on a deadline.

In another *Lassie* scene, the family gets in the car to go to church on Christmas. I have to look up at my father and talk, but the intensity of the klieg lights and reflectors on stands right behind him made it really hard to keep my eyes open. One of the producers of the show, Bonita Granville, had been a child actor in film during the 1930s and early '40s. She stepped in and said, "Okay, here's a trick to try. Close your eyes and look up at the sun. Wait until the director says "Roll it," then open your eyes, look at your dad, and say your lines." It worked.

I'm sure various precautions and standards were put into place for all of the actors, but on every series in which I did a guest star spot, there was no special treatment or pampering for kids. If you were school age, then you were expected to be prepared and put in a day's work, like any of the adult actors. I know there were restrictions on the length of time a production could work a kid during a shoot, but between the mandatory school lessons on set and the filming, it was still an eight-hour day. There were no treats or trophies for "job well done"; there was no kids' area set up for recreation; no one checked in to make sure your self-esteem was healthy. The expectation was to "know your lines, take direction, and act." I never felt deprived or mistreated in any way. It was how it was. If I needed even a glass of water, my mom was somewhere standing behind the camera line.

My episode of *Lassie* played on Christmas Eve that year. We watched it as a family and my father took photos of the TV screen when I was on it and when the credits rolled. My enthusiastic dad would always create an ad to run in *The Hollywood Reporter* and *Variety* the day before one of my guest star episodes aired. This was long before easy computer graphic designs. He had to design and create by hand an ad to the paper's specifications and deliver it before their deadline. It was his way of keeping my face in front of producers and casting professionals.

When I didn't have auditions or studio work, my mom and I would occasionally drive out of the city and look at horses in their pastures or she would take me to Jungleland in Thousand Oaks, a privately owned zoo that trained animals that were often used in the movie industry. Jungleland had camels and elephants, a giraffe or two, and cages of lions and tigers. Every Leo the Lion that roars at the beginning of every MGM movie came from Jungleland. Mom and I would stop and get a McDonald's cheeseburger, fries, and a Coke, and then go watch Mabel Stark and her big cats perform. Mabel had been an animal trainer with the circus since the 1920s and was now semiretired and working at Jungleland. It was pretty incredible to watch this woman in her seventies fearlessly stand in a large enclosed outdoor cage, surrounded by six or more five-hundred-pound tigers. She would have them do tricks as the crowd cheered it all on from the bleachers. My mother liked to stay for the lion-feeding time when the keepers would slide big slabs of raw meat under the bars of the cement enclosed cages. During one trip my mother bought a ticket for me to ride in the basket on the back of an elephant, which is not unlike riding in a jeep through a rocky riverbed, a lot of jostling. Once was enough. I'm sure none of what went on at Jungleland would have passed animal welfare laws today, but, once again, the mid-1960s were a time of slow awakening.

Being cast on a Western TV series, such as *The Big Valley* and *The Virginian*, were acting jobs that I really liked, and my mother did, too. It was fun to be around the horses, the trained animals, and other livestock brought in for the sake of realism. I loved the dusty streets with the fake facades of a saloon, a rustic hotel, and other Western town buildings and the sound of the horse hooves as they were ridden through a scene and then tied to a hitching post. My mother was thrilled to be up close to Barbara Stanwyck and Richard Long, even though I had no idea who they were.

In private, my mother was a big-time talker. As she would drive me to auditions, or to the studios and back, she would talk nonstop. She always described herself as having "nickel knowledge," meaning she knew a little bit about many subjects. On the way to my first day of filming one of my three guest star roles on *The Big Valley*, she filled me in on all of the movies Barbara Stanwyck had been in, how she was a famous femme fatale of her era, the male stars she had acted with, and the awards she had been nominated for and those she had won.

One episode of *The Big Valley,* "Hide the Children,"

was about the threat of a band of Gypsies kidnapping the children of the town, a rumor spreading like wildfire and is soon proven false.

Any character descriptions outside of Caucasian race and ethnicity, such as the Romani Gypsies or Native Americans, on a TV Western were usually played by Italian actors with shiny bronzed makeup. There were no people of color on camera or even behind the scenes in the crew. I don't remember it ever being questioned. It was sadly acceptable for its time. However, even at age eight, I could tell that TV Westerns didn't really represent the early Western life I had read about in the Time-Life books on my parents' shelves. From the photos in the books, it didn't look like the trailblazer women of the West wore blue eye shadow and fake eyelashes in 1880. Their hair was pulled back in rough buns and wasn't teased and sprayed into a cascading Tammy Wynette platinum blond country-music style. Frontier men weren't clean shaven with conditioned cuticles. But every show was make-believe and even the glaring reflector lamps in what should have been a dingy and dirty barn was how TV was made.

The older woman, Celia Lovsky, playing a Gypsy matriarch on *The Big Valley* asked me if I wanted to see the newborn kittens in her trailer. *Baby kittens?!* Sure. Why not?

I don't know if my mother was so entranced by watching Barbara Stanwyck act that she didn't see me walk off set with this character actress, but there was suddenly a panicked search at the location. It seemed I had gone missing.

Someone managed to locate me, sitting on the floor of a trailer cuddling a lap filled with kittens. Boy, did my mother ever give me the big talking-to over that unintentional disappearing act. I would never "go off, looking at kittens" without her permission, ever again.

Every guest star role I played gave me more experience and insight into what it meant to be a professional; for the "Hide the Children" episode of *The Big Valley*, I literally stepped into the dress of perhaps the most famous child actress ever to be on film. For this episode, the women's costumer brought me a dress to wear in an upcoming scene. As my mother took it off the hanger, she gasped when she saw the name tag sewn into the collar line. The dress had been worn by Shirley Temple in one of her movies. I had watched many Shirley Temple movies with my parents, from the earliest years of my life that I can remember. My parents were enthralled with her young talent and how she lit up the screen. I think they wanted the same type of fame for me. I knew I'd never be the triple talent of Shirley Temple, because I didn't possess her dance skills, but being given the dress to wear felt like the direction of "now it's your turn" to my little nine-year-old self. It was a big "dress" to step into and I knew it was my honor to wear it. The episode had me trapped in a well, so I was in an enclosed ten-foot-high set with me at the bottom, with some dirt and small pebbles dropped down on me during the takes, which made it easy to cry. The beautiful Gypsy woman, played by Louise Sorel, is lowered down to save me and the Gypsy reputation. After the scene was filmed, my mother took me to the ladies room to vigorously brush the dirt out of my hair and quickly get ready for the next scene. No time to worry about any dark, well-induced trauma, and there wasn't any. I took it in stride that I had this adventurous job to do.

About eight months after filming *Lassie,* I was cast on the TV Western *Lancer*. I played a tough-talking orphan named Pony Alice, who is being raised in a barn by my drunk uncle, who is a deceitful horse trader. He puts me up for sale, knowing he is terminally ill and won't live long enough to raise me. It was quite the plot, filled with action. I had many lines to learn and every scene required the full range of emotions. It was the first show that I earned my own credit panel on the TV screen, with my name alone: *Eve Plumb as Pony Alice*.

As word has it, the scene in Quentin Tarantino's 2019 film, *Once Upon a Time in Hollywood*, with Leonardo DiCaprio as a fading movie star discussing acting and books during a lunch break on a Western set with a small girl, actress Julia Butters, was inspired by my guest star role in *Lancer*. I asked Quentin about it, and he said the character was sort of a three-way combination of myself, Melissa Gilbert, and Jodie Foster. I appreciated the nod, but even though I was precocious for my age, I never would have been as assertive or opinionated with adult actors as the fictional little actress Trudi Fraser was in this film.

I mostly thought my guest star role on *Lancer* was a really great job because I got to be around horses and other animals. In one scene Pony Alice is yanked from a galloping horse and pulled over to the saddle of a galloping horse with the rider running parallel at a fast speed. They brought in a stunt double for the actual action, as much as I would have loved to do it myself. In that scene, shot from a distance, I was played by an adult male little person, dressed to match my character's outfit of flannel shirt and overalls. He had to wear a long blond wig pulled back into a ponytail. If you paused the screen, you'd notice that ten-year-old Pony Alice now weighs about 110 pounds and has muscular arms and an adult-sized head. Currently, with everything digitized and able to be played back in slow motion, TV viewers would point it out immediately.

In one scene I am hiding out in the barn cuddling a newborn puppy. The assistant director brought in a crate full of puppies that his own dog had given birth to recently. They were all weaned; and after one was chosen for the scene, he offered the cast and crew the chance to adopt one of the puppies. I asked my parents if I could have one.

I had already had a few pets: a couple of goldfish that lived probably longer than my parents were hoping they would, considering I didn't clean the bowl. There was a Siamese cat, Daisy, who was my parents' pet when I was born. She was good-natured enough to let me dress her up in doll clothes, but it's not like she ran to the door in excitement when I would come home from school.

My parents must have discussed it because on the last day of filming I brought home the runt of the litter, a tiny black-and-white spaniel-type puppy. I gave her my character's name and extended it out: Pony Alice Guthrie Lancer Plumb. She was my first dog and became more of my parents' dog when I left home eight years later. I guess it's true what is often said of dogs: They provide unconditional love without you having to do much at all. After a day in the car with my mother's constant chatter, or being on the set with directions and dialogue and school lessons, it was good to be around a pal who had nothing to say to me that couldn't be expressed through a wagging tail.

Pony Alice was my first dog, and Maggie was probably my last.

When Maggie began getting ill in her dotage, Ken and I knew she would most likely be our final pet. We live in a Manhattan high-rise, so walking the dog three or four times a day was a necessity. Like I've done with all of my dogs in the past, we jumped through all of the geriatric pet hoops to keep her with us as long as possible. In the end she was taking more prescription drugs than Ken and I were together. As long as she still seemed content, we wanted her to stay alive. One weekend during a trip to upstate New York, it became obvious that her organs were shutting down. We scrambled back to the city and to the vet's the next morning and said goodbye to our one-eyed terrier, who had a rough beginning to her life and then years of toys and car adventures and pampering to make up for it.

After a couple of days of grieving, Ken and I packed up her dog beds and leashes, bowls and blankets, and dropped them off to the ASPCA to be used for shelter dogs.

Despite my lifelong appreciation for the lack of verbal skills in all of my pets, it seems to be eerily quiet in our apartment now.

Every Christmas holiday season, we bring the boxes of decorations up from storage. We make the apartment festive and hold a holiday get-together in mid-December. Maggie's stocking will be in one of the boxes. It's the one thing I couldn't let go.

I usually cry and sometimes I can't stop.

Chapter Four

In 1968 I was exactly where countless women wished they could be, with my arms wrapped around the neck of an American sex symbol. I was a guest star on *It Takes a Thief*, in an episode in which the ever-handsome Robert Wagner rescues me from kidnappers. He lifts me out of an apartment-building window and then carries me piggyback down the fire escape ladder for many floors to a getaway car. I didn't mind it at all, keeping my face tucked into his neck. He smelled like expensive aftershave, stage pancake makeup, and Clubman talcum powder. The best part was that I got to be in all of the action scenes. The producers had hired a little person, a male, in a little-girl dress that matched my own costume and a long blond wig. He was, originally, supposed to be my stunt double in the scenes where Robert Wagner lifts me over rooftops and carries me down metal ladders attached to building walls. However, the director couldn't shoot the scene with any close-ups without it looking like Robert was carrying an adult man, dressed as a little girl, on his back. The stunt double stood to the side, smoking cigarettes, as I happily stepped in to do the action scenes with Robert.

In most of my guest star roles, from ages seven to eleven, I shared the screen with a handsome actor: James Drury in *The Virginian*, Peter Breck and Lee Majors in *The Big Valley*, and the exquisite Robert Wagner in *It Takes a Thief*. I was used to having to play a little girl in desperate need of saving. Because I was small for my age, most of my scenes called for me to be lifted, carried, cradled, piggybacked, and perched on the lap or in the arms of the leading man. For the directors it was easier to get the two-shot if I was lifted up, instead of the star bending over or kneeling down.

I had already absorbed my mother's "the man is the boss" point of view and had witnessed how she applied it in real life. As a 1960s wife-homemaker, and now nontypical stage mother, she was always respectful of professionals, observant and not intrusive, and made certain that I was the same. My father instructed me to shake hands with a firm, self-confident grip and say, "Nice to meet you, Mr. Last Name Only." My mother reminded me to "smile, Eve."

I wanted to avoid all criticism so I learned quickly to act in a way that the stars of the show and the director (always a man during that era) could appreciate what a miniprofessional I was. I stuck to the actual script, which told me who I was and what to say. Otherwise, I rarely spoke. I had to keep up with the adults and also stay in my lane as a child. My mother noted in one of her datebooks from that era: *Word is getting around about Eve being very professional.*

If the camera wasn't rolling, I was incredibly shy and would prefer to avoid unnecessary attention. I didn't feel like I knew what to talk about with the adult actors, especially the stars of the show, outside of responding to any question that was directed at me. Acting was easy; real life was awkward.

Attending regular public school became more socially and personally awkward as I passed on up the grade levels in elementary school. I would be absent for entire weeks due to filming schedules and return to a feeling of having missed out. I was never left out, but I knew that there was a limit to what I had in common with other children. The other children were growing up all together. I was growing up with famous faces from television: James Arness, Mike Connors, and Brian Keith. When I entered sixth grade, I had a teacher who threw shade if I was out for any amount of time for an acting job. She would vocally intone, in an eye-rolling way, to the rest of the class that I wouldn't be there because I was "an actress." Her barely disguised passive-aggressive treatment left me feeling harshly criticized. I couldn't describe to my parents what was going on or change what I was doing as a child actor, so I began having psychosomatic illnesses, like sore throats and stomachaches, to avoid going to school. My parents caught on and I'm sure my mother suffered from this teacher's attitude as well when she went to collect my school work, so they transferred me to a local private school. I doubt they criticized or complained about the public-school teacher, but I was told later that the school was refusing to accept my on-set school hours as a school day. My parents didn't get argumentative about it with the public school, most likely accepting that "regular" people wouldn't understand how show business actually works.

I don't know who researched my new school, or if they did at all, but it was more like the Island of Misfit Toys in *Rudolph the Red-Nosed Reindeer*. The students were kids who were expelled from other schools, transient foster kids, or children whose parents wanted a less-rigid environment. It wasn't pricey or elitist like other private schools could be. I'm sure it fit my mother's comfort level of not having to explain or be challenged about my absent weeks for acting jobs. It made me feel more at ease, too, as everyone who attended was stand-apart unique in one way or another.

At the conclusion of every commercial or guest star job, my dad would take me to the unemployment office in Van Nuys to file a claim. Other actors did the same and he was going to make sure I had that opportunity. We would have to fill out a form that covered two weeks of work, take it to a woman seated behind a glass window with a small opening on the countertop, who was surrounded by trays full of forms and bunches of pens rubber-banded together. She would begin the process of filling various paperwork with multiple carbon copies, then snapping open her ink pad and stamping each page with great authorizing force. After what seemed endless minutes, she would slide a piece of paper back out through the opening in the glass. We would take that form to yet another window and the clerk would count out cash into my father's hand. I wasn't sure what it all meant, but my dad would explain, "This is your money. You paid into this fund, so we are getting it back now."

"My money" was never handed over to me. My father kept a meticulous ledger of every dime I made and what I was allotted for unemployment, as well as a record of paying Helen her percentage for my acting jobs. I remember standing at his elbow one time when he registered one of my paychecks in his books. It was something like $87.50. I timidly asked him if I could have the fifty cents.

He told me, "All of this is your money and it goes in the bank for you. If you'd like, we can give you fifty cents a week for an allowance for doing things like emptying the dishwasher."

I don't ever remember being denied money for something that I really needed or wanted, despite the fact that I probably never emptied the dishwasher.

He wanted me to understand the value of money, what was necessary to spend, and what was an indulgence. One day on the way home from the unemployment office, we stopped at a newsstand that had a circular rack of comic books. I was allowed to choose one.

When we got home, my father recounted to my mother how I had looked a gift horse in the mouth and asked for several comic books instead of one. I'm sure he wanted me to hear what he was saying as a lesson in moderation, but it involved enough shame for me to remember the feeling of it to this day. He was a man who appreciated all resources and didn't allow for waste if it could be avoided. I briefly left the water running in the kitchen sink one time and my father told me to turn it off. I dared to ask why, saying that "it's just water." He replied, "Have you ever gone a full day without water? It's a precious resource." It couldn't be argued. Lesson learned. And, to this day, I watch my water usage and cringe when I see it being wasted for no reason.

I have no doubt that my parents had the best intentions for me. They never promoted my career to their personal advantage, only mine. In their motivation to preserve my confidence, I absorbed the message that they found me to be exceptional and I had to remain exceptional through their guidance and protection. I took ballet classes to be coordinated and graceful, and because my mother had studied ballet for years as a girl. My father had me become a member of the Jimmy Joyce Children's Chorus. The adult choir appeared as regulars on *The Smothers Brothers Show*, and the small group of Jimmy Joyce children, ages seven to sixteen, which I joined, sang on the *Doctor Dolittle* soundtrack. Previous chorus members had recorded with Doris Day, which is probably how my father had the idea that it would be good for me to be involved. For about a year, my dad had me take private lessons from Richard Loring, a famous vocal coach who worked with Nat King Cole, Peggy Lee, and Barbra Streisand. Richard was tall and bald, with a gaunt face and dark circles under his eyes. I was intimidated and a bit frightened of him, though he gave me no reason to be, but I would never tell my father that. It was made clear that I was fortunate at age eight to study with a professional like Richard. I don't know why Richard agreed to take me on as a student, except he and my dad had become friends through RCA and he owned the apartment building that we rented in Laguna every summer. The fear of criticism or of disappointing an adult permeated my actions, especially at work. I wanted to get it right, to do it properly.

One of our neighbors taught judo lessons to kids at a studio in Glendale and scuba-diving lessons in his backyard pool. He and his wife had two kids, a little boy about my age who became a playmate and a one-year-old baby girl. His wife was an overnight nurse at a hospital and would sleep during the daytime. I would sometimes keep the baby entertained while she napped. His son had delicate features and was small for his age and struggled desperately to be the "tough-guy" figure his father expected of him. On summer afternoons the boy and some other neighborhood kids and I would occasionally swim in their pool while his dad supposedly monitored us. Next to the pool was an open tiki hut with stacks of pornographic magazines with women in salacious and compromising positions. The other kids and I would sit on the floor and look at the images with wide, disbelieving eyes. We never told our parents of the magazines, thinking we would be scolded for looking at them ourselves. In the 1960s no one spoke of grooming a child for predatory purposes; but looking back, I'm sure this neighbor man was not unaware that we had found his magazines.

He convinced my parents that judo lessons would be "good for Eve. She's small and needs to learn how to protect herself." That appealed to my parents, so I was enrolled and would attend on Saturday mornings.

My parents decided that judo would be helpful; however, learning to ride a two-wheel bike was too high on their danger scale of injury. I was embarrassed at age ten that I didn't own or know how to ride a two-wheel bike as other kids zoomed up and down the street on theirs. I borrowed a bike to give it a go when I thought my parents couldn't be watching. Moments later I tipped over, hitting my face on the curb. I couldn't go inside with a telltale lump and a scrape on my face, so I decided to ring my neighbor's doorbell, hoping that the wife's nursing skills could make my injury disappear. The door was answered by her husband, my judo teacher. He invited me in, directing me to wait for her on the couch because his wife was still sleeping in the bedroom. As soon as I sat down, he turned me on to my back and lay on top of me and tried to kiss my mouth. I could smell his Hai Karate aftershave as his hands pressed down my shoulders. I somehow managed to slide out sideways from under him and scrambled to the front door as fast as possible.

In an industry where it was almost expected that little

girls, and sometimes little boys, should be perched on grown men's laps or be physically moved around on the set by them (see numerous photos of a young Shirley Temple on the laps of various directors and male co-stars), I had never had it cross over into any type of predatory or even sexual suggestion on a TV series or commercial set. Undoubtedly, other past child actors have vivid accounts of blatant sexual abuse that scarred their young lives, but I was lucky enough to act with and be around adults in the industry who didn't take advantage of a child. That's not to say I didn't face what was acceptable sexualization of a young teen girl in the late 1960s and early '70s. I would have to shrug away from "too-friendly" attention from men, all the while smiling. Gratefully, my mother's watchful eye was usually on the scene, so that would be the extent of it. I'm sure my parents never thought I would need protection from my own judo instructor.

After I had escaped his sexual advance, I was frightened and stunned and ran home, where I knew I'd be scolded about the black-and-blue bruise forming on my face. I stayed silent about our judo neighbor, concerned that I might make an adult angry. The next Saturday I told my parents that I didn't like judo and never wanted to go again. They didn't press it with me. Neither did the neighbor.

One day I was playing with two little girls who were sisters, Cary and Julie, in their backyard a few houses away. My mother had said that I could be there, but soon after my dad walked over to get me, saying I needed to come home. I couldn't figure out what I had done, but once outside of Cary and Julie's earshot, he explained that he was taking me to a matinee of The Beatles' *A Hard Day's Night* movie that had just come out. He didn't want to have to invite the other kids. We rarely went to movie theaters, so I was happy to spend the afternoon with my dad. The theater was full of older teen girls, and as soon as The Beatles came on the screen, they started shrieking as though the group was live on the stage. I couldn't understand why they were screaming about four boys in matching jackets as we struggled to hear the dialogue of the movie. My father must have needed to see the full movie as a record producer; otherwise, I doubt he would have stayed for the whole thing with the hysteria in the movie house. Two years later, when The Monkees began their TV series in 1966, I understood the appeal of four cute boys in matching jackets, and like millions of little girls, I had a starry-eyed crush on Davy Jones. So many kids and teens watched this TV show about a fictional band that Columbia Pictures decided to evolve them into a legit band and my father signed The Monkees to RCA.

I got to meet The Monkees more than once in the lobby of the RCA recording studio. I was invited to watch them from the engineer side of the recording booth while they recorded the single "Shades of Gray." I was intrigued by their boldness and when they used poster paint to draw peace symbols, hearts, and hip words on the glass separating the recording area from the engineers. They represented the power of the 1960s youth movement, right there before my eyes, with its freedom of expression and unapologetic break with traditional manners and style. It was fascinating to watch these four guys who believed they had the right to do whatever they chose to do, including goofing around, without concern about whether or not it appeared professional. I thought they were so cool.

My father photographed me sitting on Davy Jones's lap. It seemed perfectly acceptable and expected. At one point Davy asked my age and remarked to the room in general that he would wait for me to grow up so he could marry me.

My father enlarged that photo to an 8 x 10 and my mom included it in the valise leather portfolio case that I carried into every audition with me that was called my "interview book." It had a thick yellow brass zipper and handles that retracted into the case, which held a three-ring binder. Inside were enlarged photos of me on the set of *The Virginian*, my typed-up résumé, headshots of me smiling or looking pensive, and photos of me posing with Anthony Newley and the Jimmy Joyce singers as we recorded for the 1967 film *Doctor Dolittle*. The more my mother put into the book, the more excruciatingly embarrassed I was to hand it over to casting directors. I had zero propensity for self-promotion as a child and it has barely metered up to about 3 percent as an adult, and only due to occasional posts on social media.

I hung an autographed press photo of The Monkees sitting in director's chairs on the wall of my bedroom. Three years later it was replaced by a poster of David Cassidy from yet another fictional band.

I was having a costume fitting at the studio lot one day when my mother rose from her chair to show me an article in *Variety*. "Look at this. Davy Jones has been secretly married for almost a year!"

Did she actually believe he would wait for me to become an adult and then propose marriage?

Marriage was the theme of *The Brady Bunch* pilot in which the "lovely lady" wedded a man named "Brady," and my first day on the job was in a leased backyard of a home in the Los Angeles valley. I'm sure I had gone to

Paramount Studios for wardrobe fittings, especially the matching long pink satin gowns that Maureen, Susan, and I wore for the wedding day filming. A converted school bus was parked in front of the house and was used as our required classroom, modified with bench seats and narrow tables for desks. It was there I had a chance to spend time with my new castmates playing my sisters and brothers. For the first time in my career, I was working with a group of children on our own series and we all had equal roles. The idea of having possible pals around my age on an acting job was a fun change for me.

The backyard was supposed to belong to Carol's parents and was set up with folding chairs, covered tables holding flowers and dinnerware, tuxedoed waiters and a four-tier wedding cake. Background actors in wedding guest apparel filled the chairs. It was clear from the beginning that there was much at stake for the whole outdoor wedding scene to go off as planned. The most unpredictable elements were the trained film animals, a cat and a dog. The girls' cat, Fluffy, is chased by the boys' dog, Tiger, throughout the backyard, over the laps of guests, under and on top of tables, causing havoc and destruction. Everything, pre-chaos, was filmed over the course of a couple of days, standing in bright sunlight, holding bouquets of flowers, as our parents said their vows and all the various angles on the scene were shot. While they were setting up the cameras for the next shot, the six kids would climb into the non–air-conditioned school bus, still in our wedding formal wear, for a portion of the required three hours of schooling. There was no time to change clothes, so we had to wear light robes over our costumes to keep them wrinkle and stain-free. There were no backup dresses, so there couldn't be any accidents with food or drinks.

Each scene of havoc caused by the dog and cat needed to be shot in one take. It would be impossible to repeat actions like chairs tipping over, guests falling to the ground, buckets of ice going down an auntie's cleavage, tablecloths going askew and flower arrangements crashing. But, most importantly, the wedding cake needed to slide down the length of a table and precisely into Robert Reed's hands as everyone breathed a sigh of relief. When Florence Henderson comes to hug him, he goes off balance and the entire cake tips over, smashing into his face and tuxedo. Florence ends up kissing him and getting cake on her face and dress. There could be no do-overs for that scene. The director stressed the importance of following the blocking precisely and we took it very seriously, until the denouement moment. The cake landed perfectly on Robert Reed's face and chest. After kissing him, Florence flicked the frosting off her hand and a sizable amount landed directly on the crotch of Robert's black tuxedo pants. The whole set—crew, director, the extra actors, and our mothers—all erupted in laughter. I was perplexed. After the director yelled "Cut," I went to my mother to ask what was so funny. I didn't get the joke. She told me about the frosting, but I was still too young to get the implication. Because the scene couldn't be done over, it went to print, as it was.

The rest of the pilot episode was shot at Stage 5 on the Paramount lot, with a set for Florence's pre-marriage bedroom, the Brady boys' kitchen, and the hotel lobby that appears in the last scene of the pilot, where we all march, in order of age and size, up the stairs to our parents' honeymoon suite. My job was to handle the cat carrier holding Fluffy. I don't know why a cat who lived in a doghouse in our backyard needed to go to the hotel with us, and no one seemed to be transporting a litter box, but that's what was happening. It was a heavy carry for a small kid and I was ready for that scene to wrap. Fans often ask me, "What happened to Fluffy? He was never seen again." I'm guessing he's in "lost luggage" at thc hotel?

I must have been protected from reading the reviews of the pilot episode of *The Brady Bunch* because the cross-media panning of the episode was pretty thorough. If a show with low viewership and bad reviews aired today, its first episode would be its last. But it was 1969 and ABC needed a show to anchor their Friday-night family-viewing time slot, and so, to the delight of my parents, the show went forward.

It may have been the pacing of those first days of shooting *The Brady Bunch* that established the expectations on our young lives as actors on the show. Everything moved along quickly. There was no time to do scenes over and over again, and so our dog, Tiger, quickly became an inconvenient holdup to getting an episode in the can. The original Tiger was supposedly hit by a florist truck, according to Barry Williams, and his replacement was unpredictable and impulsive. After two additional episodes, Tiger number two was released from his contract. Only the doghouse remained on the set, supposedly to cover a burn mark in the Astroturf created by hot lighting equipment. There was no time for do-overs. Everyone needed to show up with their lines memorized, ready to go. I don't think we ever had table reads or thoughtful explorations of our individual characters. The writers weren't on standby on the set to see if their lines came off well. They were working on the next script for the next episode. Once the script was approved, we filmed it as written, even swallowing our embarrassment at having to say phrases like "far out" and "groovy."

Season 1 of *The Brady Bunch* had twenty-five episodes. For half of the next year, after ten years of being like an only child, I would spend eight hours a day with my new family, especially my new brothers and sisters: Maureen McCormick and Barry Williams, Susan Olsen and Mike Lookinland, and especially Chris Knight. Our socialization was no longer a classroom of twenty-eight other kids, or entire school yards full of children, it was with each other, the six of us. Unlike acting with adults, and being the only child on set, we became each other's schoolmates, playmates, and family members. But we were still growing kids, trying to figure out where we fit in with each other. Though we played brothers and sisters, it wasn't before long that Maureen was smitten with Barry, Susan and Mike pretended to get married at age seven, and I soon had a crush on Chris, who exuded charisma, even at age ten, along with being a very kindhearted boy. I know he was the heartthrob of many *Brady Bunch* girl fans. They've told me so.

Chris and his wife, Cara, and Ken and I still gather for monthly cocktail hours over Zoom, since we are in Manhattan and they are in Los Angeles. Fifty-five years after meeting Chris, his charisma and charm still come through on screen.

Chapter Five

Somewhere in my ten-year-old mind, I sensed that my life was about to change. I had done two previous pilots that never became a series, *The Barbara Rush Show* and *Dick Tracy*, but I had a different feeling about this one. After the pilot episode for *The Brady Bunch* was filmed, there was a drawn-out pause waiting to hear if the show would be bought by one of the networks. When Helen called my parents with the news that the show was a "go-ahead" on ABC for the first thirteen episodes, I wasn't sure how to react. My parents were over the moon that I would be a cast member on a regular series.

My mother and I went to the RCA building to meet up with my dad for dinner the next evening. About once a month, we would dress up and go as a family of three to Martoni's restaurant in Hollywood. The classic Italian restaurant, with its red leather booths, checkered tablecloths, and highly polished dark wood bar, was a see-and-be-seen place for people in the music industry. I was often the only child in a restaurant full of adults, some of them making record deals in the corner banquettes. I remembered to sit up properly, no slouching at the table. My parents were both still beaming about *The Brady Bunch* pickup and allowed me to choose whatever I wanted from the menu that night. I ordered a plate of spaghetti and a side of baked potato with butter, and spumoni for dessert. I thought it was decadent. I'm sure the waiter checked my parents to make sure that was really the order for this sixty-pound little girl.

After dinner my father returned to his office for a few hours, and my mother and I went home. She was reading on her bed when I climbed up beside her with my own book, hoping to get swept up in my *Masters of Horror* paperback. I felt unsettled, but not because a clawed skeletal hand had burst through the cemetery plot in the story I was reading or any jitters from my double starch-and-sugar dinner. It was about *The Brady Bunch*. It would be the first time I would be playing a girl who wasn't in a life-or-death situation. What would make the show interesting for so many episodes? I had a growing awareness that there were serious issues going on in the world and there was nothing serious about this new sitcom I would be on.

It was 1968 and the world seemed full turmoil to me. My brother was in Vietnam, I thought Watts was in a constant state of rioting, and Ecology, as we called the environment then, was in peril. I remember a song, "In the Year 2525," in which technology doomed us all. My sister, June, was sharing a rented house with her live-in boyfriend in Beverly Glen at that time. Despite my parents' opinion that she was "living in sin," there was no doubt that the times were "a-changing" with the social and political movements and the serious anthems of the rising folk-music artists. June became my early role model of what it would mean to be a girl and a woman in the new 1970s decade, which was right around the corner, including giving me a subscription to *Ms.* magazine in its launch year. She was into nutrition and health food supplements, and was vocal about the anti-smog and anti-pollution campaigns. I'm sure my STAMP OUT SMOG sticker that I put on my bedroom door came from time spent with June, along with the GIVE A HOOT, DON'T POLLUTE sticker that joined it the following year. My parents allowed me to plaster my bedroom door with bumper stickers because my mother didn't want them on the car. She was afraid it would attract anger from other drivers who might have a different point of view than what the sticker promoted. It was obvious that Los Angeles was being choked with smog. Driving the freeways from the Valley to Hollywood and back, you could see the thick ring of brownish-yellow air pollution hovering at the skyline. There were often weekly smog alerts where it was advised that everyone stay inside, including for school recess.

I closed my book and sat up next to my mother and told her that I had grave misgivings about this new project.

"It's not at all serious or important to society. It's not going to help people," I told her with my most earnest voice.

My mother, who had lived through the Depression and World War ll, told me in a patient way that the world may always have its troubles, but that people need entertainment, and that it was all right to do a comedy show that would make people laugh.

I let myself be reassured by this explanation. I was aware that as these acting jobs came along, it was my and the family's job to follow through. Even though my parents saw good money and a good career opportunity for me, they wouldn't have forced me to do it. However, I knew that if I made an objection, I would be reminded of the responsibility to commitment. I sensed that this one was going to be different, it was a new show with a large cast, and I would be part of it. It was a little scary.

I followed through with my commitment and soon got comfortable in the make-believe world of the Bradys, where the current war in Vietnam, rising women's rights movement, civil rights activities, environmental concerns, Watergate scandal, and other national current headlines of the year were never, ever acknowledged. If *The Brady Bunch* was put in a time capsule that people hundreds of years from now found, the most American culture they would derive from the series is that one shouldn't "play ball in the house," where arty vases might get broken. It was purposefully designed that way by show creator Sherwood Schwartz. His vision was to keep it contained to the Brady home by having one family problem, one solution, and one happy ending in every show. Our blended American family lived in an idyllic neighborhood, in a modern house with bedrooms large enough for three girls, and one for three boys, and a bedroom for a personal housekeeper, who never ate at the table with us, but seemed to be available morning, noon, and night for whatever was going on. In my personal life, I didn't know anyone who had a housekeeper or even a nanny.

Again the TV critics slammed the premise, but there were enough viewers to keep us on the air. Unlike my mom's reasoning in favor of *The Brady Bunch*, I don't think the viewers were escaping the issues of the time. I think they were kids who wished they lived a Brady lifestyle, with caring parents, a funny housekeeper to do their laundry, and food in the fridge. I'm sure no one expected the show to still be on the air daily fifty-plus years later, or to have become a part of pop culture and television history as it has. I can now see the wisdom in Sherwood's idea to keep the premise to the nuclear family, because family relationships are evergreen in relatability, despite the 1970s look of the show.

On day one of filming the show, my mother and I arrived at Paramount Studios on foot. The parents of child actors were not given parking spaces on the studio lot, at least not for season 1. We parked in a lot across the street and paid the booth attendant, who had his windows covered with photos of sexy calendar girls and double-entendre fake diamond-shaped traffic signs with warnings like CURVES AHEAD. How very 1969 that no employer questioned his decorating choices for a public parking-lot pay booth. We next checked in at the Paramount gate, where my mother introduced herself and me to the gate guards and began a five-year "nice to see you" acquaintance with the men who worked there. They were always gracious about the Christmas fruitcakes she gifted them with every December. It was still an era when fruitcake was a treat that people actually ate.

Once we made our way to Stage 5, we were shown to the dressing room for girls. It was one of 3 rooms in a hallway that had been created by putting a roof over the alley between Stage 5 and Stage 6, and the room next to it was for the boys to use. Maureen, Susan, and I had to squeeze into this very small room, along with our mothers and two female wardrobe crew members, and perhaps a hair and makeup person. We were like a bunch of nervous sardines—it was tight. After about six or seven episodes, the producers decided it wasn't working. There was no place for us to go if we weren't filming except the schoolroom, which was equally small, or to stand out in the alleyway until we were called in for a scene. We arrived one early morning to find six identical metal boxes on wheels about ten feet by eight, that were portable film set dressing rooms from 1940s moviemaking days. They lined them up like train cars between stages 5 and 6. We were excited to each have our own dressing room, with a Dutch door on the end, holding our name plaque. Inside was a small daybed, a makeup table with Hollywood style lit mirror, a chair, and a clothing rack for our wardrobe for the day. The similar dressing rooms for the adults (Robert Reed, Ann B. Davis, and Florence Henderson) were all inside Stage 5, near the set. We didn't venture into those, unless we were invited by one of them to step inside.

We filmed the opening title for season 1 in front of the bright blue background that gave the tic-tac-toe board design of the titles a uniform look. The girls were all on the right side of the screen looking out, so we had to look left to see our brothers, mother, and dad in the other squares. Nothing or no one was really there, because each person had to be filmed individually. On a galvanized steel pole frame were pieces of black electrical tape to mark where our eyes should land while pretending to see each of our siblings and parents and smiling big the whole time. The director would say, "Look up at the top piece of tape. That's Greg . . . Now look straight down at Cindy . . . Look directly left at Peter," while counting out the looks to be timed with the theme music. The first theme song was sung by The Peppermint Trolley Company pop band, and then we "kids" recorded it for the next season, sounding authentically like a bunch of kids and not very polished.

The opening titles were filmed again, four out of the five seasons, as we grew older but with our same recording. By season 3, I figured out that if I lifted only my eyes to look at Marcia, and not my whole head, the camera wasn't shooting directly up my nose

Rolling Stone magazine named our theme song as the second greatest theme song of all time, beating out *Friends*, *Laverne & Shirley*, and even *One Day at a Time*. It was definitely catchy. To this day people of all ages stopped randomly on any American street can probably sing the lyrics.

Stage 5 was the biggest soundstage on the Paramount lot and before it became *The Brady Bunch* stage, it was used to film the movies *The Graduate*, *Rosemary's Baby*, and *Yours, Mine and Ours*.

Every room that appears on the show was arranged in one long line-up across the stage floor, starting with the front door and living room through Mike Brady's office, the kitchen, the dining room, the den, and then the bedrooms. The whole show was filmed with one camera that sat on a wheeled dolly base that could be rolled to wherever needed. Unlike the current video possibilities, there were no monitors or playback opportunities with film. Every take would start with the clapboard that identified the scene number and the take letter. On scenes involving the whole cast and depending on the number of reaction shots needed, the takes would sometimes go beyond the twenty-six letters of the alphabet and start into double letters, AA, BB, CC, etc. The director, script supervisor, focus person, and sound person would all have to agree that a certain take was good for a print. The cameraperson would make a punch mark on the film and we'd move on to the next scene. At the end of the day, large canisters of film would be sent off to print for rushes the next day, which is where the director and editor can watch what was filmed the previous day to see if any scenes needed to be reshot.

I was always fascinated by how the technical aspects of the show worked, from the camera focus to the boom mics, even the props that were built to work correctly in one take. In one scene, where the girls are trying to build a clubhouse, the bag containing nails rips through on the bottom, spilling nails onto the yard. This was done with a little wooden box with a spring loaded breakaway bottom, hidden in the brown bag. On cue it could be triggered to open and the weight of the nails broke through the dampened paper. I was so fascinated by it that the props department gave it to me to take home. My dad, with his engineering training, was equally impressed.

Originally, the director, John Rich, suggested that the girls' room should have dresser drawers partially opened, with clothes spilling out, until the three of us let him know that our own parents would never allow that kind of disarray in our rooms at home. In a separate area was the front yard, driveway, and fake garage, which all had to be lit with overhead bright hot lamps to simulate sunshine. The staircase up to the bedrooms ended in a short rawwood platform at the top, with two-by-four railings. If all six kids had to go up the stairs in one scene, we had to squish together on the top platform, being very quiet until the director called "Cut." The same was true if we had to make an entrance from the second floor. We would try to stand quietly on the platform, waiting for our cue to enter. If Ann B. was "upstairs" with us, the platform would be so crowded I had fears of falling over the edge.

One of the other, slightly larger rooms in the hallway was converted to be used for our classroom. There were six school desks in two rows and the walls had bulletin boards. Every day that we were on the set to shoot an episode, we were required to have three full hours of school. The teacher was Frances Whitfield, an educator who was the mother of a child actress who had grown up. Frances understood how filming an episode worked and that we would be interrupted whenever we were needed on stage. She was a soft-spoken Southern woman with a no-nonsense attitude. At age ten I thought of her as being ancient, with her white hair and sensible shoes. She was only in her sixties. Many days our education was for twenty minutes at a time over an eight-hour day. The twenty-minute segments were required to make it count toward a school hour. Every time there was a break on the set, we would be hustled into the classroom for another twenty-minute session. It's often suspected that child actors never get much of an education. Considering how much more one-on-one attention we each received, and the lessons being crafted to the way we each learn best, I think I learned more and better than I had in public school. The school time was highly focused and we couldn't get away with anything. There was no messing around after she gave directions for the lesson. Probably the most valuable lesson I learned was to concentrate despite distractions. I might be reading a chapter while Frances was going over state capitals with Mike right behind me. Over the years other teachers would join the crew, once Maureen and Barry advanced in age to high school.

Outside of the required subjects, Frances paid attention to what we each liked to do as individuals, especially creatively. We filmed the show right through the summer months, and even when there wasn't graded work required, she kept us constantly busy. She was always enthusiastic about my art work and encouraged my learning to paint. When the walls of our classroom were covered with our artwork, Mike Lookinland's mom came up with the idea to decorate the unpainted scuffed-up doors and hallway that led to the stage. We made banners, like HAVE FUN IN '71 . . . ALL THE WAY THROUGH '72, and posters and pasted up collages of fan photos that were sent to us in the mail, along with their cards or letters. It became known as Brady Hall.

Our mothers were on the set every day as our legal guardians, and my mom formed an easy bond with the others. They were given chairs to sit in behind the cameraman and crew and out of our sight. I knew they were all watching us, but I was used to having my mom always be there, and I'm sure the other Brady kids were, too. If there was a short break for a camera reset, my mother would wave me over to brush my hair. Recently, Chris Knight told me with a laugh, "I can only picture your mom with a hairbrush in her hand."

I loved to listen in on the adult conversation between the moms as they commented about fashion, Hollywood gossip, and who said what to whom and when. I may not have known or understood the person or the subject they were talking about, but I was fascinated by their exchanges, most likely because I spent so much time with my own parents in adult worlds.

During our lunch breaks, we would have to hurry back into our street clothes and then all walk together over to the commissary on the old RKO lot, by then called Desilu and owned by Desi Arnaz and Lucille Ball. We would walk past the backlot of the Western town and the scenic department, where they painted all of the background flats, depending on what type of scenery was needed. A small door in the wall connected the two lots. The commissary was cafeteria style, so we'd get trays and order our hamburgers and grilled cheese sandwiches. The moms would have a table to themselves, leaving the kids at their own table. To make each other laugh, we'd play a game we called "Witches' Brew," by pouring salt or pepper and squeezing a mustard packet and ketchup into one another's water cups and daring each other to drink it. It would keep us amused until my mother noticed and came over to say, "Now you stop that. You're being wasteful."

On the way back, we'd run ahead of our moms to have time to race each other through the Western town and goof around to burn off energy. Then we'd have to hurry back into our on-camera wardrobe and either return to the set for filming or into the classroom for school.

The best lunch breaks were when we would go outside of the studio lot and cross the street to Oblath's Café for lunch with Florence Henderson. We would all pile into large horseshoe-shaped booths. She would always order a taco salad, which came in a big flour tortilla shaped like a bowl. Maureen and I would copy her order. If you could get through the lettuce, shredded cheese, and tomatoes on top, there was chicken and refried beans underneath. I'm not sure how much we enjoyed the salads, but we wanted to be like Florence. It was special to have time with her off the set.

Again, there really was no different treatment for the six of us than the adult actors. There was no coddling or expectation that anyone should be extra patient because we were children. No one was pampered or favored. We were expected to be as professional as the adults and we all did our best to live up to those expectations. It felt good to be treated like we were capable.

Unlike TV shows since the 1990s, there were no advertiser perks, no show jackets, no gifting boutiques, and no invitations to industry parties. The craft service table was a box of doughnuts and a coffeepot next to a tower of Styrofoam cups. Many in the crew smoked cigarettes, along with a few of the moms. There were no ashtrays, so everyone stomped out their cigarettes on the concrete floors, and the guy who handled the coffeepot was kept constantly busy with a broom and dustpan sweeping up cigarette butts.

Because it was the first season and Sherwood had to ask for every penny he got from the studio, the kids all wore recycled wardrobe from other TV shows that had been pulled from the warehouse. I was often dressed in tomboyish clothing, striped T-shirts and colored pants that were reinforced in the knee area. Susan Olsen, even though she was eight years old, had to wear little baby-doll–type dresses that were so short she couldn't bend at all without her underwear showing. Miniskirts were the fashion in the early 1970s, and before the end of the first season, the girls all had to be careful going up the stairs or sitting on the couch.

The director for the first five or six shows was John Rich, an Emmy-winning director for *The Dick Van Dyke Show* and a veteran TV director for *Gomer Pyle*, *Bonanza*, *Hogan's Heroes*, and many others. He was an excellent person to set the standard of expectations for the cast and crew of the show. Before he left *The Brady Bunch* to direct *All in the Family*, he called the six of us to the set. He had us sit, side by side, on the end of the bed in the parents' bedroom. His face looked quite serious as he advised us, "Listen, kids. This show could become big and you might become very well-known. You could become famous for a while; but most of the time, fame does not last. So remember who you are. Have fun with the show, but don't let the fame go to your heads."

I appreciated that John Rich had such optimism about the success of the show, but the truth is *The Brady Bunch* never cracked into ratings of the top twenty TV shows. In

A publicity photo of my mother, Flora, as a ballerina.

The eloping couple.

In Waikiki, 1939.

The beautiful blue tricycle.
(Author's personal collection)

With my sister, Flora June.
(Author's personal collection)

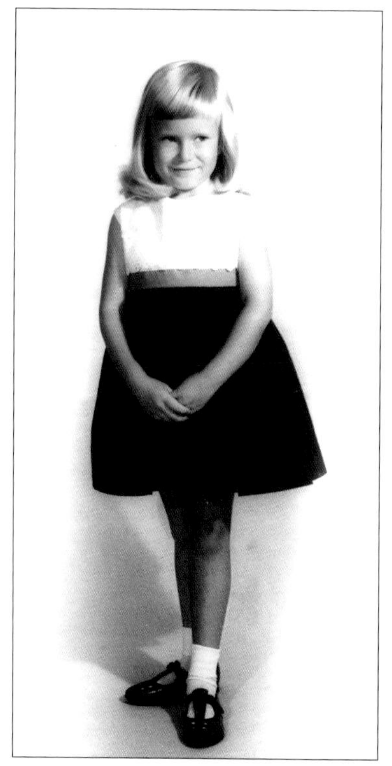

Early headshot.
(Author's personal collection)

Had to wear a bathing cap to swim in the pool.
(Author's personal collection)

Sea-Lor Apartments in Laguna Beach.
(Author's personal collection)

Favorite beach activity:
building a sandcastle.
(Author's personal collection)

Swings on Main Beach, Laguna.
(Author's personal collection)

Reading *Mad* magazine.
(Author's personal collection)

The Goya painting reproduction
that hung over the fireplace
in our living room.
(Author's personal collection)

Family Affair:
"Christmas Came a Little Early."
(Author's personal collection)

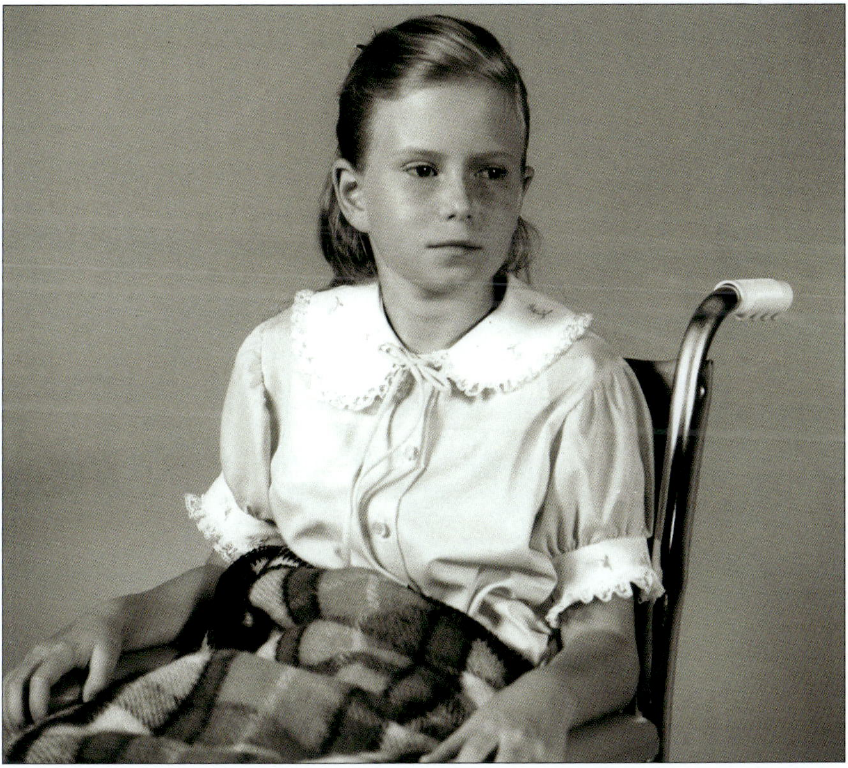

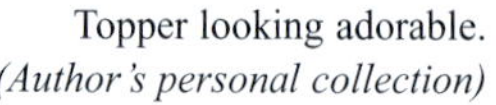

Topper looking adorable.
(Author's personal collection)

Sweet one-eyed Maggie.
(Author's personal collection)

My painting,
Woody, Woody, Woody.
He grew up to be so big.
(Author's personal collection)

At Rudd Weatherwax's house
to meet the Yorkie.
(Author's personal collection)

With Lassie, the best co-star.
(Author's personal collection)

On the backlot with
the Yorkie for *Lassie*.
(Author's personal collection)

The hungry lionesses.
(Author's personal collection)

Another western.
Am I the model for Tarantino?
(Author's personal collection)

With *Lancer* stunt double.
(Author's personal collection)

With *It Takes a Thief* stunt double.
(Author's personal collection)

With Pony Alice Guthrie Lancer Plumb.
(Author's personal collection)

With Daisy.
(Author's personal collection)

With Dick Loring.
(Author's personal collection)

Judo uniform.
(Author's personal collection)

With Davy Jones at RCA Studios.
(Author's personal collection)

"Interview book."
(Author's personal collection)

Paramount mural. Is that supposed to be us?
(Author's personal collection)

Teenage bedroom door,
now in the Valley Relics Museum.
(Author's personal collection)

My very own dressing room in the alley.
(Author's personal collection)

Kids' bathroom set for *The Brady Bunch*.
(Author's personal collection)

In the schoolroom
with Frances Whitfield
and Mike Lookinland.
(Author's personal collection)

Brady Hall, where I spent
five happy years.
(Author's personal collection)

Chris Knight in Brady Hall.
(Author's personal collection)

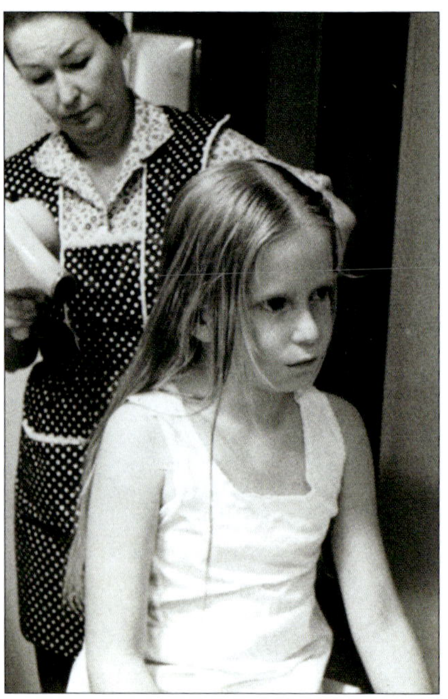

Mom was always working on my hair.
(Author's personal collection)

Oblath's restaurant matchbook cover.
(Author's personal collection)

Goofy Bradys.
(Author's personal collection)

the world of TV ratings, it was rather surprising that after the first thirteen episodes, the show was renewed for another twelve episodes for season 1. Friday was not a great night to air any TV show, at least for adult viewers, and ABC didn't have anything else that would work. However, there were hundreds of thousands of kids who were too young to go out on their own and too old to go to bed early, who tuned in on Friday nights while their parents did their own thing.

Once my parents knew that there would be an additional twelve episodes, and that we would be filming the show beyond the summer months and through the end of the year, they thought it was important to make sure I wasn't working too hard. Ballet and singing lessons ended. I only attended school on set. Since there would be no more camping trips that involved tents and driving for three or four hours each way, or two weeks away in Laguna in August, my mother wanted to find us an alternate weekend getaway. My father always subscribed to the daily *Hollywood Reporter* and *Variety*, which landed on our driveway every morning. In one issue of *Variety*, my mom spotted an ad for a tiny beach house in Malibu, with knotty pine–paneled walls and four rooms, that was for sale. It was on pillars in the sand and the ocean was about thirty yards from the deck. It was so tiny that from the road above, it looked like the garage of the more elaborate house next door. My mother thought it was the perfect weekend getaway, since it was only a thirty-minute drive from our house. My parents bought the beach property and every Friday we would pack a small suitcase and load the dog into the car and go. My parents insisted that we watch *The Brady Bunch* that evening and my father would take photos of the screen if I was in the scene. I would cringe listening to my voice and watching myself. At first, I loved the idea of having our own beach house and going to sleep with the sounds of the ocean so close. Saturdays and Sundays were spent outside on the sand and in the sunshine, where my hair got more blond and my skin was bronzed. My Malibu tan soon showed up on camera, and at one point the producers suggested to my mother that she keep me out of the sun on weekends, as I looked different from the other kids with my Coppertone-worthy face and arms. As reserved as my mother could be, she recalled the incident to my father that weekend by telling him that she had stood firm and told the producers no. She wanted me to be able to relax and have fun after a long week of school and working on the show. I'm guessing she thought it was equally good for my father to get away from his stressful job. It made an impression on me that my mother had the courage to say no to the producers. I absorbed the message that no is an answer that could be given, but it took me many years to feel comfortable using that answer to various requests.

Malibu seemed idyllic, but it was far more isolated than the beach property in Laguna. There was no place else to go besides the back deck and the sand. There were no snack stands or stores that you could walk to, since the road jutted down to the beach from the very busy Pacific Coast Highway. A small creek ran along the side of our house from the hillside to the ocean. The shore in that area was more of a cove in which the waves broke right at the shoreline. It was very private, which is what the homeowners there liked the best. The most exciting thing to happen was when a male corpse wearing a white button-down dress shirt and suit pants floated face down into the cove. I saw it, but was soon scurried into the house by my dad. One of the other neighbors had already notified the police department, so the corpse was soon fished out, not that I was allowed to watch it all happen. I never heard the story of who it was or where it came from, which was probably for the best.

My father was always busy. He wasn't one to sit in a chair and stare out at the sea. He had a small workshop in the garage section of the beach house. After a high storm tide tore apart the steps leading from the deck down to the sand, my father built a set of stairs that could be raised up by ropes every night, for both protection and to keep them out of the water during a storm surge. If he sat still, he was at the small electric keyboard he brought to the beach to orchestrate some music. My dad taught me how to make little whimsical sculptures out of found materials, like a little café table from a bottle top and some wire that he twisted for the legs, and tiny characters made by soldering a hex nut as a head onto a washer body with twisted wire arms and legs.

He hung a swing on a rope from the overhang on the house and I would swing out over part of the narrow deck, making sure my feet faced away so I wouldn't crash into the plate glass window. The whole setup seemed remarkably dangerous, considering how cautious they were with me. Amazingly, all six Brady kids made it through five seasons of filming shows without a broken bone or even a sprained ankle from an accident that happened away from the set.

The weekends that my sister, June, came to spend the day with us in Malibu were the best for me. From the kitchen window, you could look up the sloping hillside to the road where cars turned off from Pacific Coast Highway. I would stand there for an hour, waiting to see her car come down the road to our little cottage. I adored her so much that I would never talk about *The Brady Bunch* or any of my guest star appearances. I knew she was always trying to find work as a stage actress and I felt embarrassed about my success, especially since my parents thought she should only be pursuing television and film and not focus on the stage so much. June was my touchstone of what it meant to stay true to oneself. She did what she wanted to do, without looking for anyone else's approval. I wasn't there yet at age ten, but I hoped to be one day.

With the purchase of the Malibu cottage, the Science of Mind Sunday Services at the Encino Community Church also came to an end. My dad wasn't up for driving back for church on a Sunday morning, though my mother continued to believe the "thoughts become reality" premise of the teachings. My father was never particularly religious; he was more philosophical. He was always interested in the ideas of those BCE guys: Socrates, Aristotle, and Plato, along with inspirational people from the last two centuries. He would keep note cards with famous quotes and "words to live by" on them. One kept on his desk was Calvin Coolidge's famous quote that begins, "Nothing in the world can take the place of persistence." My father was definitely a "stick-to-it" person. Following his own career as a musician, he dedicated himself to being a great A&R person for RCA records, bringing in The Limeliters and Jefferson Airplane, and earning the label gold records, as well as producing and conducting a single called "How Will It Be?" that he had me record after my first year of *The Brady Bunch*.

Since my brother, Ben, was an officer in the Vietnam War in 1971, my father was very aware of the waste of young lives and the purposelessness of the war dragging on and on. I knew of the Vietnam War as much as a sixth grader could absorb its reality happening almost eight thousand miles away from me. In my spoken-word segments between the chorus, one detailed how my friend's big sister held a GIVE PEACE A CHANCE sign and didn't live to be age twenty-two. I guess it was a Kent State shooting reference. No wonder I was a serious kid. Even though the new release was promoted by Jim Lange (*The Dating Game* host and a popular Los Angeles DJ), the single hovered low on the Billboard charts. It seems the only blond-haired, blue-eyed female singer who could pull off a protest song was in the group Peter, Paul and Mary, and not the 4' 9" prepubescent blonde who was co-starring as the middle child, Jan, on *The Brady Bunch*.

Though my father rarely expressed anger outwardly, he had ethical issues with the way RCA handled musical artists and finally resigned. When he came home with the contents of his desk from his corner office, he took the small ceramic dog, Nipper, the symbol of the RCA Victor logo, and smashed it on the front deck of our house. When my father found people to be unethical, he would be all the way done with them, without looking back. He persevered until he couldn't stand behind the company any more. He soon launched a successful record-producing company out of our house, helming the soundtrack for Franco Zeffirelli's *Romeo and Juliet*, which earned him another gold record.

My mother was eternally curious about many things, including astrology and tarot, mostly because it gave her some way to try to figure out people and situations. Long before there were computer programs that configured a person's astrological chart, my mother would use the American Ephemeris, an almanac with data of where the planets were in the sky the time you are born, to get insight into situations or people. It was annoying to me when she would say things like, "You're impatient because Aries is in your house of (something or other)." She always scoffed at the newspaper horoscopes, saying, "There's much more involved than a person's sun sign."

My mother must have subtly acquired the birth information for the cast members of *The Brady Bunch* early in the first season, as she told me while driving to the studio one day, "Well, I look at all of these charts and it makes sense that we are all together because of the way the charts work together. We will be together for a long time and always involved in each other's lives." I used to think it was all wishful thinking on her part, but it ended up being true. She was right.

When I was old enough to date, I would instruct my boyfriends not to tell my mother their birthdate, as she would look up their chart and then give me all the reasons why he wasn't the right boy for me. As my mother continued to withdraw from situations that might have intimidated her, my sister devoted her time to theater and her love of the stage. If she did possess any envy about my career, it never showed. In my personal life, I looked to June to understand what was possible for women.

In my career, I looked to my three exceptional adult castmates, Robert Reed, Florence Henderson, and Ann B. Davis, who demonstrated for me what it means to be respectful, professional, and to put in a day's work. If a ten-year-old child is to spend the next five years of her growing-up years around three adults who would become family, then I won the kid-actor lottery with Florence, Robert, and Ann B.

Chapter Six

Realism was the goal in season 1 of *The Brady Bunch*. The kids went in and out of the house to the backyard through the kitchen sliding door. We were loaded in and out of a station wagon if we went somewhere as a family. Our clothing looked like it had gone through many wash-and-dry cycles and the styles were rarely in; they were very out. The girls all looked like they could be Carol Brady's daughters and the boys looked like their dad, Mike. The director of the initial episodes, John Rich, had the set crew spread dirt on the Astroturf under the swing set, because that's what it would really look like under the swings where kids play. And typical of houses in 1969, the kids shared bedrooms and there was one bathroom for all of us.

Our trusted housekeeper slept in a tiny bedroom that also contained the utility closet with mops and cleaning supplies. Apparently, Alice didn't need a closet for clothing, as she wore the same blue uniform, with white apron, for all five years, as if she were a hotel maid. How's that for the women's liberation movement of the 1970s?

As every child actor can tell you, TV realism is very unreal. The sliding door opened and closed with incredible ease and barely a muscle needed as if it were only an aluminum frame, which it was. There was no glass in it. The station wagon was rolled into the fake driveway up to the plywood carport. We had to use whatever station wagon happened to be available on the Paramount lot on the day a car was needed for the episode. Sharp-eyed viewers noticed that in some episodes we would depart in one car and come home in another. Mike Lookinland had his strawberry blond hair dyed dark brown to match Robert Reed's hair, who had his naturally curly hair straightened, which meant Barry Williams had to straighten his hair, too. Susan Olsen had her sandy-colored hair bleached out platinum to match Florence Henderson's blond wigs so the three girls all looked like "Mom." No one seemed to question why the girls' bedroom window was only waist high to a child and a wide-open frame with no glass or screen. The bathroom had no toilet, two sinks, and only one or two towel rings for all six kids. The food we ate in the dinner scenes was mostly real, but some couldn't be consumed. Irving, our prop master, would fix the food on a regular household stove in the corner of the stage. Even Irving looked a bit unreal with his swollen, pocked red nose and walrus moustache. He dressed in velour jumpsuits that zipped up the front, with some type of sash or wide belt around his waist, like a cross between Avery Schreiber and Liberace. He would put plates of food on the table for the dinner scenes and say, "Kids, you can eat the little round potatoes, but don't eat the fruit salad in that bowl. It's coated with fly spray."I now think it was his way of keeping us from messing up the plates of food. Having to eat for the dinner scenes was rarely realistic, as you had to time when you could take a bite, chew, and swallow, as you couldn't have food in your mouth if it was your turn to say a line. It was also important to remember what you did so you could match it for every take. The dinner scenes were first shot with a wide angle and then it would all have to be repeated four or five times to catch the close-ups of whoever had the next line, and then three or four more times to catch the reaction shots. Those were the most time-consuming filming sequences, which is why you rarely see all the Bradys at the table together. When it would get frustrating to be on the tenth take of the same line and people would feel impatient, Cosmo Genovese, our script supervisor, would break the tension by saying, "God, this is fun!" in an over-enthusiastic way that would make us all laugh.

The closet in the girls' bedroom was filled with clothes from the costume department to make it look real, but it held unreal garments for young kids, like negligees or adult 1950s dresses. The phones were real, but the lines were dead. To do a scene with a phone call, the script supervisor would read the line from the side of the stage and you'd pretend you were listening through the phone, or you had to imagine it yourself and hope the timing was realistic. The bedside lamps were never plugged in. The TV in the den was real, but not plugged in. One late afternoon it did get plugged in so we could all gather to watch the 1969 moon landing, which many to this day still think is unreal.

Fortunately, Robert Reed, Florence Henderson, and Ann B. Davis were very real with us six kids and became great role models in our young lives. It was established early on that we could use their first names: Bob, Florence, and Ann, but we also knew we weren't on equal terms with the three of them. We were still "the kids," and they were the adults, dependable adults at that. No one came to work hungover, or went off to their trailers to get high or take pills. No one seemed moody or hungover. The shooting schedule was never changed because of any personal issues that the kids were in on. All three of them were phenomenal people for a child to look up to.

When the regular series episodes began, I didn't know of the accomplishments of Ann B. Davis. She had already won two Primetime Emmys for *The Bob Cummings Show* and had been recruited by Sherwood Schwartz for the role of Alice based on her talent and brilliant comic delivery, no audition needed. As funny as she was on *The Brady Bunch*, she had a serious, businesslike nature when the camera wasn't rolling. She played the kindhearted intermediary between the kids and the parents on the show, but it was soon pretty clear that, off-camera, being around children wasn't really her thing. We all treated that respectfully. When she was at work, she was there 110 percent. No one ever had to wait for Ann B. to be ready. Once in a while if we started cutting up or got giggly while shooting a scene, she would clip out a somewhat-firm "Okay. Straighten up now."

In one of the early weeks of filming, I noticed that Ann B. carried her script around in a leather notebook. *The Bob Cummings Show* was stamped on the cover with the year 1958. I must have found it amazingly coincidental because I said to her, "Hey! That's the year I was born!" She peered at me with her crystal-blue eyes and said, "That's great, kid. Really great. Thanks." It wasn't said in a way that belittled me, but it was a reminder to stay in my lane as a kid and that I didn't need to remind adults about how long they've been around.

We often filmed twenty-two pages of script in one day,

and except for the longer twenty-minute breaks when we would have to be in the schoolroom, everyone stayed nearby on the set between takes while the camera or lights were reset. Ann B. would sit in her chair and needlepoint while she waited between takes. One by one, we each became intrigued with needlepoint, and Ann B. didn't seem to mind teaching us her favorite hobby. Florence Henderson would be working on her own needlepoint during the breaks and soon all nine principal actors had a project going, including Bob and the Brady boys. Needlepointing in the early 1970s was catching on as the hot hobby since L.A. Rams star player Rosey Grier needlepointed for relaxation. If a huge defensive tackle football player could needlepoint, it seemed to open the door for other men and boys to give it a go. For Christmas one year, Ann B. made us all little needlepoint pillows with our names on them with a satin ribbon border. I still have mine.

Like me, I don't think Ann B. Davis ever aspired to be an actor; the acting world chose her. As a young woman, she hoped to be a doctor, but eventually admitted that she couldn't keep up with the academics of pre-med. She had done some stage shows and enjoyed it, so she switched her college major to drama. She only auditioned for *The Bob Cummings Show* because her friend knew the casting director and encouraged her to go read for the role.

I wasn't surprised that she semiretired following the final season of *The Brady Bunch* and moved to Colorado to join a religious community that served the poor and homeless. She always seemed aware of the challenges or hardships of others. In one episode we were all dressed in pilgrim costumes for a student film that Greg made for a school project. Susan and I were minorly complaining about how hot and itchy the dresses were under the hot stage lights. Ann B. turned and said, "You only have to wear them for a few hours. It must have been tough for the pilgrims. One dress would have been all they had to wear for both summer and winter."

Ann B. did a commercial or informational PSA for a detergent company about how to do laundry properly. "Always button up your buttons and zip your zippers so your clothing doesn't get wrenched around in the washer." She did it so effectively that I still can hear her voice, see her face, and think about that line every time I do a load of washing, despite her having passed away more than a decade ago. Ann B.'s willingness to give it her all on *The Brady Bunch* taught me about contributing 110 percent to every acting job. Her integrity about making the most out of whatever line or action she was given imprinted my own work ethic and is a part of my own outlook on any role I've played as an adult.

The Christmas episode in season 1 was the first time I realized that Florence Henderson was an incredible singer and a previous Broadway star. It was the only Christmas-themed episode the show ever did, but the nation got to hear Florence Henderson sing "O Come, All Ye Faithful." The established pattern with the show was that each episode would feature an issue for one or more of the kids, and the parents would be in reaction to the children. My first Jan-featured episode is when it seemed I was allergic to Tiger, but, spoiler alert, it was really only to his flea powder.

The Christmas episode featured Carol Brady's problem, and the children's reaction to it. Carol had lost her voice and it looked improbable that she would be able to sing her solo for the Christmas Eve service. The kids set aside their own problems out of concern for their mom's laryngitis.

This show in particular opened my young eyes to Florence's immense talent. Florence, as did the three adults on the show, role-modeled professionalism and leadership. She taught us how to show up for work with no complaints and a great attitude.

After a few seasons on the show, I learned that she had grown up on the Kentucky border as the youngest of ten children in a situation that was close to poverty. She knew what it was like to struggle every day and she was determined to never go back to that way of life. I imagine she was also in a position of having to help out her brothers and sisters along the way, once she started making money. I doubt Florence ever turned down an offer to work unless it conflicted with a contract. She certainly never took the job for granted.

Florence overflowed with exuberance on a daily basis. If she had her own problems, they got left in her dressing room and were never brought to the set. When the critics bashed the show, she shrugged it off, saying that they didn't understand the point of view of looking at life through childlike eyes. She honored Sherwood Schwartz for creating the show and being the bridge between the network, the studio, the crew, and the cast. She defended the original series and every subsequent revival of the Bradys. She knew everyone's names—cast and crew—and usually knew the names of their spouses and kids, too. Because we spent so many hours together on the set, she did become like a second mom to the Brady kids. She was warm and beautiful and always smelled good, so it was never difficult to let myself be "mothered" by Florence as Carol Brady.

She and her first husband, Ira Bernstein, and their four children lived in New York, but during the months the show was filming, she would rent a house in Beverly Hills with a swimming pool and her children would live in LA for the summer. If there were additional roles for kids in an episode, her daughter Barbara would step in. Over the first summer of the show, she and I became friends and still are today. Sometimes, on a Saturday, Florence would have the Brady kids come to her house for a pool party with her own kids. She always had a warm smile, hug, and a good word for each of us. But it wasn't reserved only for the people she knew. She was old-school in the best possible way: She never turned her back on her fans. She would stay and sign every autograph, give out hugs and encouragement to anyone who approached her. She would teach us, "Be kind to your fans, they're the ones who put you where you are."

I would walk around her home and admire her impeccable decorating style and how it was personalized with her own needlepoint pillows. Her home office had all of her awards beautifully framed and displayed, and her desk had boxes of her stationery with her name embossed on each page. She would make sure every fan who sent her a letter got a response from her. I could tell that Florence was really good at being a celebrity and I wanted to be like her. I thought, *Okay, when I'm a grown-up person, I'm going to need an assistant, because I'm going to be very busy and fancy like Florence.*

It was obvious she had very good business sense. When I asked her about it, her advice to me was: "When you're an adult, always sign your checks. Your assistant can fill them out, stamp, and mail them, but you need to sign the check. Make sure you know where your money is and where it is going." Considering that it was 1970, and women couldn't even have their own credit cards without their husbands co-signing on it, Florence really knew how to run every aspect of her life. She may have played the housewife mom who didn't have her own career on TV, but the only person writing checks from her earnings was Florence herself.

Florence talked to us like we were really her children, and Bob, treated us as if we really were his flesh and blood. He wasn't one to toss a football in the alleyway or play a card game of Go Fish on the sidelines, but when you did a scene with Bob, there was an authenticity to his fatherliness that came through on the screen. He was the same person off-screen for each of us. He was a great listener and gave good advice.

The long-told tales from the set are true that he would not be happy if the script had unbelievable elements to it, or he felt it didn't have enough integrity for his standards, like in the first season where he installs a pay phone in the house to decrease the phone bill charges that came with six kids. Who could blame him, really? We often overheard his frustration, but it was never, ever directed at anyone other than the producers. He was always gentle, respectful, and loving to every cast member.

Where Florence had done morning talk shows, TV game shows, and a variety of guest star spots, Bob had only done professional stage acting and television dramas. He wasn't used to performing in a way that wasn't absolutely true realism. Florence was willing to follow the vision of the producers, turning in the best performance possible, without complaint. Bob saw every far-fetched moment or stretched possibility as below his standards as a legitimate actor. Despite being unhappy with many of the scripts, he seemed to love and appreciate Florence and Ann B., and we knew he cared about the six of us.

One morning we came to work to find invitations from Bob in our dressing rooms. He wanted to take the six of us kids on a fishing boat to Catalina for the day on a weekend morning. He rented a bus, large enough for all of us, and off we went to San Pedro to board a fishing boat he chartered just for us. Our moms gave Mike and me some Dramamine to prevent seasickness, but about an hour into the trip, he and I were below deck, napping in a couple of berths. The others probably caught some fish. Mike and I caught a long snooze.

It never registered with me that Robert Reed was gay. I once overheard the word "homosexual" from one of the crew members on the set. That evening, when I was in the car alone with my mother, I asked her what that was. She told me that it was a man who wanted to be a woman. *Yikes, Mom! Bad answer.* Based on that misleading definition, I knew Robert Reed was obviously a very handsome man who didn't seem to want to be a woman, so I never thought it applied to him. In the early 1970s, being out as a gay person would mean the end of an acting career. Of course, he had no options except to hide it and not be caught in any situations that might endanger his career.

Florence said that she knew Bob was gay from the very first scene they did together, but she kept it to herself and it didn't stand in the way of playing a happily married couple. Robert had been married and had one daughter, who would also appear on the show where the girls are having a slumber party. Karen lived with her mother on the East Coast, and I only remember being around her for that one episode. She described her parents as having a bitter divorce, and being estranged from Robert for a decade. As I got older, I grew to have sympathy for his daughter not having him present in her life. It must have been hurtful to watch your father playing "America's dad" on TV every Friday night, perhaps especially the episode where Marcia nominated him for "Father of the Year."

After we wrapped filming on the first season, my parents and I went on a trip to London, Paris, and Florence. My father needed to do some recording in London and decided we should all go and use it as vacation time. We had no idea if *The Brady Bunch* would be given a second season, but it looked hopeful. My dad, being a photography buff, took hundreds of photos as we went from England, through France, to Italy.

I had celebrated my twelfth birthday a month before this trip, but in my mind, I would tell myself that I was still only eleven. We had watched the "What happens in puberty" short movie at school when I had returned to a regular classroom for a short time that year, and I saw Maureen McCormick, who is two years older than me, was starting to show evidence of what was to come. Most of the girls I knew looked forward to the changes. I wanted to put on the brakes. The changes would mean that I was no longer my parents' little daughter. No one would bend low to remark about what a cute or pretty little girl I was. It would be harder to play younger parts when I had breasts and hips. If I was no longer "sugar and spice and everything nice," then what would I be? As unrealistic as the possibility was, I knew that I was in the sweet spot of childhood, and I wanted to make it last.

Chapter Seven

The Brady Bunch was never supposed to be about what's going on for the kids. According to Lloyd Schwartz, Sherwood's son who started out as our dialogue coach and ended as a producer on *The Brady Bunch*, the original focus of the show was about two single parents who marry and the trials and triumphs of blending two families into one large family. As the title song goes, how this group "somehow formed a family."

Then it became clear that the viewing audience was mostly children at home on a Friday evening, so the fulcrum shifted more to how the kids interrelated in their new family dynamic and with their stepparent. If Florence or Bob questioned that shift in focus, I never knew about it.

Since the writers had no idea who we were as individual children, many of the first season scripts had a boys-vs-girls theme, one prime example being the Brady's season 1 camping trip. As working kid actors, we were all pretty happy to be filming an episode on location and out of Stage 5. A few days of being outside in the wild world of nature was an exciting prospect, especially since we were filming every week of the summer months. As it turned out, the "wild world of nature" was a mere three miles from Paramount Studios.

The Franklin Canyon Reservoir in Los Angeles is where many Western movies and outdoor scenes for TV and movies are filmed because of the Wild West look of the landscape. There are no electric poles, car-jammed freeways, or corporate office buildings within view that might get caught on camera. There are flat expanses of park with brush and natural grass areas, and the man-made reservoir that passes for a lake in the background if the camera doesn't get too close. This was where the Brady Bunch family pitched their tents in 1969, illegally if it were real life. There are no other campsites or campers around in any scene, no stone firepit or picnic table. The Bradys appear to be going rogue, establishing a campsite on private property.

In the boys-vs-girls theme, this episode is loaded up with gender stereotypical language that went unquestioned in TV scriptwriting in 1969. Carol comes into the girls' bedroom to tell her daughters that the whole family is going camping together. The girls describe it as a "fate worse than death," and Marcia declares, "Camping is for boys!" As Jan, I wrinkle my nose and say, "Do you really expect me to sleep in a tent?!" It's an ironic protest, considering that my Malibu-tanned face and arms from beach house weekends, compared to Susan Olsen's porcelain doll skin and Maureen McCormick's fair pink blush, made me look like I've been backpacking along the Pacific Crest Trail for four months. It's rather hard to believe Jan is an anti-outdoors girl.

At the campsite Greg blames Jan for freaking out while touching fish scales and scaring away all the fish the boys planned to catch for dinner. When Bobby and Mike return from fishing, Mike is carrying a soaking wet Cindy, who . . .

being a girl . . . fell into the lake and needed rescuing. The girls are obviously ruining the whole trip and are the reason the boys couldn't catch any fish for dinner. Mom makes it all better and redeems her daughters' gender shortcomings by presenting a pre-made picnic basket full of food, oddly not in a cooler or containers, but displayed plates of chicken and lunch meat at the bottom of the basket.

The boys and Mike sleep in their own tent, leaving the girls, Carol, and Alice to be together in another tent. Alice, true to the stereotype of middle-aged women in 1970, puts her hair up in curlers before crawling into her sleeping bag and one of her bobby pins pokes a hole in her air mattress. Alice, Carol, and the girls all shriek loudly, believing that the hissing sound of escaping air is a rattlesnake. Mike, to the rescue of the hapless and helpless females, runs over and deduces that the problem is Alice's damaged air mattress and instructs the female tent to "calm down."

After being directed by the gentle and soft-spoken John Rich for the first seven episodes, this was our first time working with director Oscar Rudolph, a hefty man with a big personality. If he felt the scene was slumping at all, he'd yell out from behind the camera line, "Kids!! Up! Up! Up!" Along the same boys-vs-girls theme, Oscar thought it was perfectly fine to lift the three girls off their feet and move them, like chess pieces, to where he wanted them in the scene. Susan Olsen got the worst of it, being physically picked up by Oscar and deposited on the next mark, instead of letting her walk to it as she had successfully done for seven episodes already. At one point, while impatiently transporting Susan, he asked her, "Did you start acting yesterday?!" Being a good girl and in obedience to adults as we all were, Susan refrained from telling him that she had been acting for half of her eight young years of life.

The nighttime scenes were filmed at about four in the

afternoon because we had to be released by six-thirty under the child-actor law, and the film crew had to break down equipment and be out of the park before dark. It looks pretty obvious in the episode that it's either daylight or a super-bright full moon. For the daytime scenes under the California summer sun, there were still crew members holding giant mylar reflectors to catch the sunlight and bounce it toward the actors. It made it twice as challenging not to squint in the glaring light, and twice as hot as evidenced by the sweat forming on our foreheads. Any scene inside the tents and all close-ups were filmed back at Stage 5 the next day, but having a few days outside was a rare treat.

Every twelve or thirteen episodes, we faced a very strong chance that we might be out of Paramount Studios permanently. The network would wait until the first batch of episodes had aired before we would be granted the second half of the season and an additional twelve episodes. I never felt all that worried about a cancelation, and probably Robert Reed was secretly hoping it would be over and he could go back to one-hour dramas; but our mothers, the crew, and producers, they all seemed both happy and relieved when we were renewed for more episodes and then another season.

It would also give the producers reason to believe the show would go on when ABC would request group publicity photos. We would have to dress up and meet at a certain location to be photographed. In one eye-rolling staged photo session, we had to pose in a grassy field with huge Easter baskets adorned with giant bows on the handles. Robert Reed stands behind us, holding a three-foot-tall stuffed rabbit, doing his best to grin. I'm surprised he was talked into doing that. Florence and Ann B. are not in any of the Easter photos. After the Christmas episode in season 1, the show never acknowledged another holiday, so the Easter-basket theme was odd and misleading. There are additional promo photo sessions of us holding obviously empty cardboard popcorn containers next to a hot, buttered popcorn cart, with nothing inside the boxy glass compartment. Was it supposed to look like we ate it all?

The next year we were taken in a van to LA's "Train Town," a place where vintage locomotives are on display in Griffith Park. Florence and Ann B. joined the full cast for this photo shoot, as we all posed with our heads protruding from the engineer's windows or lined up on the front footboard, near the smokestack, in our elephant bell-bottoms, and Florence in a sleeveless blouse with a collar as big as the Flying Nun's winged wimple. It's anyone's guess what trains had to do with *The Brady Bunch*, especially since we rarely left the studio. The most enduring press photos were always the ones where we lined up on the staircase of the house on the second floor in order of age. That one was repeated for *The Brady Brides*, every sequel, and endless memes and take-offs.

Once the studio figured out that the kids on *The Brady Bunch* were little pros at coming to work prepared and ready to film, because we became known as the "One-Take Bradys," they tried to push the producers to film two episodes per week. Each episode would have to be filmed in two and a half days, no time to do anything extra or even film the scene more than a couple of times. The producers gave it a go to appease the studio executives and it resulted in a lot of on-set tension and confusion. Doubling the workload was actually slowing down the entire process. Sherwood Schwartz had already cut as many corners financially as he possibly could and was now being asked to shorten the filming season to save costs. As my mother observed, Paramount had their brand-new show *The Odd Couple.* The opening titles needed to be filmed on the streets of Manhattan, which was an expensive process and would deplete their budget. They decided to make up the money on a show with a bunch of wise-child kids.

In season 3 we were granted the go-ahead to increase the miles between the Stage 5 set and a remote location. The show was going to the Grand Canyon as the Brady family vacation. We were thrilled at the chance for a real adventure! It was my first time at the Grand Canyon. We arrived the evening before the first day of filming, and the dark abyss of the canyon at night, and the splay of brilliant stars like a dome from horizon to horizon, was both scary and breathtaking. The crew, cast, parents, and producers were all housed at the Thunderbird Lodge near the south rim of the canyon and had our meals all together in the rustic log-cabin-designed Bright Angel Lodge.

The information sheet given to everyone in the cast by our unit production manager stated: *All shooting will occur at 7,000 feet above sea level and running or playing could cause unpleasant puffing and shortness of breath.* Of course, the very first scene we shot was the whole family jumping out of the station wagon and running to the nearest lookout point. The camera crew was positioned on a lookout ledge directly below us. Also listed on the sheet is an explicit bit of precautionary advice: *Head coverings, dark glasses, and protection from sunburn and windburn are advised.* There isn't a hat, sunglasses, or scarf on any cast member in any scene, except for Mike Lookinland, who wore a ball cap, probably to protect his dark hair dye from fading. It wasn't until season 4 that Mike talked the producers into letting him have his actual strawberry blond hair color. They relinquished because he had been touching up his roots with dark hair dye for three years already. Children's hair usually gets darker as they age, not lighter, but it didn't seem to matter, as by then Robert Reed and Barry both got to wear their natural curls, instead of straightening their hair. Poor Susan didn't advance past pigtails until season 5 when she finally got to wear it down. She still had to bleach it out, though.

One early morning we rode on nine sure-footed mules down the side of the canyon, supposedly to camp in tents in the basin. We actually rode about one hundred yards to the first turn-around point, only long enough for the camera crew to catch the action. As the story goes, the guide leaves us all at the bottom of the Grand Canyon and takes all the mules back up with him, supposedly to return in three days so we can ride the mules back up. Considering that there was no way to contact anyone if something went wrong, it was pretty daring stuff for the family who never went anywhere. Carol has ridden her mule down in a lovely peach-colored polyester pantsuit, which remains pristine after setting up tents and sleeping bags on the dusty canyon floor. She agrees to help Alice cook dinner at a full standing barbeque range that must have been left by previous campers, though it's sparkling clean. That's showbiz!

Because I grew up doing TV shows and commercials, being around actors was part of my everyday experience. In my first season on the Paramount lot, we would walk by the man who played H.R. Pufnstuf, leaning against an outside wall of their stage, the head to his costume lodged under his arm so he could smoke his cigar. I saw up close how television was made and the ways each person contributed to that effort. If I had been older or an adult, I probably would have had much more appreciation for the time I spent with incredible character actors, like Jim Backus, who played Thurston Howell III on *Gilligan's Island*, another Sherwood Schwartz show, and who was featured in our Grand Canyon episodes; and Imogene Coca, from *Your Show of Shows*, who played a great-aunt that Jan resembles in the photos from her great-aunt's youth. I do remember listening to the distinctiveness of their voices and how they used them to make their characters memorable.

Season 3 is when the writers began to characterize Jan as a bemoaning middle child who struggles for visibility between her boy-charmer big sister and the parent-charmer baby sister. I was never told it was Middle Child Syndrome, and didn't know of the phrase until I was an adult, although it had been around since the early 1900s, coined by an Austrian psychotherapist. Susan, Maureen, and I were all the youngest children in our birth families, so we didn't really have to compete for attention at home. It wasn't difficult for me to play the feelings that might accompany coming in second or not doing something as well as someone else, but I never considered the impact of Jan's character on millions of middle kids who watched the show. One of the comments I hear most, post-Brady, is from adults who tell me that they, too, were an underappreciated or overlooked middle child in their family. Wishing to be kind, I don't remind them that I only played one on TV. *The Brady Bunch* is still such a cultural phenomenon that in the business world midlevel managers, mid-earning employees, and midsized companies are referred to as having the Jan Brady Syndrome in some articles and the press.

The "Marcia, Marcia, Marcia!" line was never singled

out as a middle-child complaint until actress Melanie Hutsell first parodied the character Jan in the stage version of *The Real Live Brady Bunch*, originating at Chicago's Annoyance Theater, and later when she became a *Saturday Night Live* cast member in 1991. Everyone thought it was hilarious, understandably. After it went viral, I couldn't go anywhere without people asking me about it or wanting to know my reaction.

So here is my true reaction: Although the *Saturday Night Live* sketches were a parody of a TV character, it still felt like harsh mocking of me as a child. I was a young girl who was given lines to say and a scene to play. The parody made me feel like the child actor I once was had to undergo schoolyard taunts two decades later. It bothered me more than I would like to admit, comparable to when you have an uncontrollable blush or feeling of shame when remembering something regrettable, even if it was two decades ago. At that time there were very few other instances where it was acceptable for an adult to make fun of a child, in a professional setting or otherwise. My physiological reaction was embarrassment about being seen as an idiot and an open target for ridicule. I was already a thirty-three-year-old adult when the *Saturday Night Live* parody happened, so I know my reaction isn't exactly reasonable, and I've been constantly reminded that imitation is the sincerest form of flattery, but it didn't feel that way. Growing up, especially through the puberty years, on national TV was a very exposing experience. Like every preteen and teenager, I was coping with all of the uncertainty and the struggle to individuate, but the six of us went through it all under the scrutiny of millions of TV viewers. The *Saturday Night Live* parody is still one of the first questions the media will ask me about, though I had nothing to do with it. If I'm recognized on the street, more often than not, people will say to me, "Marcia, Marcia, Marcia," and expect me to laugh. When I get asked to repeat that line for an appearance or a show, I always decline. It lives on in film. Should I really have to feel the pressure of revoicing a line from a script from 1971 when I was a child?

There's a long-lived rumor that I have bitterness about *The Brady Bunch*. Nothing could be further from the truth. Being on that series has gifted my life in countless ways, including the sequel series. I have a deep appreciation and gratitude that I could be a part of it. However, there has been a relentlessness to the "Marcia, Marcia, Marcia" thing that I've had to learn to live with, hopefully without offending people when I change the subject. I imagine Jimmie Walker who was on *Good Times* had to deal with countless pleas for him to say "Dyn-o-mite," and Henry Winkler probably spent years having *Happy Days* fans request "Ayyyy." The difference is, Jimmie was twenty-six and Henry Winkler was twenty-eight when they both played teenagers.

I know my unwillingness to still perform or rehash young Jan Brady lines is seen as humorless, but I've had to learn to be okay with letting people think whatever they will think. From my personal point of view, "Marcia, Marcia, Marcia" isn't a chart-topping song. It's not one of my greatest hits. I know it still remains a viral phrase that is instantly recognized by millions of people who grew up watching the show.

I truly have no resentment about my years as a child actor. I learned to work hard and work together with people who were very different from me. I have heard many, many times about what *The Brady Bunch* has meant to people, including other celebs, who didn't grow up in loving or calm households. It's a privilege to bring comfort to people through the medium of television. I feel honored to have been a part of an American classic that mattered to millions of kids for decades. For myself, I have no need to repeat that one line or any others from decades ago. Also, I've never watched *The Brady Bunch Movie* or *A Very Brady Sequel* from the mid-1990s, which I understand were send-ups of the '70s and of every character. They are another instance of the enduring *Brady* phenomenon.

Every new season came with many changes for all six of us as we all grew taller and more mature-looking. The show producers still tried to maintain our "little kid" status as long as they could. After all, for the first episodes, Susan had to play age five, though she was almost eight, I had to play age nine at age eleven, and Maureen was playing eleven or twelve at age thirteen. Barry was fifteen when the show started and his leap in height was very noticeable after season 2. The scripts were written as though we were younger, which was most likely the hardest on Susan and Mike, who were relegated to speaking lines that actual eight-year-old kids would never say. This worked out fine for the first season or two, until the physical changes became more of a reality. I didn't worry about it, but I was not looking forward to getting older, especially since the messaging from the adults who surrounded me was to remain a cute little kid as long as possible.

One of the reasons Sherwood Schwartz wanted to cast "real" children is that we came with our own growing-up experiences that could be incorporated into the show by the writers. One of the first life passages for me, personally, was having to wear glasses. In the tiny schoolroom at the studio, I could see everything clearly. When I returned to regular school in the spring, and the blackboard was twenty-five feet away from my desk, it was discovered that I couldn't see well at all. My days at the studio moved along at such a rapid pace, I didn't notice that anything more than ten feet away had become blurry. When I got my first pair of glasses, it was like one of the videos of the little nearsighted babies on YouTube who have the tiny pink or blue glasses on a band pulled over their bald heads, and they look around first in bewilderment and then in joy. I was thinking, *Wait! What? Look at all of that!* Driving home from the optometrist was similar to the scene from *Little House on the Prairie* when Mary and Pa are in the wagon coming home, and she revels in the stunning beauty of the landscape all around her that she can see with her new glasses. With my glasses I could see all the leaves on the trees and read the signs way down the street. I didn't realize what I was missing until I got the correction.

My having to wear glasses meant that Jan also had a problem that needed to be solved. The script was written that Jan could no longer see well, but that included both far away and close up, which would be a very, very rare vision problem in children. When Mike has her read a letter from her teacher, she struggles with seeing the words inches from her face. According to the scriptwriters, poor Jan needed bifocals at age eleven. The problem was that she needed the glasses, but refused to wear them outside of the house because she didn't want to look like "a drip" around Bernie, a boy in her class. After returning from a library date with Bernie, she crashes her bike into the back of the garage, smashing a family portrait that was to be a gift from Mike to Carol. Jan eventually decides it's safer to wear her glasses after she sells her bike to pay for a second photo shoot and a framed photo for Mike to give Carol. The glasses I wore in the show were identical to the ones I wore in real life—with one exception. The show glasses were only frames. Real glasses could not be worn on TV as the lenses would reflect the stage lights. I would wear my real glasses to the set and then Irving, the prop master, would replace them with the frames-only version. Luckily, everything on the set was less than ten feet away because, for the sake of the camera, I still couldn't see well at work.

Thankfully, I didn't have to deal with teenage acne or extra-oily skin or hair, like many teens have to do; and unlike the high-pressure and shaming stories from other female child actresses on other sitcoms, no one ever mentioned maintaining a certain weight to me. I don't think Susan and Maureen were ever given any warnings, either.

It was always an adjustment to return to regular school in the springtime. School events, dances, club activities, field trips, and parties had gone on without me. After *The Brady Bunch* had been on the air for two years, it became harder to interact socially in real life. Other students at my school either liked me only for being on television, or they decided that I was a television actress snob and often didn't speak to me. I was far more comfortable on set and with my TV family than I was trying to figure out the social structures of junior high school.

For the most part, I didn't want to be recognized or draw any extra attention to myself. I always felt embarassment when my mother would have me go into a store with her when my hair was in curlers for the show or an audition. She would tell me, "You're an actress and this is what actresses do. We'll put a scarf over it." Her reasoning wasn't exactly comforting to hear as a twelve- and thirteen-year-old.

Around the same time, my father became the proud

owner of one of the early editions of personalized car vanity license plates in California. He ordered one for his Cadillac that said EVE 1 on it. The irony of them wanting me to always be safe and then advertising that I was in the car did not escape me.

Also ironic, considering my parents' penchant for keeping me protected from any possible physical harm, is the fact that I was sent on an audition for *The Exorcist*. I had read the book, surprisingly, even though I was young. Jamie Lee Curtis wanted to audition as Regan, but her parents objected to the storyline and what would be required of the child actor. It's rather surprising that my parents did not. I don't recall much of the interview except that I tried to lower my voice and deliver the lines with a gravel-crunching tone. As I read later, they had auditioned over five hundred girls for the role, including Laura Dern, Kim Basinger, Anissa Jones, and Melanie Griffith. When the movie was released, I went to see it and was so terrified by it all that I had to sleep in my mother's bed for the next couple of nights. I have compassion for what the movie did for Linda Blair and how it would be the role the press would never let her leave behind.

On certain weekends, Maureen McCormick or Florence's daughter Barbara would go along with my family to our beach house, which made it more fun for me. One weekend, when I was about thirteen, my mother became intoxicated and began slurring her words while making dinner. Maureen was in Malibu with me that weekend, and when she saw how embarrassed I was, she had the social grace to tell me, "It's okay. I think she's cute." If no one went with me, I'd spend hours reading books or *Mad* magazine, painting or swimming alone. Instead of it being relaxing, which was my mother's plan, I began to dread the isolation of the beach house and would look forward to getting back to the set.

The fourth season started out with the best possible news from the producers. The cast and crew were going to Oahu for a week to shoot a double episode of the Bradys' vacation in Hawaii, and we'd stay at the big pink Royal Hawaiian hotel on the beach. I'm guessing it was all a gratuitous exchange for the free advertising of being featured on a national TV show. Off we went with an airplane filled with cast, crew, producers, and many of our family members, who jumped aboard at the chance for a Hawaiian getaway. My parents went with me and it was special for them to return to the hotel they stayed in the week after they eloped, before they found a place to rent and live while Dad played in the big ballrooms. Hawaii wasn't even a U.S. state at that time, before World War II, and the hotel was only a decade old. This was their first time back. My sister, June, joined in for the week, along with my mother's best friend from Oklahoma, "Aunt" Ethel. Aunt Ethel was never my favorite person to have around. I was already self-conscious about having to be on camera wearing a bathing suit. In her cutting Southern drawl, she commented, "Well, c'mon, with those two little mosquito bites you don't even need to wear a bikini top!"

Both Maureen and I were used to wearing miniskirts on the show by season 4, but bikinis were another thing. In *The Brady Bunch* in Hawaii episodes, it is obvious that Maureen and I are both self-conscious as we hold our folded beach towels or large beach bags in front of us despite neither of us being overweight. I guess a prop person had sympathy for our embarrassment and accessorized us with the towels and beach bags.

Following the final season of *The Brady Bunch*, it seemed that almost every movie or guest star spot I did, from *Wonder Woman* to *Telethon*, a movie set in Vegas starring Red Buttons, I was required to wear a bathing suit, usually a bikini. I was never, ever comfortable doing that, but I never challenged it, either. At that time I didn't even know actresses who seemed to take issue with that demand. Not much seems to have changed over the years, as evidenced by current magazine covers featuring actresses, music videos, and TV shows. It still seems to be a subtle but continuous pressure from the media and entertainment industry.

Hawaii is where Barry really kicked up his flirting with Maureen, a not well-hidden pursuit, which made the producers uneasy. There couldn't be any "smitten" expressions coming from either one on camera, as they were brother and sister. In my attempt to keep pace, I wanted to hang out with Chris as much as possible. I'm pretty sure Chris was oblivious to my confused and hard-to-decipher flirting. The only attention I was getting from a boy was from Mike, who would circle me like an eager puppy. He was darling about it and I didn't want to hurt his feelings, but I thought of him as a friend and a little boy compared to Chris, as I had the wizened age difference of being nineteen months older than Mike.

The first episode is more like a tourism film for Hawaii, with a lot of voice-overs, going to see statues and Pearl Harbor, and plenty of B-roll, probably courtesy of the tourism department. The family goes to a luau, hosted by Don Ho, where we each take turns sounding the horn of a conch shell for about ten seconds. I guess they had to fill some time in that episode. All of the outside scenes took place in Hawaii and then we headed back to the studio, where anything that occurred inside was re-created. The

Hawaiian episodes were some of my favorites because everyone was more relaxed, which was not unexpected, since it's paradise.

I am often asked if the six of us became friends during the run of the show. Like with all children, there were moments of snide comments and a bit of teasing among us, but we all instinctively knew that we were in a closed pressure-cooker world. We only had each other as peers and pals for most months of each year during the majority of our growing-up years. Beyond that, we understood what each other was experiencing as child actors.

When I look at the press photos of all of us together, even the ridiculous Easter Bunny ones, I see the genuine relationships of a blended family. Not the Bradys, but individuals from nine separate families who came together to make up one large extended family. Only the six kids remain from the original cast of nine, but, like siblings who lost their parents, we don't spend a lot of time together and we don't share many points of view, but we are still bonded and will continue to be. I'm pretty sure of it.

Chapter Eight

Every family has issues. Who is the favorite kid? Who is getting less attention? Who let the pet mouse escape? In television sitcom land, issues are the refillable slushie cup of flavors that look different, but taste the same. Issues were prevalent, commonplace. By season 3 there needed to be some additional flavor to the show. It was time to up the stakes for the Bradys.

In the early 1970s, a new moneymaker in entertainment was appearing on stages across the country and on the pop music record charts and radio. Good-looking families of multiple siblings who could sing and perform together were rising in popularity. There was no doubt that the Jacksons, the Cowsills, and the Osmonds were selling out venues and getting TV offers due to their wholesome good looks and stress-free entertainment value. Happy families, singing together, who appeared to have no issues with each other, were selling albums like mad and booking concerts that couldn't be canceled due to viewer numbers.

Lucille Ball, being the savvy businesswoman that she was, knew how to bump up her ratings with younger viewers by having Donny Osmond on her sitcom *Here's*

Lucy. I was the other guest star on her show that week. I know I didn't audition for the part, so I'm guessing she summoned me from Sherwood Schwartz, since our stages were a short walk away from each other. My mother was very excited to have me be selected to play Lucy's niece and to have the chance to watch her in action. The storyline of the episode was that Lucy had taken me and her daughter, played by her actual daughter, Lucie Arnaz, to a dinner club to watch Donny perform. I was to play a smitten twelve-year-old who is beside herself when Donny approaches our table. But Donny gets one look at Lucie Arnaz, who is years older, and becomes infatuated with her. Thus, the comedy of errors begins.

I'm sure Sherwood Schwartz was thrilled to cross-pollinate the two shows, and my parents saw it as a great opportunity. Lucy reminded me of Ann B. Davis, very professional and slightly reserved. I'm guessing she wanted to work with a girl who wouldn't have palpitations getting to have Donny Osmond lip-sync a foot from her face. As always, I went in, did the job, and left with kudos.

The Brady Bunch continued to air on Friday nights, and by 1972 on Saturday mornings, children could watch *The Brady Kids* cartoon. Our animated selves required voice-overs, so once a month we would go into a studio to record our lines. The show also featured a sheepdog, two twin panda bears, and a talking wizard crow who made magic happen, but usually not without fumbling it to undesired results. My mother thought that my cartoon Jan was cute, and that the artists had even captured my round John Lennon glasses and how I usually stand with my feet in ballet third position. The opening title lyrics must have been written by a second-grade contest winner or something because they were a very remedial version of the original song, with lines like, "There's another boy, by the name of Peter. The youngest one is Bob."

My most distinct memory of recording for the cartoon was a promotional film we did for ABC's Saturday-morning lineup of cartoons, ours as well as the Jackson 5 cartoon. My mother had picked out a special red, white, and blue outfit for me to wear—a short culotte, white sandals, and a matching red, white, and blue purse to complement the look. We appear to run into the Jackson 5 brothers, all dressed up in matching outfits with white newsboy hats. We all shook hands and shared one of those brief moments of recognizing that we were all working kids in the public eye and it was a life that few understood. Only a few photos remain from the promotional film, which played once and then was somehow lost.

I don't know who had the idea first, but someone took notice of this golden goose of the performing family template and asked, "If it's working for the Osmonds, the Jacksons, and the Cowsills, why not the Bradys? Why not form a singing family group that could tour and sell albums?" After all, we had managed to pull off singing the theme song for the opening titles and everyone loved it.

It seemed to be too good of an idea not to pursue, overlooking the obvious reality that we didn't have an abundance of musical talent among the six of us. Barry could sing and play guitar, and Mike was learning to play guitar, but none of us had ever performed in a musical or in a band. In the case of Jacksons, Cowsills, and Osmonds, their great sound came from years of rehearsing, seasons of touring together, and skill in playing musical instruments. Their success included countless hours in recording studios and promoting their singles to radio stations. Also, actual genetic family siblings have a tonal quality that blends together perfectly for harmonies. We had a lot of catching up to do.

The Partridge Family was premiering, a TV sitcom featuring a family band. Wisely, the producers had cast Shirley Jones and stepson David Cassidy, knowing they already had professional singing careers and could lead the cast who didn't have band experience. Not wanting to miss out on a secondary income and a career opportunity, the Brady kids were sent into the recording studio. Our first album, *Christmas with The Brady Bunch*, was recorded twenty years before the invention of Auto-Tune, the software system that can correct both key and pitch for a singer.

The whole album sounds like a performance by the Sunday school at the five-thirty service on Christmas Eve, something only relatives should have to endure. Most of us could sing on key, which made it passable; and surprisingly, *Billboard* magazine gave it a kind review in November of 1970, saying it was a "first rate collection of Christmas carols and songs." It's true, the songs were first-rate classics; the delivery of each was regrettable at best and left us all chagrined. Whoever decided to have Susan Olsen sing "Frosty the Snowman," with all the *s* sounds in her lisp, must have thought it was endearing.

It was drilled into us from the start to "be nice." Nice meant to acquiesce to whatever the adults thought would be a great idea for us. We didn't think of it as relinquishing our free will at the time. We didn't really know we had a choice.

The only chart *Christmas with The Brady Bunch* ever made it onto was a deficit sales chart for Paramount Records. Still, the challenge to have us become a commodity beyond the sitcom was so tantalizing to the adults, and most of our parents, that we pressed on. Another album was recorded, this time we had all matured another eight months and the tracks resemble actual music more than an Alvin and the Chipmunks sophomore album. In our spare time—or, as I remember it, on scheduled Saturdays—we would have to meet up to get in a van to go to a White Front discount department store somewhere in the southland area to promote the album and sign autographs. The store managers were rarely prepared, setting us up at the end of an aisle with lawn chairs and folding tables that they sold at the store. They were always surprised at the size of the turnouts, lines of parents and raucous kids, mostly little girls, waiting for us to sign their record with Flair felt-tip pens supplied by the store.

There may have been a time cutoff for how long we had to stay, but some of the signings were chaotic and potentially dangerous, with ten-year-old girls shoving their way to the table to have Chris Knight and Barry Williams sign their albums. While they waited for them, they would ask Mike and me a million questions as we signed their records. I've never been a big crowd person, so I would dread when these Saturday mornings would roll around. When the crowd got overwhelming, we'd have to hightail it for the van that had pulled up behind the store for our getaway, making the parents still in line very angry. Mike and I would be happy that we got to take home the Flair pen we were using, as if that were an equal trade for a loss of our Saturday mornings.

After seeing the turnouts at the album signings, it was next decided that we should not only sing, we should dance to group choreography so that we could go out on tour when there was a hiatus from filming the show. I thought it would be something different and fun. I had dance training before *The Brady Bunch*, so learning choreography didn't intimidate me. Barry always loved performing live, so he was into it. Mike knew how to turn it up and was cute and energetic. Susan and Maureen went along willingly, but I know poor Chris dreaded the whole leap into the singing-family idea from the beginning.

Our parents collectively chipped in to hire Ray Reese and Joe Seiter, regular cast members and writers on *The Andy Williams Show*, who had helped the Osmonds develop a Vegas stage show and a touring act. They agreed to build a touring show for us. They came to the Paramount lot and at the end of our film day we would meet up with them in a rehearsal room with a mirrored wall so we could see what we were doing. It was before wireless microphones, so Joe set us up to rehearse with wooden dowel rods with a long piece of jump rope taped to them, so we could get used to holding microphones and not tripping over the cords. I never saw any looks of hopeless despair on their faces, but I'm sure after working with the Osmonds, who were already trained to move in step with each other, we were a true challenge. Joe was acerbic and liked his sexual innuendos, I guess to see if we caught them. He never outright screamed at us, but his voice would get a lot more animated as the rehearsal went on. He would slap his forehead and say, "Come on now, kids!" and "Chris! Move your ass!" We could see them through the open doorway having to step outside for a cigarette break, probably to defuse. Somehow they managed to put together an hour-long show with four different segments, dance elements, and clever patter in between the songs.

At one point, when it was determined that we might be able to pull off a stage show, we all trooped off to the famous Fred Segal store on Melrose Avenue to find some outfits that could be customized to look like stage costumes, one being a stretchy knit white-and-blue turtleneck and matching blue pants with a white stripe. We also wore these costumes while performing our original "Keep on Movin' " as The Silver Platters on the sitcom. For the opening of our stage show, we had long, wide-legged jumpsuits made for the girls, and the boys wore button-down shirts to match our colors. Susan and Mike wore the same lemon chiffon color, I matched up with Chris with a light orange, and Maureen and Barry twinned up in a darker apricot color. We even dared to include three costume changes within every show. Our mothers fancied up our big closing-number outfits by buying bags of plastic door-hanging beads and stringing them onto the long fringes from our arm cuffs and from the knees down on our bell-bottoms. A few times we became entangled with each other on stage and would have to exit like a couple of chain gang prisoners. I was tangled with Chris one time, and in a panic to change clothes, he shouted, "Just rip it!" I did it for the sake of timing. We had to get off stage and do a quick change before the next number.

To promote *The Brady Bunch*, we first rode in the Hollywood Christmas Parade. The klieg lights and the fan-filled bleachers, along with the press and cameras and red-carpet area, are at the beginning of the parade. The six of us squeezed into one convertible car, three sitting on the backseat and three of us sitting up high on the back. Someone slapped a hand-lettered paper sign saying *The Brady Bunch* on the side of the car. Once the parade leaves the grandstand area, it's a couple of miles of the more depressing aspects of Hollywood and Sunset Boulevards—many accordion-gated closed souvenir shops, bars, a few hookers, and only streetlamps illuminating the nighttime parade.

On New Year's Day, we rode in the televised Rose Bowl

Parade in 1972. The "Joy of Music" was the theme and Lawrence Welk was the Grand Marshal. We had to be there at about five in the morning, dressed in our Sunday best and ready to go. We didn't perform, we only smiled and waved, and smiled and waved some more, for five slow miles, while strapped to a plywood plank seat to keep us from flying off the float if it stopped abruptly. The television hosts of the parade were talk show host Steve Allen, sitting next to his wife, actress Jayne Meadows.

My mother was at home watching the parade live on KTLA and told me that Jayne said: "Here's The African Queen. And that's her boat," not understanding that the boat itself is called *The African Queen*. She followed that up with commenting, "And who are these lovely children on the float?" Not a single mention of the TV show or who we were beyond "lovely children." So much for promotion. The best part of the day was being invited to Robert Reed's huge Spanish-style Pasadena home for a brunch following the parade. He didn't ride the float with us, but we celebrated New Year's Day together at his house.

When the show finished filming for the third season, we went out for our first summer tour as a song and dance act. We did a southern tour for a couple of weeks and then a northern one, ending in Atlantic City. We mostly played state fairs—cow barns with bleating sheep and trains whizzing by in the background blasting their whistles—and some outdoor festivals and large community halls. We were almost always packaged in with other acts, as we only had a one-hour show, and a half-hour show if we were the opening act for another performer. At the fairs we opened for country singer Mac Davis a couple of times. And in Atlantic City, we were the opening act for The

Fifth Dimension. Unbelievably, we opened our portion of the show with "Proud Mary," which, of course, makes sense, since a group of Hollywood child actors knew all about "cleaned a lot of plates in Memphis, pumped a lot of 'tane down in New Orleans." I'm sure Joe and Ray were hoping the audience would clap and sing along and drown out our panting vocals as we sprinted around the stage in our "rollin' " choreography.

Joe Seiter's brother was a drummer and he formed a backup band of rugged road-warrior types to play for our sets. It was probably a pretty easy gig for them. We did our thing as kids and they did theirs as thirty-plus-year-old musicians who were making a paycheck. One day when Barry Williams was feeling his oats about our growing popularity, he was verbally asserting that we weren't being treated well enough by the venue organizers. I don't remember what the issue was, but I do recall one of the band members sighing, lighting a cigarette, and saying, "Oh, Barry. Fuck off." I'm sure they thought this cocky eighteen-year-old kid had no idea what life on the road was really like. I thought it was pretty cool that someone would dismiss his complaints so casually.

Chris Knight's mother did all of the bookkeeping for our tour, and Susan and Mike's moms came on the road with us. They helped us organize our costumes and do our quick changes backstage. I'm sure they volunteered because both Mike and Susan were only eleven years old and probably too young to be sent out on tour without a parent. The initial leg of the tour was the most difficult for me. It was the first time I had ever been away from my parents for more than a few days, and I found myself being incredibly homesick, especially after a trip to Atlanta, where we arrived at ten-thirty at night, with no transportation to meet us at the airport to go to the hotel. Someone from the crew finally wrangled a van to take us to a Holiday Inn and then had to go back to the airport to get our luggage and equipment, which had missed the flight. It was Mother's Day and we were tired and hungry and needed to be at a local radio station by seven the following morning to promote our show. By one in the morning, Maureen and I both ended up having a good cry in front of Mike Lookinland's mom. She was kind and comforting and assured us that it would pass. And it did.

By sheer growth in television viewers, our tour also grew in popularity. The crowds got bigger and different requests came in. Sometimes the enthusiastic fans would wait for us to head back to our hotels and surround the car or van we were trying to leave in to go back to the hotel. Once in a while, we would find fans outside of our hotel room doors and someone would have to call security.

All of the Brady kids had our photos on the cover of teen magazines, like *Tiger Beat* and *16*, at one time or another. They would arrange a photo session through my agent and then send a photographer to our house to get some original photos. In one magazine there's a photo of me, sitting with my legs up on the wooden bench that encircled the large tree in front of our house. My feet were bare. I received a number of letters from men asking if I had any other photos of my bare feet.

Chris Knight was the big heartthrob for ten- to fifteen-year-old girls. He would have to outrun his adoring fans while out on tour. I found myself relishing a bit of a taunt by waving to the girls from the backseat of the enclosed car, where I was sitting right next to Chris.

My personal favorite booking was performing at the

then–brand-new John Wayne Theatre at Knott's Berry Farm, which we could travel to from our own homes. It had a fancy rain curtain that looked like a semicircle fountain that would open to reveal us. The shows were so packed that they extended our booking for a second week. An Old West–looking locomotive ran behind the theater and around the amusement park. Between shows Susan and I would dash out and leave pennies on the tracks to be smashed flat. One afternoon between shows, Susan and I wanted to take a break to go on a few of the park rides. We took the opportunity to play dress up in a couple of calico bonnets bought at the Western souvenir shop, which kept us from being recognized and gave us some time in the park as regular kids.

The Brady Bunch Kids began to get more bookings and even shared a Sid and Marty Krofft televised evening at the Hollywood Bowl, with Jack Wild from *H.R. Pufnstuf* and Johnny Whitaker from *Sigmund and the Sea Monsters*, both Sid & Marty Krofft Pictures TV shows for children. Like anything that garners great attention, people came out of the woodwork wanting to represent us and be involved. One man, Harvey Shotz, wanted to take us all on as our manager, agent, and tour booker. He was convincing about the great heights to which he could take The Brady Bunch Kids and each of us individually. His aggressive manner in trying to get all six of us to sign contracts with him is what eventually ended our touring as The Brady Bunch Kids. My father, with all of his experience at RCA and producing records, saw Harvey as a big-talking salesman who was looking for large percentages. Both Susan's and Mike's parents felt the same way and the group became divided. After performing as a singing family on the TV show a couple of times, with songs written for us, and recording four albums together, it appeared that our fifteen minutes were ticking down. Before going back to film season 5, we no longer had future bookings as a singing group. I'm sure there were some hard feelings about it, and it appeared to even cause a small rift among our parents and a few heated phone calls. But the truth was, with the exception of Barry, performing in a musical group or band was never an aspiration for any of us, especially Chris Knight. Let's be real, even the Jacksons and the Osmonds had their breakout family members who went their own way after they grew up.

When you've been working since age six, it can make you feel pretty grown-up by age fourteen or fifteen. By season 5 Barry had already graduated from high school and was driving himself to work. Maureen drove to work, too. Smoking cigarettes seemed a very adult thing to do, so I joined Barry and Maureen in taking a tobacco break between filming scenes. Maureen and I would go off to smoke in the large women's restroom at the end of the alley. Then we would use breath drops to hide that we had been smoking, as if no one could smell it on our clothing.

On the weekends I would ride my bike to a nearby gas station, buy a pack of Marlboro Reds, and tuck it into my sock, under my bell-bottoms. One weekend at the beach house, Barbara, Florence's daughter, was spending the night. We had got a hold of some cigarettes and decided to crawl under the beach house for a smoke, not thinking that it would go up through the floorboards to where my dad was sitting inside the house. My father called me out on it, saying, "You know better than that."

The next time we decided to sneak a cigarette, Barbara and I took a walk down the beach. We pocketed an aerosol can of some type of deodorant, thinking we'd spray it on our sweatshirts so my parents couldn't smell the smoke. My father saw us leaving with the aerosol can and chased us down the beach, making us come back to the house. He was so angry, he pounded the can down on the table, causing my mother to ask what was going on.

"We were going for a walk to smoke cigarettes," I confessed.

"Then what was this for?" my father asked, holding up the spray deodorant.

I explained that it would hide the smell of cigarettes on our clothes. What I didn't anticipate was that he thought we took the aerosol can to use for "huffing" or "sniffing," which was getting high by inhaling the fumes from an aerosol can. I'm sure he had seen his share of substance abuse as a touring musician, but I didn't really know a thing about huffing.

After that day my becoming a smoker was never discussed. They probably thought it was the least problematic way a teenager could go through a rebellion phase. And they were right. I was too afraid to have a drink after watching my mother's nightly dependence on it, which seemed to get more pronounced with time, or I was just old enough to call it for what it was.

Robert Reed bought us all Super 8 handheld movie cameras for a Christmas gift and then invited us to go with him and his parents on a voyage on the *QE2* out of New York City and into London. I think he wanted to make sure we all experienced the culture and the actor training he had enjoyed before becoming a TV actor. Frances Whitfield went with us as an extra guardian. The first stop was New York City, where Robert put us all up in the Plaza

Hotel. Maureen and I shared a room, as did Barry and Chris; and Susan and Mike, too young for a room on their own, had to bunk up with Frances Whitfield. I'm sure we all hid our disappointment at being supervised by her non-stop. She was very good at her duties, while being strict, proper, and polite in that Southern gentlewoman way. Bob took us to the top of the Empire State Building and to see the Broadway show *Pippin*. Maureen and I would step around the corner of a building for a quick smoke when we thought we could get away with it.

In our room at the Plaza were framed prints of Gibson Girls, the pen-and-ink drawings of elegantly costumed women from the early 1900s. I really liked one of them, so, with a "no one will notice or miss it" attitude, I took the frame off the wall, undid the back, and lifted out the print. To make sure the empty frame wouldn't draw attention on the wall, I used the paper drawer liner from the desk and sketched a reasonable replica of the print I had removed. I centered it in the frame and hung it back up. After having stayed in hotels many times in my young life, I have no idea why I thought it was okay to do that. I imagine at one point either a housekeeper or a guest must have said, "One of these things is not like the others."

Before the trip to New York, my mother had figured out that I could switch from wearing glasses to hard contact lenses. It took a while for my eyes to adjust to the feeling, but I was willing to try, as I wanted to wear mascara and eye shadow. One afternoon, at the Plaza Hotel, I took an afternoon nap in our room without taking the lenses out and woke to find that they had become somewhat adhered to my eyes. I managed to get the lenses out, but my eyes felt as if sand had blown into them and my vision was still very blurry. As grown-up as I thought I was, I went to find Frances Whitfield, trembling in fear that I had permanently damaged my vision. She got out the Yellow Pages and made a phone call, consulting with an ophthalmologist, who told her my corneas would return to normal after a few days of wearing my glasses.

Being on the ship for five days was a huge adventure. I had never been on a boat where you couldn't see land in the distance. Mike and I would run around on the windy deck, filming each other. Every night we would all dress up and eat together with Bob, his parents, and Florence Whitfield in the formal dining room. I don't know what was happening between Bob and his ex-wife at that time, but I imagine there was some sadness for him about looking at a table filled with his TV kids and not having his own daughter with him on this extravagant trip. Maureen and I would stay up late into the night, roaming the carpeted hallways and going up on the deck to smoke a cigarette. I had never stayed up until three in the morning before.

When we arrived in London, England, Bob took us to see the changing of the guard, Shakespeare's home, the Globe Theatre, and to a West End show, *The Mousetrap*. London was the first time I heard the music of David Bowie and fell in love with it. My days of being a David Cassidy fan ended in one visit to a Soho record store. My parents were probably a bit surprised by my quick conversion from David Cassidy's band attire—black vest, white shirt, and shag haircut, singing "I Think I Love You"—to David Bowie's formfitting gold, red, and blue outfit, exposing his bare chest, calf-high boots, and spiky auburn hair and "Starman" music. Down came the David Cassidy posters and up went the David Bowie ones.

By season 5, my body had changed to the point where I could no longer play a younger child. There was no hiding the new developments in my life. I found a photo of my older sister and me in Hawaii and noticed that she still had long blond hair, but wore long, loopy side curls that framed her face. I don't know if I had asked to wear my hair like that or if my mother had taken notice and decided to update my look with the side curls. I was finally allowed to wear eye shadow and mascara on the show, training myself for "my perfect shades" through the pages of *Seventeen* magazine, which I scoured like a life manual for teenage girls. There was the knowledgeable advice of actress Angela Cartwright, who wore shades of blue shadow as a brunette. As a blonde I was advised to wear shades of pink. I wasn't looking for more attention from anyone, so when Maureen announced to the cast and crew, "Look! Eve is wearing mascara for the first time!" I felt embarrassed and humiliated, like I was trying to become someone I couldn't pull off. Going through the process of maturing on camera and in the public eye was not easy, especially getting a whole different type of attention from boys and grown men, too.

The fifth and final year of the show was the height of style and fashion for us—what you might call "Rococo Brady"—the hippest hip huggers, the highest platform shoes, the best hair. Jan had stopped wearing the glasses she went through such angst to get, and I felt pretty for the first time. Now we had a budget for current clothes and a wardrobe department to fit them to us. One morning, before filming, Maureen suggested that the two of us go braless, which was quickly becoming a statement from the growing feminist movement, especially with halter tops being a hot fashion trend. Cher, Helen Reddy, and . . . the Brady girls? I guess I agreed and it went unnoticed for the entire day of shooting, until the editor showed the footage to producers. From that day forward, Lloyd Schwartz would approach Maureen and me to say hello with a friendly hand on our backs. We could both tell that he was checking to make sure we were wearing bras because there was no time to reshoot questionable footage. We didn't speak up about it because no one questioned an adult man hugging or touching a teenage girl. Most often we would try to smile and shrug away from men who became too familiar with us when we had to greet guests on set or take photos with them.

However, when Joe Namath was the guest star, Maureen and I both found ourselves flattered at the attention of this very handsome older man. It was never aggressive, only obvious, as he wrapped his hands around our upper waists, almost at breast level. I even wrote in my calendar that week, in large cursive, *Joe Namath kissed me!!*—as if having a thirty-year-old man's attention was a highlight of the week. After watching Florence Henderson be starry-eyed and subtly flirt around him, it seemed a kiss from Joe was quite the score. I can't imagine that our mothers weren't standing by and observing, but no one seemed to have an issue with it.

The Hawaii episodes had been a success in season 4, so we were anticipating another remote location for season 5. In every script for the past four seasons, any announcements in the dialogue from our TV parents would be followed by an all-kids stage direction. For good news: *shouts of enthusiasm!*—like when Mike Brady announces that the whole family is going to Hawaii. And bad news: *groans of disappointment*. Rumors were swirling around the set that we would be packing up our hip threads and heading to Japan. Then the announcement came that we would be filming episodes in Warren County, Ohio, near Cincinnati. Off-camera we six kids definitely had groans of disappointment. We had no idea why Ohio would be the destination, but soon found out. Kings Island, a big amusement park, offered to pay our expenses in exchange for the in-show advertising that would happen with the Brady family having fun at the park. Nothing against Kings Island, but it was a bit of a let down after the idea of the Far East. Truth to tell, I was still kid enough to get excited about it.

We arrived to stay at a hotel near Kings Island a day before filming began. Being restless, Maureen and I wanted to go into the park and go on some rides, but we were concerned we would be recognized and maybe followed around. We asked Lloyd Schwartz what we should do and his advice was for us to say, "What would the Brady Bunch be doing in Ohio?" We were only recognized a few times and the line worked. We were always recognized far quicker if the six of us were together than any of us alone.

Though the park paid our way, what they didn't want to have to do is shut down the park to real customers and pay for background actors, so it stayed open to the public while we filmed. It was such a strange sensation to have people watching the scenes being filmed as we never had a live audience in the studio, and I'm sure the crowds weren't crazy about us being ushered to the front of the lines to be filmed on the rides.

There were no dressing rooms or backstage areas for us to go in between takes. We only had a roped-off area, like a small corral for actors and crew. While we waited for the next scene to be set up, we would sit on folding chairs inside of the ropes. Curious fans and customers stood along the ropes staring at us like we were an exhibit. It was unnerving to be in a fishbowl.

In one of the scenes, the family is riding a roller coaster together. Before we filmed it, Robert Reed took a close look at the camera mounted on the first car that would be catching our reactions as the coaster drops over the highest point. In one of his "disagreeable moments," Robert insisted that the roller coaster be sent around the track empty to test the safety of having a camera attached to it. The producers relinquished, sending the coaster on a test run, and it came back with a fragmented brace on the front car and no camera. Mike and I were the kids in the first car, so I'm pretty certain that Robert Reed being difficult prevented us from being badly injured or killed.

As 1974 began, it was obvious that the Brady "kids" were no longer the impressionable or impressive sprouts we had been at the start of the show. Barry was nearing twenty, Maureen almost eighteen, Chris and I were sixteen and fifteen, and Susan and Mike were fast approaching puberty. The ABC executives must have thought that it was time to "cute" up the show again by bringing in a brand-new tot. Introducing Cousin Oliver, played by ten-year-old Robbie Rist. Robbie was a brainy child who, like me, could play a seven- or eight-year-old at age ten. He was a very quick study; in fact, so quick, he had the whole script memorized and would tell everyone their next line. As patient as Florence was, I could see that she was annoyed by the boy genius being thrust into the show. Ann B. would grimace and say, "Thank you, Robbie. I know my own lines. I don't need your help."

Through no fault of his own, the addition of Cousin Oliver shifted the tone of the show and it didn't improve the ratings at all. *The Brady Bunch* was one of the first shows to try reviving declining ratings by bringing in a new kid, but certainly not the last. *The Partridge Family* tried bringing in a little brunet four-year-old boy, supposedly a neighbor, and *All in the Family* brought in the youngest orphan girl from the Broadway hit show *Annie*. It's become almost a harbinger of "the beginning of the end."

At the end of season 5, there was no wrap party, no tearful goodbyes, no final walks through the *Brady Bunch* set. There were no shouts of enthusiasm or groans of disappointment. We had no idea that the show was over. No one did. I'm sure the writers and producers were trying to gather up more family issues that could be handled in season 6. Would Greg go off to college? Would Marcia get the attic room? Would Jan get a nonimaginary boyfriend?

Chapter Nine

My husband, Ken, and I hopped into the golf cart driven by Courtney, a young tour guide who happened to be a fan of *The Brady Bunch*. She drove us to the front gate of the Paramount Studios lot, stopped to take our photo, and then drove us to Stage 5. Much had changed for the better, and some for the worse, at this soundstage where I spent so much of my youth. I found myself unexpectedly sentimental about the pathways my childhood shoes had roamed more than fifty years ago.

I was in Los Angeles to take part in a charity event that Chris Knight and Barry Williams had helped promote for No Kid Hungry. My agent called to tell me she had arranged a private tour of the Paramount lot, and Ken and I were to meet Lindsay, with public relations, the next morning. Lindsay asked me how much time we had and then set us up with Courtney, who was well versed in Paramount, both past and present.

At the end of the tour, Lindsay brought out a handled shopping bag. "We just wanted to give you this gift."

"Is this full of residuals?!" I asked.

There was laughter all around and no need for explanation on my part.

I appreciated the swag bag, with Paramount ball caps, cookies, and a framed photo of Ken and me at the Paramount gate.

People often think that the six Brady kids now coast through life on our residuals from the hundreds of thousands of times the five seasons of *The Brady Bunch* have been in reruns since 1974. If only it were so. The reality is that we each had a contract that would pay us residuals for the first ten reruns of each episode only. Once again, no one questioned it, including our agents. Obviously, it was never expected that the show would rerun more than three, maybe four, times. Needless to say, that faucet of residuals income ran dry before I even graduated from high school.

A few months after season 5 of *The Brady Bunch* had wrapped, I was a guest star on *Sigmund and the Sea Monsters*, a live-action kid show, starring Johnny Whitaker. It was a one-day shoot on Soundstage 5, but not on the Paramount lot. This day we were on the Samuel Goldwyn Studio lot in West Hollywood. Earlier in the week, we had heard from Sherwood Schwartz that there would be no sixth season of *The Brady Bunch*. The show had been canceled by ABC. My parents were far more disappointed than I was, and I remember my crestfallen mother remarking that if there had been one more season, I would have made an enviable salary bump. For myself, I thought about what it would be like to attend tenth grade in an actual high school. I didn't feel concerned for my acting career. I had already filmed a small role on *Sara's Summer of the Swans*, an after-school movie, and now had booked this *Sigmund* guest star spot.

As my workday on *Sigmund* ended, I got dressed in my

street clothes and went to find my mother. She was on the stage and deep in conversation with the prop master. Between them was a folding director's chair, and when I got closer, I saw that Florence Henderson's name was on the arm plate of the chair. My mother was in negotiations to buy the chair from the prop master.

As I stood by, waiting for her, I looked up to see smoke rising from the top of the two-story-high set that was decorated to look like a beachfront sea cave. Most of the set was painted Styrofoam, carved to look like the inside of a rock cave.

At first, a crew member, alerted to the smoke, got on the scaffold to see what was going on. I think he tried to slap out the smoking embers, but it had already progressed farther than was reachable. The next thing I knew, he was shouting, "Run for your lives!" The entire top of the set was catching on fire and it was tearing through the foam cave walls rapidly.

I grabbed my mother's arm and headed to the exit doors to escape as shouts of "Run! Everyone out!" reverberated from wall to wall on the soundstage. The exit was two heavy doors, separated by a vestibule, for the purpose of minimizing sound and light coming in from the outside. When the doors were pushed open, the rush of air pushed us out into the alleyway as the fire grew in intensity inside. My mother tripped and fell to her knees in the doorway and I turned to see that she was trying to drag the director's chair with her. I tried to get her to let go of it, but she had an iron grip, got back to her feet, and we escaped into the fresh air.

The oldest soundstages, built in the early 1900s, were soundproofed with mattress material studded to the walls and covered in canvas, which was now brittle with age.

Some areas of the canvas were covered with chicken wire to keep the padding from collapsing. All of it fed the blaze quickly. Everyone stood stunned as the entire stage became an inferno and the roof collapsed. One crew member had some minor burns from trying to rescue the film camera that was near the set. He had to leave the camera, worth tens of thousands of dollars, and escape, but somehow my mother had managed to save her twenty-five-dollar Florence Henderson nameplate chair.

As the fire trucks arrived, and we were ushered farther away, my mother noticed that Steve McQueen was at the edge of the group, observing what was going on. I later found out he had been cast as the fire chief in the movie *The Towering Inferno*, which was going into production that month, and had rushed over from his meeting on the lot to do some background research. Smoke billowed into the air as we walked to the parking garage with the chair. It was a frightening experience; a classic Hollywood soundstage that seemed so permanent was gone within minutes, not unlike the waning days of my career as a child actor.

For most child actors, when you reach your midteen years, audition opportunities become far less frequent. It's less costly for TV producers to cast young adults who can still play teenagers. Eighteen-year-old actors don't need guardians. They can work more than eight hours each day. No need for production to have to pay for a schoolteacher to be on set. In looking through the résumés of many child actors, you can see the teenage gap where they were no longer working in television until they turned eighteen, if they stayed in the business at all.

I looked at Johnny Whitaker as we did our scene that day, thinking that he had grown tall at age fifteen. His voice was deeper and his face was no longer little-boy cute. I had watched the same happen to Barry Williams and to Chris Knight. Gone were the days of playing wide-eyed innocents. Screen star Mary Pickford may have played a teenager in her thirties, but that was film. No one was going to believe that time stood still on a sitcom. I knew that my own competition for roles had increased dramatically, from the four or five other little prepubescent fair-haired girls whom I once auditioned against for a role, to gorgeous young actresses who moved to Hollywood after high school to pursue their dreams and could easily play ages fifteen to twenty.

Perhaps it was knowing that our days playing kids on *The Brady Bunch* had ended, or only needing the familiarity of someone who really understood what it was like, that became the reason Chris Knight and I tried to go out on a regular date. My younger self would have been so excited, and I still was, but I also knew that we had spent too many years as friends, growing up side by side. Any attempts at making out that evening ended with laughter and resignation that we'd always be sister and brother, even in real life. In actuality, Chris wanted to jump feetfirst into being a regular high school kid and so did I. I knew, somehow, the two of us would remain friends.

My parents still held firm to their conviction that I would be cast continuously, which is not what happened. At age fifteen I didn't feel any dismay over it, personally. Not yet. No one prepares you for the obvious when you're a child actor, that within a matter of months you may no longer look like a child. Everything that had brought you success as a "cute" or "precocious" kid evaporates into the reality of being one more actor in a city flush with other adults all vying for a limited number of roles.

That fall I became a regular high school student and the auditions were few and far between. For the first time in my life, I participated in regular teenage social activities. I went to the roller rink with girls from my class to spend the evening on four-wheel skates that laced up above the ankle, going around and around the rink, our eyes on the boys who zoomed past us. The field of possibilities for a boyfriend was so much more expansive than I was used to having and I fell into the natural teenage drama created in the pairing up of girls with boys. The stakes seemed monumentally high in who was getting the most attention and who was being ignored that week. It was almost guaranteed that you would find a girl sobbing in the bathroom before the evening was over. One week it was me. I had been dating a boy for a couple of months who broke up with me. He told me, "I didn't believe it when you were crying because you're an actress."

Having this boy essentially call me a liar and manipulator was far worse to me than losing him. It wasn't the first or last time that someone denied that I could possibly be a real person living in a daily reality—and not only an actress playing a role. In the long run, one night of crying in the roller rink bathroom was nothing compared to being the woman I knew that he abandoned at the altar on their wedding day a handful of years later. I consider myself spared.

I became a cheerleader, though my private high school was so small, all of the games were away games, as we had no football field or basketball courts. The high school was an old converted motel with a fake front that looked like an antebellum mansion from Civil War days. There were additional rooms, simple brick or cinder block structures that branched off to the sides, which served as individual classrooms. It was both odd and awkward, as you had to go outside to get to the next class.

Any type of physical sportslike activity took place off campus. I signed up for tennis, as my best girlfriend, Ellen, and I could smoke cigarettes courtside, and in the car going and coming back. At some point horseback-riding lessons were on offer and my parents, surprisingly, allowed me to sign up. We were trained in English riding, which I loved. Beyond my wanting to be around animals since my early childhood, I was now able to ride horses on a weekly basis.

In junior high at a different school, our PE class included being taken on a school bus to a bowling alley in Van Nuys once a week. We formed a small girls' team and called ourselves the Gutter Balls. My mother thought that was a terrible name and had negative connotations. We thought it was clever. (As it turned out, we were pretty good bowlers, a skill I was able to use for the TV show *Celebrity Bowling*, where Chris Knight and I competed against Barry and Maureen.) One afternoon a classmate and I were trying out eye shadow in the bowling-alley restroom and probably smoking cigarettes. When we came out of the bathroom, everyone was gone and the bus was no longer in the parking lot. Either no one seemed to notice we were missing, or it was funny to them that we were left behind.

There was a pay phone, but neither of us wanted to call our parents or the school. We would have to be responsible for getting ourselves back to school, so we decided to hitchhike. Neither of us had ever tried that before, but we figured there was safety in numbers, as if two ninety-four-pound girls could overcome potential danger from grown men in a moving vehicle. Luckily, we made it back safely and, more importantly, I escaped my parents finding out what we had done.

In 1974 some of the other girls in my high school began to frame virginity as something to "get over with" before the old age of seventeen, a compulsory rite of passage. The country was on the heels of the "free love" years of the 1960s, and the 1970s had ushered in radical changes in attitudes about sex. Virginity wasn't something to worry about or rush into marriage to have a legitimate reason to lose it. One girl in my class had parents who both worked during the day, so often a group of us would go hang out at her house unsupervised. It was there, one afternoon, when I decided that my day had come. I had been flirting with a boy and we found ourselves in her brother's bedroom, and before long, as is often the case with young men, the whole thing had happened and was over. I recall thinking, *Is that all there is to this?* Still, being an invincible teen, there were some tense countdowns hoping I wasn't pregnant.

I certainly didn't tell my parents, but I think my mother sensed it. She scheduled an appointment with a gynecologist, who set me up with a diaphragm. My mother gave me no knowing look and it certainly wasn't a permission slip from my parents. In fact, she barely mentioned the reason for the visit. The only time my mother ever explained sex to me was when I was ten years old. We were in the car, heading to an audition, and I asked her how babies were made. She calmly told me about intercourse. Being a little kid, I listened to her answer, looked out the passenger window in a mixture of bewilderment and embarrassment, and didn't ask a second question. After that day we never spoke of sex again.

* * *

For my sixteenth birthday, my parents surprised me with a car—a new Audi Fox. I probably wouldn't have picked out a beige four-door sedan if given an option, but they must have thought it was conservative enough not to draw unwanted attention and also safe. With my own car came even more freedom. My best friend, Ellen, also had been given her own car, so that spring and summer we were out and about from the Malibu beach to Hollywood to wherever we wanted to go.

One day we were traveling from Malibu, back to Ellen's home in Encino. For some reason we each had taken our own cars. Instead of taking the freeway, Ellen suggested I follow her on Mulholland Drive, winding through the Santa Monica Mountains, to go home. To do that, we would have to travel unpaved miles along what was called "Dirt Mulholland," driving through steep-sided hills with no guardrails and only a flattened surface. Ellen roared on ahead of me.

At one turn I drove too close to the edge, where a gulley had been carved out by rainfall. The tires on the right side of the car went into the trench and my car tipped up onto its side, leaving me suspended by my seat belt in the driver's seat. Fortunately, it didn't continue to flip over and slide down the rocky slope. The engine was still running and the radio stayed on. I unhooked the seat belt and managed to climb out of the driver's-side window. I was sure that Ellen would realize that I was no longer behind her and turn around. I leaned against the side of the car and smoked a few cigarettes. After fifteen minutes it was clear that she wasn't returning to see what had happened to me.

A couple of guys on motorcycles came along and stopped to help me. The two of them managed to rock the car back and forth until it tipped back onto all four wheels. Then they followed me as I carefully navigated the rest of the dirt road to Encino. Ellen's car was there in front of her house. I parked and went inside. I wanted to use her phone to call my parents, as I was now late getting home.

"What the hell, Ellen? Where did you go?"

She said, "I was nervous. I couldn't turn around on the dirt road."

"Did you think I was dead? Were you going to leave me there?"

I called my parents to explain why I was late before I drove the car home. The headlight was broken out and the front right tire rim was bent and the paint on the right side was scratched, but for the most part, it wasn't too damaged to drive.

I thought they'd rush out to the driveway and hug me and say, "Thank God you're all right." But the second I saw their faces, I knew that wouldn't be the reaction. They were both really pissed about it. They thought I had taken a foolish risk and let me know it. The next day my car was taken to a body shop to be repaired and I was stuck at home until it came back.

As teenage trial-and-error experimenting would have it, I wasn't done taking risks. One day I was enlisted to be the "getaway" driver for my longtime neighborhood friend and a girl from her high school, a petite blonde with doelike eyes. They decided to go on a shopping spree at the mall in Topanga Canyon, but not to buy anything. They were going to steal it. They each brought with them large leather satchels with stiff sides. The plan was that if one of us got stopped, the other two would scatter, in order not to get caught. If I had not driven them there, I probably would have left right away, but I couldn't leave them.

In the large department store, both girls rolled up pants they had tried on in the dressing room and shoved them down in their bags. I pretended to browse nearby, but I was nervous. I knew it was wrong to steal and didn't even want to try it. We went to a record store and the pretty blond girl stacked some albums in her arms and walked out with them. As we left that store and were walking down the mall, I caught a glimpse of a man in a dark suit and rubber-soled shoes coming up behind us. I had read enough detective novels in my early teen years to know that this was an undercover cop. As per the plan, when he stopped the blond girl with the albums, I kept walking. I walked down the mall and out of a side door and then around the buildings to where I had parked my car.

My neighborhood friend had gone the other way and soon joined me in the car. We weren't sure what to do or how long to wait. I nervously watched for a police car to pull up, but none arrived. About fifteen minutes later, the blond girl appeared, with who knows how much of the stuff she had stolen. She had somehow convinced the undercover cop that she had switched bags and must have dropped all the receipts. At least that's how she told the two of us she got away with it. I have to admit that it never crossed my mind that if I had stolen something and been caught, it would have been a tabloid story.

You would think that close call would have scared me straight, but age sixteen had a few more truth-or-dare moments—and for some reason, I always picked the dare. My parents allowed me to take a trip to Hawaii with this same neighborhood friend and the girls from her public high school. It must have been a spring break trip, but I don't remember adults being around to supervise. We stayed at the famous Moana Hotel on Waikiki Beach, three girls in each room.

Streaking was a big trend in 1975 and we decided that going out on the fire escape steps naked was a hilarious and worthwhile dare. We would also go down to the beach late at night and skinny-dip in the warm Pacific waters, which felt both luxurious and bold. One night some teenage boys came along and stole one of the girls' clothes she had placed on the sand near the water, and we had to make our way back to the room with the few articles of clothing we had left among us all. As a self-imposed challenge, in one of the hotel gift shops, I pocketed a pair of seashell clip-on earrings and a pen, trying to be a brave burglar, but I was scared to death of being caught. I wasn't. I gave the earrings to my mother when we got back to LA and felt guilty and strange about it. I'm sure she would have never worn them if she knew they were hot property.

Before my junior year of high school was over, I decided that my boyfriend should be the bad boy of the senior class. He had probably been kicked out of a couple of public schools and ended up at Montclair Prep as a last resort before juvie lockup. He was one of those "rough" types who could afford to be a bad boy because his parents divorced and he lived with his fashion-conscious single mom in an upscale condo in Encino. He drove a souped-up green Mustang, loaded with all the amenities, given to him when his mother upgraded her own car. He kept a knife in his glove compartment, which seemed daring and temporarily interesting in a *West Side Story* kind of way, although our high school didn't have gangs and I never really noticed anybody claiming turf in Sherman Oaks. I dated him for a few months and we would cruise Van Nuys Boulevard, a popular pastime for teenagers not old enough to go to a club. At the stoplights he would bare-ass other cars full of kids. No wonder I found him so very sexy. *Really?* I still went to his senior prom with him. He had a fancy pale blue tuxedo, with a ruffled shirt, and I bought a long dress that was black on one side and white on the other and found accessories to match.

Then one day in a drunken rage, he pulled up in front of my house and decided to smash his eight-track tapes on his steering wheel, causing the horn to honk continuously. I looked out the front window, seeing the ridiculousness of it all, like the neighbor girl smashing her tea set on the driveway, wasting perfectly good music tapes in an immature tantrum. The neighbors started to step out their front doors to see what was going on, looking to me for an answer. I wised up quickly and told him we were over. After he graduated from high school, I asked my parents why they allowed me to see him. My dad told me, "I was worried that if I told you no, you'd go off and marry him instead." Thanks, Dad. Spared again.

The only bad boy I cared to be around after that was Tim Curry, the star of *The Rocky Horror Show*, the stage play, prior to the movie retitled to *The Rocky Horror Picture Show*. A producer had bought the American theatrical rights to produce the show at the Roxy on the Sunset Strip in West Los Angeles. Tim Curry was one of the original cast members as the lead role, Frank-N-Furter. My sister took me to see the show in one of the first few weeks, as one of her good friends was playing the square guy, Brad. I had never witnessed anyone like Tim Curry in character, or anything like this radical and funny show. I bought the cast recording and played it in my car. My friends and I would drive to sit in the parking lot because at the beginning of the show, Tim, in full-drag regalia, would have to walk from the stage door to the front door to make an entrance through the audience. The show grew quickly in popularity and soon there were no tickets to be had. That's when the movie producers took notice. *The Rocky Horror Picture Show*, of course, is history, and continues to be.

In my senior year, I was voted homecoming queen, which seemed ironic, since our high school had no home field to be on. We were at a different high school for the homecoming game. I and the cheerleaders who were princesses had to change out of our cheerleading outfits in the bathroom and into formal dresses and ride around the quarter-mile track that encircled the football field, waving from the backseat of a convertible. I had no idea how or why I won and was sure that other girls deserved it more. I can only guess that the twenty-three students and parents who were sitting in the bleachers were quite impressed by my win. Fifteen minutes later we had to run back to the bathroom to change into our cheerleading uniforms and smoke a quick cigarette. It was all very high class.

When I turned seventeen, if an audition came along, I would drive myself to it. One summer day my agent called to say she had set me up with an audition that would take place in a few hours. I was sitting in the backyard in some shorts and a halter top, which was summer fashion in the mid-1970s. I decided it was too much of a hassle to change clothes, but my mother disagreed. She didn't want me to show up at a casting office wearing a halter top. We got into a heated argument about my being old enough to wear whatever I wanted. I knew she was probably right that it was tacky, but I was determined to exercise my free will.

Soon enough my father came out of his home office and

stood in agreement with my mom. I argued my case that it was current fashion and every girl wore them. My father went into the bathroom and, in his anger, put up the toilet seat with such force it smashed the tank, sending porcelain shards to the floor and water out into the hallway. He was so rarely mad to that level that I changed into more appropriate clothes quickly and left for the audition. It's good that I swapped out outfits because it ended up being a Kodak commercial with the very cute Mark Hamill, who would soon go on to *Star Wars* fame. Even though he was already twenty-three years old, he easily passed for a teenage boy. The camera featured a switch that went from a regular shot to a zoomed focus for "only thirty-six dollars."

Being seventeen, I still had to have my mother with me as a guardian and attend school for three hours on the set, though all I wanted to do was hang out with Mark. He was talking about his upcoming Oscars party at his house and I was hoping he would invite me. He didn't. *Sigh.*

No longer being considered a child actor was a new world for me and I was reminded when I attended events that my place in the television acting world had changed, especially when people like Ted Turner leaned forward to leer down the neckline of my dress and remarked, "You've really grown up . . . and *out.*" Hilarious.

By the time I was in my late teens, I was very self-conscious about my breast size. They seemed disproportionate to my frame and attracted unwanted attention from men much older than me. In my senior year of high school, my biology teacher asked me to stay after class one day. I had no idea why. When he came around from behind the desk and stood close to me, I became worried. Then he whispered, "I am very attracted to you, Eve. I feel I needed to get that off my chest." I can guess the reaction he was hoping for—

is that why he saddled me with his confession? I giggled my way out of it, side-stepping to the door with my books hugged against me under my crossed arms. I never thought I was signaling a message of availability and, if anything, tried to downplay sexuality. I never reported the teacher or told my parents. Girls were so reluctant to speak up for themselves, grown men had no fear of retribution or rebuke for their actions. They counted on it. Gratefully, that is far less true now.

Months before my eighteenth birthday, my agent sent a script for me to read. It would be a TV movie about a runaway fifteen-year-old girl. It had controversy in that the girl is a sweet teen, in her skirt and buttoned-up blouse, who runs away to Hollywood and is coerced into becoming a young prostitute. Since I would soon be an adult, it seemed like a good time to break away from the Jan Brady image. Even my parents agreed. I auditioned for *Dawn: Portrait of a Teenage Runaway*.

Chapter Ten

I had read *The Happy Hooker*. It was a huge bestselling book in the early 1970s, selling 20 million copies. There were obviously a lot of people who were intrigued by the life of call girls and this madam who was the author. It begins with a jail holding-pen fight between different brothel houses following a police raid and language that I had never heard anyone use before, but I was still impressed by this woman who took a harsh early life as a prostitute and turned it into a profitable life for herself. And she was funny about it. Later, as an adult, I had a much clearer understanding of how difficult, often degrading, and dangerous the sex worker occupation can be. However, in 1976, having read *The Happy Hooker* was the total of my background research heading into playing the lead role in *Dawn: Portrait of a Teenage Runaway*.

My dad thought it was a good transition role for moving me past my midteen years between child actor and working as an adult. I was soon to be eighteen, which meant I could now play the teenage roles that went to adult actresses. Since it would be a made-for-TV movie, we knew it wouldn't be pornographic in any way. I was told that the producers were screen-testing three young couples to play Dawn and Alexander. It was the first time I had auditioned with a film camera running, instead of only reading in front of the director and producers.

Then my agent called to say I was being offered the role of Dawn. It was a big career step for me, from playing a supporting role as a child to being the lead role now as an adult. I was ready for a challenge and maybe a bit naïve, believing that I was cast on talent alone. In retrospect I'm sure the producers had television ratings in mind and thought America would tune in to see Jan Brady as a teenage hooker—in no way a happy one. They did. The ratings were so impressive that a TV movie sequel, *Alexander: The Other Side of Dawn*, went into production soon after.

I didn't realize the gravity of having the lead role until the first day in production. The hair and makeup crew gave me a T-shirt when they met with me. My name was on the front of the shirt and on the back it read: *This is Dawn.* I wasn't sure when or where I was supposed to wear it. It felt too flashy. The production team asked my opinion about things like my hairstyle and if I wanted anything in particular in my trailer. I had never had anyone ask about my preferences before. It was a new world.

For the first four days of production, I was still seventeen years old and treated as a minor. I had to do three hours of school during the day. The teacher, whom I had worked with many years before, and I mostly chatted, as I already had enough credits to graduate from high school, and so three days of school on the set were pointless. She would say something like, "Name all the state capitals," and mark that down as a lesson. I was released at the conclusion of eight hours and my mother and I went home.

Then the calendar ticked over and I was eighteen. I

thought, *This is it. I'm an adult actress, free of school hours, and it's no longer required that my mother be with me as my guardian.* The cast and crew threw me an eighteenth birthday party on the set and then I was an adult, required to work at least a twelve-hour day and responsible for getting myself to the set, signing in, and following the schedule.

It seems that I was so wrapped up in stepping into this lead role that I didn't take into consideration what it meant for my mother to no longer go to work with me. She had devoted twelve years to my career and suddenly her daily hours of being on the set with me had ended. I know the same happens to parents whose eighteen-year-old children go off to college, but I'm sure it must have been more of a shock to her system to lose both time with me and her interesting outlet for social interaction. It wasn't until I was well into adulthood that I have had great pangs of sorrow about what an abrupt life change it must have been for her due to my lack of attention to her feelings about the situation.

To credit her selflessness about it, she never once brought up that it might have been hard for her or that she missed our time together. She was very stoic about the change, never once saying she wished she could go to the set with me. Either because I felt the pressure of carrying the lead role or because I had been led to believe that my acting career would go on and on, I never looked back. I was encouraged that my parents saw this role as a breakthrough into an adult acting career, galvanized by having the lead role, and I thought that meant I had to move on as an adult as well.

Randal Kleiser was a young up-and-coming director at

that time who had directed episodes of TV dramas, like *Family* and *Marcus Welby, M.D. Dawn* would be his debut with a full-length movie. I don't know if he was nervous about it, but he seemed to have some big names that were confident about his talent. He invited me to a dinner party at his Hollywood Hills house. At the table was famed film director George Cukor, who had directed many megahit films, including *The Philadelphia Story*, *Born Yesterday*, and *A Star Is Born* (the 1954 version), to name a very few. I had watched all of those films with my parents on TV, but didn't quite understand the importance of this elderly man at the table. Who knows who else was there that evening? I was doing my best to act as if I belonged there, but I felt very out of place at this dinner party filled with movie professionals. I stayed silent most of the evening, only speaking if spoken to directly.

Early in production, the costume designer, a distinguished-looking older gentleman, took me into Frederick's of Hollywood, the famous lingerie store that originated on Hollywood Boulevard and then grew to be in malls across America, eventually overtaken by Victoria's Secret. The clothing there was sexy and racy, exactly what the costume designer needed for when Dawn tries her luck at being a prostitute. I'm not sure if we told the clerk why we were there, but I'm sure they took a long look at the two of us and thought the designer was my sugar daddy or pimp and I was being outfitted for his pleasure or the street life. I had never worn clothing like that and I'm sure my face matched the skintight red vinyl jumpsuit I was given to try on when I had to step out of the dressing room to get his approval. It was a huge departure from any previous costume I had worn that never showed even a quarter inch of cleavage. Yet another big transition to adjust to on my own. I knew the clothing was right for the character, but never felt comfortable in it.

It was impossible to shut down Hollywood Boulevard for hours to film for the movie, so the sidewalk scenes were shot with mostly real people walking up and down the street. I think the crew posted signs saying that if you walked into a certain area, you were giving permission to be filmed as background in the movie. Some people avoided the area and some stood along the periphery watching what was going on. During one scene I was at the side of the street, wearing the red jumpsuit and a white rabbit-fur jacket. I was waiting for the camera crew and trying to pick off pieces of rabbit fur that had shed and were sticking to my large, black false eyelashes. The regular traffic was still traveling along the boulevard. A man, driving a Corvette, pulled up to the curb and waved for me to come to his passenger window.

"Let's go. Get in," he said, obviously thinking I was an actual prostitute for hire.

It freaked me out. Terrified, I sprinted down the sidewalk toward the film crew, where Randal Kleiser was standing, going over notes.

Breathless, I told him, "A guy pulled over and tried to pick me up!"

I'm sure I literally looked like a scared rabbit in my bunny-fur coat.

Randall looked at me and calmly said, "Use it."

I stepped back, stunned by his response at first, and then smiled. I had just received my very first real acting lesson. Here I was, eighteen years old, having worked for twelve years on camera, and had never taken a single acting class or lesson. Before that time I had only been given line readings by a director or a producer if they felt I needed it, if my own interpretation of the line was far off. Otherwise, it was noted in the script what I needed to do. If it was to cry over something, I could cry on cue. If it was to be amused, I could make laughter sound authentic. The thought of actually allowing an experience to affect my performance *authentically* had not been part of my understanding of the craft. I had never considered it a craft because it was just something I could do, something that I had been told came naturally to me.

My other on-set acting lesson came from the woman who played my mother, actress Lynn Carlin. The production had gone to Arizona to film the family home and the scene of Dawn's high school dance, where her mother confronts her. Lynn played my mother with such intensity of purpose and desperation that I found my own performance elevated in reaction to hers. Coming out of five years of sitcom acting, where everything was delivered with more of a wink and a smile or a furrowed brow in reaction to the situation, Lynn's performance was like a tutorial in dramatic acting for film. She wasn't a character actress; she was the character.

I wish I could have been as in sync on camera with Leigh McCloskey, who played Alexander, but it never felt like natural chemistry. We didn't have much to say to each other off camera, so on camera was more of an acting challenge. There were no problems between us, but also no connection. It was difficult for me to act in an intimate way with someone who was an acquaintance. I had never had to kiss on camera or act out a physically romantic scene. Randal had most of the crew leave the set so I would feel more comfortable. Since it was television, there was no nudity, but I was wearing only a skin toned "modesty garment" under the covers, and still felt very exposed and uncertain to be in bed with a man not my boyfriend. I don't know if I ever relaxed enough to make it believable.

One of the strangest scenes to film in the movie is when Dawn goes to a motel room to turn her first trick. She meets a middle-aged businessman at a mini golf course, and when he whispers to her what he wants, she utters the saddest line ever—"Can I have a sandwich first?" The script really wanted to portray this girl's predicament. The scenes fit the movie fine; it was the actor who seemed like the wrong choice for the role. As we rehearsed the motel room scene together, he made a joke or two about it, obviously equally uncomfortable. The producers had cast William Schallert, the actor who had played the warm, patient, and benevolent father of a teenage girl on *The Patty Duke Show*. Now, he was playing a creepy guy who gives Dawn (who was also Jan Brady) twenty dollars and tells her she must be new at what she does because a real hooker puts the money in her shoe.

Coinciding with filming *Dawn*, Fred Silverman, the president of ABC Entertainment, decided he wanted to do a Brady Bunch variety hour. Maureen, Susan, Mike, and Florence had made an appearance on Donny and Marie Osmond's popular variety show and the ratings were really good. Sid and Marty Krofft offered to develop a variety show on *The Brady Bunch* premise of a singing-and-dancing family. They wanted the entire cast to reunite. Through the advice of my dad and my agent, I offered to appear in five shows, but didn't want to sign a contract that could go on for another five years as Jan Brady.

My dad said, "You have a lead role as Dawn now. Let's go on to new opportunities."

The network gave me an "all or nothing" ultimatum,

so I passed. They recast the role of Jan Brady through a nationwide search for a girl who looked similar to me and could sing.

I had no problem with it or regrets about it, and even visited the set one afternoon to cheer them on and wish them all well. I couldn't quite see how it was going to work out in the same way *Donny & Marie* had succeeded. The Osmonds had been singing and dancing together since they were toddlers and it showed in the musical numbers. The only true musical performers on this stage were Florence and Barry. Barry left behind his climb on Broadway as the lead role in *Pippin* to do the variety hour.

I think everyone involved was surprised that Robert Reed agreed to do the show, considering he found so much of the regular sitcom to be unbelievable and simplistic. I know I was. He did try his best, but you could almost hear him counting out the dance steps in his head. Geri Reischl, the girl who was cast in my role, became known to the press and fans as "Fake Jan." It seems that she willingly adopted the moniker, as she signed her press photos with it, and still refers to it on her social media.

For years after that show was canceled, the press asked me why I was the only Brady not to do the variety show. They often imply that I was rejecting my Brady family, out of bitterness or embarrassment. It wasn't a rejection of them; it was a redirection for me. To this day most of the other Brady kids regard that time as a regrettable line on their résumé and laugh about the attempt at a variety hour.

Right before the TV movie premiered, my father took me to meet with a new agent. Creative Artists Agency was relatively new on the scene and growing quickly. One of the agency founders, Ron Meyer, took a meeting with us in their modern offices and wanted to sign me. They seemed to be excited about the possibilities and ambitious about what CAA could do for me, despite the fact that they wouldn't receive any commission off *Dawn*. That would go to my childhood agent, Helen. My father was all for it and thought it would be helpful for me to leave the child agent and enter the adult world with an up-and-coming, hardworking agency. He wrote a letter to Helen, explaining that I would be moving on, now that I was eighteen. She wrote back, asking my father to reconsider, as she felt she had arranged many good opportunities for me and more were to come. I still chose to move on, knowing that she was mostly contacted for casting children's roles.

When *Dawn: Portrait of a Teenage Runaway* premiered that fall, the ratings were impressive and there was a lot of buzz about it. I think my parents thought the phone calls would start coming in, requesting me for upcoming projects, one right after the other. If that was happening, Ron Meyer would have told me about them, I'm certain. As it was, my next acting job was to revive the role of Dawn for the sequel movie. I was happy to do that, but it didn't feel so much like moving forward as running in place.

As it was explained to me by a casting director, "You're too well known as Jan Brady and not well enough known as a dramatic or movie actress."

My whole world had revolved around my parents' belief that my career would keep going, one role following another. There was no talk of going away to college or pursuing a different career. My sister, June, had moved to New York years before to work on a short-lived soap opera and I remember my parents' comments after she moved back. "She should be here doing film and television."

I knew about some of the colleges in the East, like Harvard. But that only seemed to be for intellectuals. I never looked into the wonderful liberal arts schools. I honestly didn't know it was an option. No one encouraged me to explore other careers. I had no plan B. I felt no agency over my own career. It was always more of an attitude of "What's next? What other roles are on offer?"

Because college was a given, I enrolled at California State University, Northridge, to take theater arts classes, since that was what my sister had done. I didn't want to live in student housing, but I also didn't want to live at home anymore. My mother found a small two-bedroom tract house for me to rent in Encino. For a while I lived alone and went through a reality-check type of awakening. I had to learn how to set up a house, figure out utilities, and write checks for my bills. My father had always demonstrated fiscal responsibility, but I had never even written a check on my own. I took my childhood bedroom furniture with me and decorated the place almost as if it were a college dorm, with posters and odds-and-ends furnishings.

I had to learn to do my own chores and pick up after myself. It seems strange to admit, but when you grow up on camera, there is always a crew member there to make sure your costume is washed and ready, clean up the dressing room, and make sure you have an available lunch or dinner. At home my parents didn't really push the chores on me, as they felt I had enough work during the day. I never thought about it. It all seemed to be magically in place when it was needed. Now that I had my own place, I got hit with the cold facts that there was no one to make sure I had clean clothes or empty the wastebaskets. If I didn't shop for groceries, then there would be nothing in the fridge. It was like a life-prep crash course.

I started classes at Cal State Northridge, a short drive from my rental house. I signed up for drawing, astronomy, Acting 101, stage design, and a class that became my favorite: History of Styles. Like my mother, I was curious about how and why certain cultural changes happened. One of my classmates, a very handsome, semicloseted boy, with a funny outlook on life, moved in with me. It worked out great for me, as there were no expectations of romance and we could hang out together without hooking up. It all seemed to be so much fun, to be with a young and enthusiastic group of theater students. For the first time in my life, I felt like I had peers who didn't set me apart because of my years on *The Brady Bunch*.

I decided to audition for the university musical *Jesus Christ Superstar*. I was happily cast in the ensemble as a zealot, which ironically mirrored what was going on for me personally. The young man who played Jesus was so talented and attractive that I decided that he should become my perfect new boyfriend. He never hid the fact that he was gay, but, in my blinding desire, my zealot uncompromising pursuit of what I wanted, I was sure I could make him realize that he was actually heterosexual. Turns out it doesn't work that way. Most often the scenario is the complete opposite. Perhaps if I had been more focused on the rehearsal process, I wouldn't have dislocated my knee during a choreography session. I fell to the stage floor and couldn't stand up on my leg at all. I guess out of caution the director called an ambulance and I was rushed to emergency, where they cut away the leotard and tights I was wearing. I lost all hope of Jesus being mutually attracted to me while being wheeled out of the theater on a gurney.

* * *

One morning I got a call from an agent at CAA who told me that Universal was going to shoot a two-episode miniseries of *Little Women* and they were looking for an actress to play Beth, one of the teenage March sisters. They had already cast Meredith Baxter Birney, who was on TV playing the oldest sister in the TV drama *Family*, as Meg, and Susan Dey, fresh off *The Partridge Family*, as Jo; Amy would be played by one of the few Universal Studio "contract players," Ann Dusenberry. They were looking for someone who looked similar enough to be a sister. I think I said "great," but then remained silent. The agent took the clue that it was a book that I had never read.

"Beth is the quiet, innocent, shy sister and rather sickly. She dies of complications from scarlet fever."

I dug in my closet and put on a long skirt with layered ruffles and a high-necked blouse. I wore my hair down, with sides pulled up in modest twists gathered in the back, very little makeup, and went off for my interview. I had learned through years of auditioning to dress the part so the casting people don't have to make a huge leap to see you as the character. When I met the director, I spoke softly and smiled demurely.

An hour later the agent called to tell me that I was in. I would play Beth March.

I can't imagine that anyone enjoyed going to work on that miniseries more than I did. It was so many of my favorite things, beginning with working on the Universal Studios lot. So many great movies had been filmed there, you could sense the history of the creative endeavors emanating from every corner of the lot. The director would be David Lowell Rich, who was the brother of our original *Brady* director, John Rich. I was especially excited when I heard that the person overseeing our costumes from the Civil War period would be none other than the multi-Oscar-winning designer Edith Head. She had costumed Audrey Hepburn and Gloria Swanson and so many more stars and had become a legend in her own right. I was a bit intimidated by her at first, but I appreciated her perfectionism.

Our fittings took place at Western Costume, the huge historic costume shop that, sadly, is now a parking lot. We used a downstairs fitting room that had a small stage and mirrors. Outside of the dressing area was a group of chairs for the director and some of the production staff to sit and give approval to what I would be wearing in the miniseries. I was so happy being dressed in the big full, rounded petticoats, skirts, and shawls of that era. Edith made sure I wore the dress correctly and that it fit as it should. She would ask, "Is this comfortable, dear?" and I would say, "Oh *yes,* Miss Head." I felt like Vivien Leigh in *Gone with the Wind*.

One day, early in the filming, there was a costume issue for Susan Dey. Edith Head had her remove the outer layer of her skirt and Susan stood by waiting for it to be fixed and lit a cigarette. I was smoking in the dressing-room area on set as well. I noticed that Susan's belly was protruding and thought that she might have been gaining some weight. I looked away, but Susan saw that I had noticed and explained to me that she was three months pregnant, but didn't want the producers to know. The character Jo had to climb down a tree, ice-skate, run through the snow, and do other physical stunts. Susan didn't want the producers to tell her she couldn't. She knew it would be fine. And it was. I imagine Edith Head must have figured out that Susan was pregnant, but she didn't let on that she knew. I'm pretty certain that it wasn't the first pregnant actress that Edith Head needed to costume in a way that no one could tell.

When I was about seven, my father took a photo of me in front of the makeup department building on the Universal lot. There I was, thirteen years later, getting to enter that famous building every morning to have my hair and makeup done. It was like a moviemaking wonderland for me. Everyone was a professional in their specialties. There were rows of salon chairs and shelves full of hair products and makeup of every shade. There was a kitchen attached, and a production assistant would ask what you'd like for breakfast. They would make eggs and toast and whatever else you wanted and bring it over to the chair where you had your hair done.

As Beth I often wore a fall on the back side of my head, which could be styled and attached to prevent wear and tear on my real hair. Many mornings I would see actor Jack Klugman come in with his German Shepherd dog to have his makeup and hair done for the TV show *Quincy, M.E.*, which was also filmed on the Universal lot. Like Edith Head, the hair and makeup people were perfectionists. One day a production assistant came to the building to take me to the set. One of the hair professionals stopped him before I got out of the door.

"Wait. She can't leave. That fall doesn't blend in well enough with her real hair. She has to come back."

The production assistant told her, "It's fine. It's for a short scene where she's wearing a hat."

I went back to the chair to have the hair blended in the way it had been for every prior scene. I admire this about the creative venture of making a movie or a TV show. It's a community of specialists, each in their own skill, creating one product. You might be the best director going, but if you don't have a lighting designer who knows exactly what is needed to light a scene, then you can't capture it on camera. As many actors attribute during award shows, there is no dialogue to speak without a writer who has told the story of the film. There is no point in speaking the lines without an expert soundperson, who is making sure you can be heard and there's no noise from overhead airplanes in a movie about 1860s America.

From the time I was a small child, I've always been fascinated by how it all comes together. I can often be found on a set chatting with the crew about what they do and how they do it. I've never understood when actors approach their work as if they are the most important aspect of production. I am grateful for the years I spent growing up on camera where I quickly learned how every job on the show is a link in the chain, and if one area is weak, it can affect the results. It's especially bolstering when you can sense that the other actors are watching out for you, and you for them, which was true on *Little Women*.

One day Meredith Baxter Birney was waiting for her next scene and she called me over to her before I went on camera.

"Eve, come over here for a second. You have something all around your mouth. You look like you've been sucking on a tailpipe."

Sure enough, I had some gray shadowy stain around my mouth. I'm not sure where it came from; perhaps I had put my hand down in cigarette ash and then accidentally wiped it across my mouth.

She made me laugh and helped me to get it off my face. I was grateful she caught it before I went on camera and they had to stop the take.

There were other incredible veteran actors in the miniseries who were fascinating to watch: Dorothy McGuire as my mother, Robert Young as the Scrooge-like neighbor, and Greer Garson in the role of the elderly wealthy aunt. I especially took note at how Greer put aspects of her character into every scene, like walking in the house with her cane and pausing to adjust a crooked frame on a painting, even if it wasn't called for in the script. I felt too shy to engage with either Dorothy or Greer personally, which I regret now. I'm certain I could have learned valuable insights from each. I left them alone, a holdover inclination from my child-actor days on the set with adults.

I didn't feel as reserved or shy around the crew and would joke around with them on a daily basis. I noticed one crew member, Rick, who was with the lighting team, began finding more opportunities to talk to me. I thought he was handsome, and when he asked me out on a date, I said yes.

Rick was ten years older than me and had also grown up in a Hollywood family. We had that in common. His father had worked for a film development company and was a World War II vet. When the Vietnam War happened in the late 1960s, Rick had felt a family obligation to follow in his dad's footsteps. During basic training in the state of Washington, he was bunkmates with someone who became his good friend. After about six weeks, the buddy was called up to be transferred to Vietnam. He confessed to Rick that he was actually a conscientious objector and didn't want to see or be involved in battle. Rick, feeling the generational pull to represent, somehow convinced the higher-ranking officers that he was more qualified as a door gunner and should be the one to go. He was sent instead of his buddy to operate a machine gun, sparing his friend from seeing active duty.

I soon came to understand his daredevil personality, but saw it as a good characteristic for being protective. He began doing deep-sea diving photography and loved surfing. He eventually went to the police academy to become an officer. We dated for about six months and then became engaged.

I believed that I had fallen in love and, more than that, I thought it was the natural progression of how life goes. My mother married at nineteen. My sister got married at twenty. I thought it was literally "my turn" to go into married life. My mother encouraged me to wait until I was twenty-one, which I did, but she didn't have much ground to stand on, as she had married young and it had worked out fine.

During my engagement I was cast in a made-for-TV movie, *The Night the Bridge Fell Down*. I played a woman who was leaving the young policeman she had been dating to join a convent after working in a Catholic orphanage. A damaged bridge has been opened without being inspected and it collapses on both ends, trapping some cars in the middle. The movie co-stars James MacArthur, Desi Arnaz Jr., Leslie Nielsen, and Barbara Rush, whose daughter I had played in the pilot that didn't make it to series years earlier. Most of the movie takes place at night, so the soundstage was dark and eerie, with large metal beams to represent the collapsing bridge. There isn't a single intentional laugh line in the entire three hours, though anyone watching today would probably laugh at the improbability of most of what happens. I don't know what young nuns are supposed to dress like, but I'm in a shapeless over vest, long brown skirt, and very sensible grandma-ish shoes.

Before the television and film industry realized that Leslie Nielsen was comedic gold, prior to *Airplane* and *Naked Gun*, he was cast in very dramatic roles. All of the humor was done off camera, but he was great at breaking up everyone in the cast and crew. Early in the filming schedule, as the cast would be waiting to go on the set, he would squeeze a rubber fart-sound-making bag hidden in the palm of his hand; and then, with a deadpan face, he'd look in disgust at whoever was next to him, as if they had farted. At first, everyone tried to pretend they didn't hear someone fart loudly, which made us laugh even harder when we realized what was actually going on. From that point on, if there was a new "victim" on the set that day, we'd have Leslie torture him with the fart maker as we all turned to stare at the newcomer in disbelief and they would struggle to defend their innocence. Leslie could keep a straight face like no one else.

If I had a day off from filming, my dad and I went together to look for a venue for the wedding reception, which was at the Universal Hilton, in one of their ballrooms. On the evening of the dress rehearsal, I was held over on the film set and didn't make it to the chapel on time. It went on without me.

The next day Rick and I married in a chapel at the church that my parents had helped to found, Encino Community Church. It was a small gathering and I chose not to invite any of *The Brady Bunch* family. I knew that I was the first Brady kid to get married and I really didn't want to make it a press event, only a private ceremony.

And so I was married. My final thought right before the

pastor declared us to be husband and wife was this one: *Well, if it doesn't work out, I can always get a divorce.*

I'm not proud to admit that truth, but it is the truth. I had my reservations while the wedding was being planned. I was still continuing to live my life with the belief that if I had already committed to do something, then I must follow through. Only this time it wasn't a two-month miniseries shoot or a sitcom that would eventually be canceled. It was, supposedly, "till death do us part."

Chapter Eleven

The *Little Women* miniseries had very good ratings and NBC decided to turn it into a series. At first, I thought, *Well, I'm out. Beth died in the miniseries.* Then my agent called to say the producers wanted me to be in the series as Cousin Lissa, who was coming north from her destroyed manor in the Deep South following the Civil War. I signed on, delighted that the character may have looked just like Beth, but she was very different. She was crafty and feisty and had a bigger personality than Beth. I was given a dialect coach to help me with that particular Southern accent.

Dorothy McGuire returned as Marmee and Robert Young signed back on for the series, but Susan Dey and Meredith Baxter Birney had both moved on to other projects. Susan had given birth to her daughter. The roles of Meg and Jo were recast. It was fun to film the eight episodes—I got to wear actual hoop skirts—but the competition to get viewer numbers was tough because our show ran opposite the TV sitcom *Mork & Mindy*. NBC tried to hang in there, but Robin Williams's comic rising star sealed the fate of our one-hour drama. I tuned in myself to watch Robin bounce off the walls.

* * *

Sherwood Schwartz had come up with a reunion idea for the Brady family. What if Marcia and Jan both found men they wanted to marry and their engagements and wedding plans were happening simultaneously? *The Brady Girls Get Married*, the TV movie, would be the first and the last time the entire original cast would ever be together on a TV project. The house set was rebuilt, true to its original look, and we all went back to work. My agent, my parents, and the other cast members were all for it. Sherwood had not been a part of, or in support of, the misguided Brady variety hour, but he never gave up on the Brady brand. He had decided that people would be interested to see the Brady kids grown up, and he wasn't wrong.

The ratings were great, although the critics pointed out every unbelievable twist and turn, which were numerous, beginning with a double wedding. I'm pretty sure even grown-up Jan wouldn't be excited to share the spotlight with Marcia. Nevertheless, they decide to get married in the backyard, half traditional for Jan, and half modern for Marcia. It's a gorgeous day until a massive thunderstorm rolls in after five seconds of the Wedding March, with Marcia and Jan each on an arm of Mike Brady. The happy ending takes place with us being married inside the house, near the famous staircase, and concluded with the four-tiered wedding cake being dropped and landing on the face of Marcia's new husband. Why not? It's a Brady tradition.

Like *Little Women*, I thought it was a one-off line on my career résumé, only to get a call from my agent that they wanted to turn the idea into a sitcom. This time it would be Maureen and me, with other Bradys making occasional guest star appearances, if possible. It's not like my phone was ablaze with other offers, and the idea of having another series seemed like a happy relief. Jan was now an architect, which I liked. No one was expecting the submissive housewife role. Maureen and I were each given a dressing room on the set, like grown-up lead actresses, and were asked how we would like it decorated. It felt decadent to be able to pick out the fabrics and paint colors and pieces of furniture for our dressing rooms.

The Brady Brides sitcom was the first time I had acted in front of a live TV audience. It was an interesting change, as I had to quickly adjust to the audible reactions of the audience. It gave me more opportunity to understand comic timing and stay focused on the scene, while at the same time pausing for laughs. We would meet up on Mondays, do a table read of the script, rehearse on Tuesdays, get our costumes, and decide on hair and makeup. On Thursdays we filmed the show in front of an audience, usually tourists to Los Angeles.

Maureen and I reconnected on a certain friendship level as well, spending time outside of work to go shopping or see a movie. She had a darling one-bedroom apartment that she had impressively decorated and we would hang out, drink coffee, and smoke cigarettes. Maureen thought it was a great idea for us to be seen in public together as press for the sitcom. She thought we should go to restaurants and some clubs, where the paparazzi might catch photos of us. I was up for it in a promotional sense, though I never went to clubs. When I would ask her when she wanted to go, she would put it off. I didn't know why, until later.

I never drank any alcohol at all in my twenties and thirties, most likely because I saw how it affected my mother almost every night when I was growing up. No one spoke of it out loud in my family, but shortly before I moved out, my father took a bottle of vodka and dumped it all down the sink while saying, "The problem in this house is that there's too much drinking." I loved my father for never making my mother feel humiliated about her alcoholism, at least not in front of me, but I also felt sorry for him to have to come home from work, knowing that she would probably be tipsy, at the least. In my childlike mind, I thought that you can't have alcohol without having a personality change or becoming embarrassing or sloppy.

I had also never taken drugs. I didn't go to clubs or Hollywood parties, so I wasn't around it much, although it was very prevalent in the television, film, and sports industries at that time. I was oblivious to the fact that Maureen had acquired an addiction to cocaine, which she made public for herself later in life in her own memoir. She never did drugs around me, and if she did them on the set, I didn't notice.

What was noticeable is when she wouldn't show up for a day of rehearsal or when we needed to do some pickup filming, perhaps for shots or reactions that they didn't get during the live taping. The entire cast and crew were called in to work on Christmas Eve, to capture a few scenes that needed to be shot for the next episode. There were a few grumbles, but Lloyd Schwartz, who was also producing, said, "Look, I'm Jewish, and I've always had to work almost every Jewish holiday, so this time you all have to work one Christmas Eve."

The set was ready, the cameras in place, the crew on standby, but Maureen did not arrive. One hour went by, then two. Finally, the director moved ahead, getting the re-

Beach house.
(Author's personal collection)

Soldering at beach house.
(Author's personal collection)

Dangerous swing.
(Author's personal collection)

PRESS ON

NOTHING IN THE WORLD CAN TAKE THE PLACE OF PERSISTENCE

TALENT WILL NOT: NOTHING IS MORE COMMON THAN UNSUCCESSFUL PEOPLE WITH TALENT

GENIUS WILL NOT: UNREWARDED GENIUS IS A PROVERB.

EDUCATION WILL NOT: THE WORLD IS FULL OF EDUCATED DERELICTS

PERSISTENCE AND DETERMINATION ALONE ARE OMNIPOTENT

A quote Dad posted over his desk.
(Author's personal collection)

Myron, the mouse from the *Brady* episode that they let me keep as a pet.
(Author's personal collection)

EVE PLUMB

CREDITS

Age 14, Born April 29, 1958
Blonde, Blue Eyes, 60 inches tall
Student of Judo/Karate, Ballet & Guitar
Singer in addition to her Acting Career

Representation:
JUNIOR ARTISTS UNLIMITED
Helen Mayer Bruce 763-9000

Featured as JAN in THE BRADY BUNCH, ABC TV(Just Completed 4th Year;over 100 Episodes)

Has had feature and guest starring roles in the following shows:

IN NAME ONLY (Feature for TV)	LASSIE
THEN CAME BRONSON	THE VIRGINIAN
LANCER	THE BIG VALLEY (Explosion Pt. II)
GUNSMOKE	THE BIG VALLEY (Brother Love)
FAMILY AFFAIR	THE BIG VALLEY (Hide The Children)
HOUSE ON GREENAPPLE ROAD (Feature for TV)	THE DICK TRACY SHOW (Pilot)
MANNIX	THE SMOTHERS BROTHERS SHOW
ADAM 12	THE BARBARA RUSH SHOW (Pilot)
IT TAKES A THIEF	BONANZA
THE BRADY KIDS (Animated Series Sat. AM)	LUCILLE BALL (Co starring with Donny Osmond)
THE BRADY KIDS (2 ABC Specials)	THE DATING GAME

COMMERCIALS

Glad Bags	Allied Van Lines
Mattel Toys (10 Commercials)	Kool Aid
Lever Brothers	Pream
Kellogg's	Interstate Bakeries
Nalley's Potato Chips	Biz Bag
Proctor & Gamble	
One-A-Day Vitamins	

Singing Credits

RCA RECORDS SINGLE: (SOLO ARTIST) "HOW WILL IT BE?" c/w "THE FORTUNE COOKIE SONG"
RCA RECORDS "Dr. Dolittle" LP with Anthony Newley/Jimmy Joyce Children's Chorus
20th CENTURY-FOX "Dr. Dolittle" Soundtrack with Jimmy Joyce Children's Chorus
RCA RECORDS "Oh Dad, Poor Dad" with Neal Hefti/Jimmy Joyce Children's Chorus
CAPITOL RECORDS with Soupy Sales/Jimmy Joyce Children's Chorus
NANCY SINATRA TV SPECIAL with Jimmy Joyce Children's Chorus

EVE IS THE YOUNGEST VOTING MEMBER of NARAS (National Academy Of Recording Arts & Sciences)

PARAMOUNT RECORDS - 3 ALBUMS with THE BRADY KIDS

THE BRADY KIDS (Song & Dance Act)

The DICK CLARK SHOW (3 appearances ABC TV)
The MERV GRIFFIN SHOW
The ED SULLIVAN SHOW, AGVA Awards

THE BRADY KIDS (Song & Dance Act)

IN CONCERT ON TOUR - 1972-1973 Season

1972 résumé.
(Author's personal collection)

My brother Ben, my sister June, and I.
(Author's personal collection)

Needlepoint was all the rage.
(Author's personal collection)

Signing albums on a Saturday.
(Author's personal collection)

Brady Kids' outfits for our act.
(Author's personal collection)

The three girls in our opening number costumes.
(Author's personal collection)

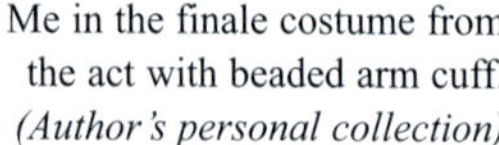

Me in the finale costume from the act with beaded arm cuff.
(Author's personal collection)

We performed at the AGVA awards show with Ed Sullivan. *(Author's personal collection)*

Susan and I at Knott's Berry Farm in our prairie hats. *(Author's personal collection)*

100th show party cake with Robert and Florence. *(Author's personal collection)*

It was fun to be a cheerleader.
(Author's personal collection)

Ellen and I went to the Renaissance Faire as mimes.
(Author's personal collection)

Homecoming. I'm in the middle, no surprise.
(Author's personal collection)

Prom dress.
(Author's personal collection)

High school graduation.
(Author's personal collection)

EVE 1 license plate.
(Author's personal collection)

With Mark Hamill,
shooting the Kodak commercial.
(Author's personal collection)

With my horse, Ace.
(Author's personal collection)

Little Women wardrobe continuity photo.
(Author's personal collection)

Harry Langdon photo with appropriate props.
(Author's personal collection)

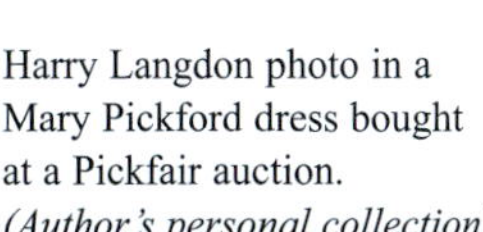

Harry Langdon photo in a Mary Pickford dress bought at a Pickfair auction.
(Author's personal collection)

'80s headshot.
(Author's personal collection)

Bucks County Playhouse, where I played Nellie in *South Pacific*. *(Author's personal collection)*

Me and Broadway's John Bolton when we met during summer stock. *(Author's personal collection)*

Florence and I on the *Fudge* set.
(Author's personal collection)

Florence and I at
Broadway Backwards.
(Author's personal collection)

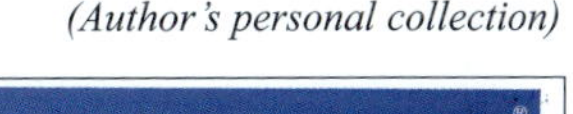

Flo telegram.
(Author's personal collection)

FLORENCE HENDERSON PM
MARINA DEL REY CA 90292 28AM

Western Union Mailgram

4-0151733119 04/28/88 ICS IPMRNCZ CSP LSAB
6158891000 MGMS TDRN NASHVILLE TN 43 04-28 1239P EST

EVE PLUMB
NORTH HOLLYWOOD CA 91607

DEAREST EVE

30. I CAN'T BELIEVE IT. I WAS 34 WHEN WE STARTED THE BRADY BUNCH. I HOPE YOU HAVE THE BEST BIRTHDAY EVER. WISH I COULD BE THERE.

GOD BLESS AND LOVE.
FLORENCE

12:43 EST

MGMCOMP

Kelley and I: Feminine HiJinks.
(Author's personal collection)

Feminine HiJinks.
A social media post in the '80s was a paper flyer.
(Author's personal collection)

A fave pic of me and Chris Knight.
(Author's personal collection)

Cynthia Szigeti
invites you to
. . . cause how often are girls this funny?
starring
Lisa Fineberg, Lisa Kudrow,
Stacey Michaels, Eve Plumb, and
Audrey Rapoport
with Tim Bagley and Chris Darga
Tuesdays & Thursdays
July 10, 12, 17, 19
8pm
at the Groundling Theatre
7307 Melrose Ave.
for reservations and information call . . .
213/285-7746

Girls Club postcard we sent out.

Ken and I when we first met.
(Author's personal collection)

A note Mom sent before the wedding.
(Author's personal collection)

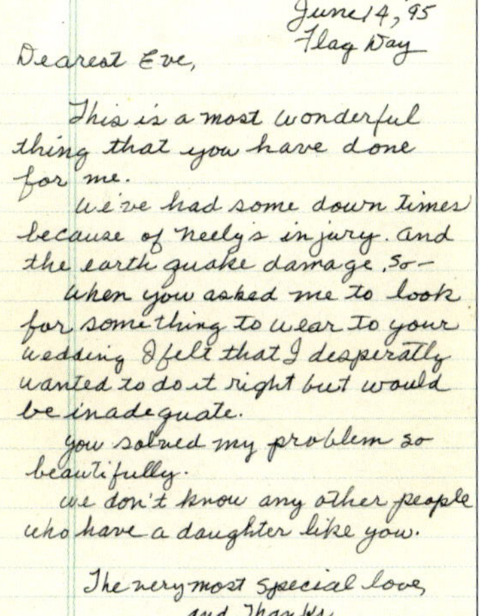

June 14, '95
Flag Day

Dearest Eve,

This is a most wonderful thing that you have done for me.

We've had some down times because of Neely's injury. and the earth quake damage, so—

when you asked me to look for something to wear to your wedding I felt that I desperatly wanted to do it right but would be inadequate.

You solved my problem so beautifully.

We don't know any other people who have a daughter like you.

The very most special love,
and Thanks
your Mom

Wedding. Left to right: Jann Goldsby, Stacey Michaels, me, Ken, Jim Fithian, nephew Kyle Johnson, Rich Chasin.
(Author's personal collection)

Palette I painted for the Laguna Beach holiday decorations. *(Author's personal collection)*

Mom and the "Minnie Winnie," her home away from home. *(Author's personal collection)*

Our Happiness Included Coffee.
(Author's personal collection)

One of the original daisy patterns.
(Author's personal collection)

Now That's Done film noir oil painting.
(Author's personal collection)

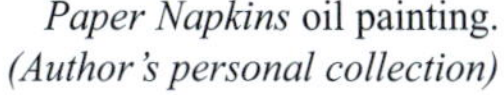

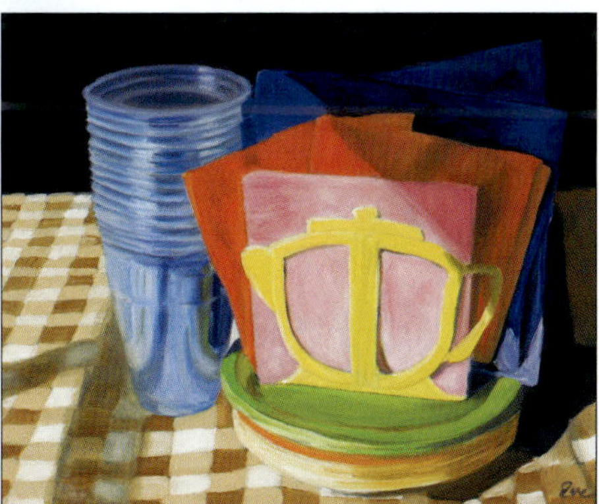

Paper Napkins oil painting.
(Author's personal collection)

Me and June. *(Author's personal collection)*

Neely and Flora June Plumb. *(Author's personal collection)*

action shots from me that he could. A few more hours went by and then the day was canceled. The cast and crew were silently angry, and someone had been sent to Maureen's apartment and found her completely strung out and unable to work.

The *Brady* cast has, for the most part, had a code of silence among us and I've tried to honor that. If Maureen had not spoken of this time in her life, neither would I. *The Brady Brides* was canceled due to ratings, not because of Maureen. The cancelation for me coincided with taking a step back from an ongoing friendship with her. For me, the issue was her disrespect of others by not showing up for her obligations and costing everyone on the show both time and money. I'm still that way, probably too much so, but it's the reason I don't commit to anything, even a social event, if I think I won't want to follow through when it is time.

My parents remained encouraging following the cancelation. My dad offered to call the agent to help in making sure I was being seen for other opportunities.

Before Rick and I married, he had lived in Hermosa Beach. He wanted to stay close to the sea, so we found a house in Redondo Beach we wanted to buy, one where we could walk down to the beach and he could surf often. I would go with him and take my boogie board. We both were happy spending hours in the ocean. My parents were not for the move to Redondo Beach. They thought we should stay in Los Angeles not an hour's drive away, reminding me that I had a great career and had made the transition from child to adult roles. My mother would say, "Work begets work. If they see you on the screen, then they see your value as an actor and want you, too." The idea of it is true, but there are a million factors that go into casting a show and it usually centers on the performer they want as the star of the show.

Redondo Beach became a fun fix-up project for me and took my mind off the truth that the phone wasn't ringing off the wall with acting opportunities. For the first year or so of our marriage, I was content learning to snorkel and taking trips with Rick to Hawaii and Europe. At one point he kindly encouraged me to buy a horse to ride. I did, and named him Ace. I boarded the horse nearby and went to learn to ride almost every day. Horses need a lot of attention and exercise. After a while I got very relaxed being on horseback, and one day decided to go out on the trail by myself with just the saddle pad, which is merely a padded blanket strapped under the horse's belly. On a down slope, the blanket slipped and I went over the side and fell to the ground, startling Ace. He took off running without me and never came back. It was a long walk back to the stable.

Being a smart guy, Ace knew the way back to the stables. When I finally arrived, the barn manager told me that he had been prancing around, trying to eat the other horses' hay, and misbehaving as loose horses do. They caught him and put him back in his stall—the one he could manage to get out of until I changed the latch. I was amused by his sassiness. Every holiday he would allow me to dress him in a Santa hat or bunny ears so I could take his photo. He would hold perfectly still, as though he were in on the whole joke.

Over the next three years, I did three *Love Boat* and three *Fantasy Island* episodes as a guest star. I was always hoping that one of the shows would require my presence in Hawaii or on an actual cruise ship, but everything was shot in the studio. It seemed I was always there when the location manager would come in with photos of their next fun location. It was still interesting to work with the other guest stars who were famous for their TV and movie roles, like Peter Graves and Marion Ross.

In one very dramatic *Fantasy Island*, I played a young woman wanting to contact her dead twin brother through a séance. She didn't believe that he had actually committed suicide and it turns out he comes through to say he had been murdered by the cousin third in line to inherit the family fortune. I played the twin brother as well, dressed in an overcoat with a moustache. The special effects were very rudimentary, with flashes and swirls and sheets of pelting rain coming down on me. It was one of the more fun weeks of production, as the unpredictable Leslie Nielsen and I were reunited, with him playing my rich uncle.

The best part of being on those shows is that I didn't have to audition. It would be an invitation, since they always wanted to have TV or movie personalities as the guest stars. I know Florence Henderson and Robert Reed appeared in an episode of *The Love Boat*, actually playing Carol and Mike Brady. Maureen and Barry were also in other separate episodes. It was always a yes from me when my agent would call to see if I wanted to do one of the shows.

There was no exact turning point where the marriage began to disintegrate. Rick was happy to have me work as much as I wanted. He didn't seem to mind that I didn't do any of the typical homemaker things, like cook dinner or take care of all the laundry. When he wanted to train as a policeman, I was for it, but it made me take a closer look at my own life. I had only been on a few shows, which added up to about three weeks of work per year. I was twenty-four years old and couldn't imagine what I would do with my life, married to a police officer and living in Redondo Beach, an hour away from Hollywood and most of my friends.

My sister, now living in LA, was directing two one-act plays, each with two men and a woman, at a small ninety-nine-seat house in Hollywood. She wanted me to be in them. I drove daily up to LA for rehearsals and began to feel like some life blood was pumping through my heart again. It was invigorating to be participating in something creative. Rick didn't seem to mind and would remind me, "There can only be one star in this family and you're it."

As I went toward rehearsals in LA, I found myself moving mentally away from being a young wife. One day my sister and I went to grab a bite to eat in a Beverly Hills restaurant, and June asked, "What's going on with you?"

I told her, "I'm not sure. I have a great house in Redondo Beach that I've enjoyed fixing up. I have an adorable horse to ride whenever I want. I can go to the beach at any time. But I'm not very happy in my life. I don't know what to do about it."

Being fourteen years older than me, she advised me to take some time, figure out what I really wanted for my life. That would have been the wise thing to do, I agreed. That's not what I did right away, because a new catalyst of change entered my life in the body of one of the stagecraft guys hired on by the theater. He wore flannel shirts and grungy jeans; had long, shaggy hair and a creative nature. He began to flirt with me and I soaked it up. He wanted to be a filmmaker and looked at life with a "what's interesting to me" attitude—one that I found wildly attractive. He invited me to hang out with his friends, who lived in an artist-hub shared house in Echo Park, and we'd go to Gorky's, a bohemian-style coffeehouse and brewery in downtown LA that was open twenty-four hours and hosted open mics for performers. The unpredictable nature of being around artists who didn't follow the rules of expected behavior gave me a sense of freedom that I had never felt before. After growing up with protective parents, working in a structured studio environment, a year of formal college classes, and now a married life, I had followed the rules so well, I had no idea what I *wanted* to do outside of what I thought I *should* do.

I didn't tell Rick about any of this. Instead, I began to concoct made-up reasons I needed to go to LA, when it was really only to hang out with this crush and his artist pals. One afternoon the crush wanted to make a short film and we all jumped in as actors, wearing some type of aluminum foil hats. I played along, thinking that it must be what really creative people do, without ever wondering if there was a purpose to any of it.

Over a sticky table and overflowing ashtrays at Gorky's at one a.m., I would say things to his friends, like, "I don't know what to do with my life." And they would tell me, "Well, first you have to figure out how to contribute. How do you want to get out there and contribute to society?" Sadly, I had never thought of it that way. No one had encouraged me to be introspective about what I might want for my life up to that point. It seemed like an eye-opener to realize that I could ask it of myself and also decide for myself.

Some of this group was heading off to New York City for the one hundredth anniversary of the Brooklyn Bridge. I wanted to go, too, and planned a way to be a part of it.

Late at night I would drive back to Redondo Beach, thinking, *My crush on this guy proves that I shouldn't be married. Otherwise, I wouldn't be feeling this.*

I told Rick that I was going as part of a future project,

which was not altogether false. I thought my upcoming project was to see if I really wanted to be with this crush guy. I decided to treat him to this trip I knew he couldn't possibly afford. I bought both of us round-trip plane tickets and reserved a hotel room for a long weekend. In my logical mind, I was thinking, *This is wrong. I'm married.* But my impulsive heart was feeling that if I didn't get to kiss this guy in the rain that I would forever regret it. I had a different movie playing out in my head, not unlike Sir Lancelot and Guinevere, forbidden love that is inevitable. My movie didn't involve aluminum foil hats and bad lighting.

He was very late getting to the airport, in a sour mood, saying he had been delayed by traffic. We still made the flight and I hoped his mood would switch to flirtation and romance. It didn't. He stared out the window for most of the six hours, barely speaking. In New York he walked way ahead of me, down the sidewalk, to the hotel. Trying to lighten the heavy atmosphere, I joked, calling out, "Hey, what am I, an anchor on your ass?"

He snarled back at me, "Well, yeah. It looks like you're gonna be."

The hotel held no reprieve or flicker of romance, especially when he invited the bellhop who had brought our bags to the room to come in and get high with him. As the two of them sat on the couch smoking pot, I tried to keep my thoughts from scrambling about what this meant and what I had done to make him so suddenly indifferent. The weekend held almost no physical contact at all with him—seeming to take a giant step back from the flirtatious guy from the week before. When I sat on the edge of the tub to watch him shave in the morning, he asked me, "What are you looking at? Why are you watching me?"

Despite the earlier part of the weekend being a blur, illuminating clarity filled my mind. This dude isn't a cool, free-thinking artist. His art is to pursue what he thinks he can't have; and once he does, to reject it as a power move. That's what was happening here. I'm sure it was a game for him to see if he could get the married woman to stray. Once I set it up where something might actually happen, he turned into a jerk. I know, in the big picture, I was spared, but it didn't stop me from feeling like a hurt fool who had actually paid for an expensive weekend, only to feel rejection. I canceled the rest of the hotel weekend and called my friend, Jann Goldsby, who lived in Manhattan, to see if I could stay with her for the next couple of days. I don't know where he disappeared to, and I didn't care.

On the morning I was supposed to fly back to Los Angeles, I called Rick to say that I was going to stay in New York for a few more days to visit with my friend Jann. She lived in a small one-bedroom apartment in Hell's Kitchen, on the fifth floor of a walk-up apartment building. Hell's Kitchen in the early 1980s was gritty and not considered a desirable neighborhood as it is today. I arrived with a glistening smile, mostly beads of sweat on my upper-lip area from climbing five flights with a suitcase. I pushed my suitcase into her closet and made a bed on her couch. Four weeks later I was still there.

Jann and I would talk every day about my unhappiness and what to do about my marriage. She was a great friend and never made me feel like I was in her way, despite her apartment being small. I spent my days walking around New York, going to a few galleries, and mostly sitting in a café or on a bench with a notebook, drawing or writing down thoughts. I considered all the ways I could stay in New York, how I could get an agent and perhaps audition for theater or one of the soap operas that filmed there every day. The buzz of the Manhattan streets took me farther and farther away from my life in Redondo Beach. I rarely called Rick, though he would reach out to ask when I was coming home. He let me know that my parents were asking about what was going on as well.

On the weekends, Jann and I would go dancing at a gay nightclub, surrounded by beautiful men and the scent of Calvin Klein cologne. We'd walk back to her apartment, bypassing drug dealers and people passed out on the sidewalk from drinking.

I didn't want to go home, but I knew I couldn't stay in denial about the life and the husband I had left behind. I decided to tell him about my original reason for coming to New York and getting a hotel room with the guy I had a crush on. I think I was hoping he would say that he wanted to have an affair as well, and we could both admit that the marriage no longer worked and part ways peacefully. Instead, he told me he could forgive me for doing that and he really wanted to give our marriage a go, so would I please come home.

I booked a flight, back to our marriage and my Redondo Beach neighborhood. I got back on the horse, literally and figuratively, hoping the phone would ring with another audition, bought some canvases and began to paint for myself. Rick continued his police training and scuba diving. One weekend a guy I had dated for a short while in college, and continued to remain as friends, came to see me at my invitation. We went out for the day and talked, a simple and fun catchup with each other. That evening we were going to go out to see a play together. Rick had to go to work, and when my friend saw his gun in the holster, he got worried. Rick had been silent and withdrawn, and my friend thought it was about him.

When I got back later that night, Rick said to me, "Well, I forgave you for that first guy you told me about, but it looks like the same thing is happening with this guy."

Instead of having the courage to tell Rick that absolutely nothing was going on, and I just didn't want to be married anymore, I said, "You're right, it's happening. So I'm going to move out."

I knew that there was an open apartment in the Echo Park building that was more of a converted old mansion. The crush guy was gone, and some of the other arty people as well. Different, interesting people had moved in and I wanted to be a part of it. The building was awkwardly divided into various apartments, but I knew the two rooms and small kitchen I would rent would be enough for me. Dave, the guy who managed the building, told me the apartment was mine if I wanted it. I moved before I told my parents, as I knew they would both worry about my relationship with Rick being over, as well as my new living situation, because the building was located near to downtown LA which seemed dangerous to them. I took a few pieces of furniture, and because of the small size of the place, I bought a futon that would double as a couch and a bed.

The industrial look was very popular then, so I painted the bathroom floor red with stamps of different colors in circles and triangles in gray and black. I began to paint more and made my own Christmas tree from two large pieces of intersected cardboard, painted it green and hung red glass ornaments into punch holes in the cardboard.

When my parents visited, my mother looked with disappointment at my homemade spruce as she perched uncomfortably on the edge of the futon couch. "Oh, Eve. Don't make fun of Christmas," she said. She didn't see any need for improvising on tradition. I wanted anything but tradition.

At some point along the way, I did a guest star spot on *The Facts of Life*. I played Blair's stepsister, once a wild goodtime girl, who decides to do a one-eighty with her life, join a convent, and become a nun. As irony would have it, I personally felt that my life was going one-eighty in the other direction. I had lived a structured life, mostly around career professionals; functioned with the rules of the business and not strayed far from what my parents would approve of for me. Now I wanted to be free of my long Jan Brady hair, speak up with my own voice, and dip my arms in paint up to my elbows.

I don't know if this passage of change for me could be coined a midlife crisis, since I was only twenty-five years old, but within months I was driving a red Mustang convertible. Also, within months I accidentally backed it into a garage pillar, crunching a rear light and knocking off a side mirror, then having to stop short in traffic on the freeway and rear-ending the car in front of me. Nothing like a flashy red Mustang that looks beat-up. The soft top would stick going up and down and I would have to push or pull it. The trunk could hold two shoeboxes and that was about it. It really was not the car for me.

I boldly cut many inches off my hair, which felt like releasing years of long-hair obligations. Then I began questioning if all of the positive thinking mantras that I had taped up around my apartment were really doing anything at all. Did it really make sense that I could think myself successful or protected from harm or even healthy through making statements out loud, as though it would make it so? Did other people deserve misfortune or ill health simply because they didn't know the tenets of metaphysics and speak powerful statements? Could I really memorize lines by sleeping with my head on a script? Suddenly, it all seemed so subjective, as if the world operated differently for some of us than it did for all of us. It was freeing not to have to watch my language anymore, to be able to admit that I was sad or angry. I treaded carefully into some new thinking, allowing myself to question everything that I had wholeheartedly believed before.

I dated a bunch of different men and took classes in Brazilian capoeira, a style of fighting dance. As I kicked my leg in a force-filled arch through the air, I felt an emergence of a new aspect of myself. I knew I still wanted to be an actress, but now I also wanted to be a woman who was no longer striving to fill an expected role in my real life.

Chapter Twelve

On my own, yet feeling a part of the artists' house in Echo Park, I let myself explore what I thought had been missing from my life. Without a TV to distract me, I had plenty of time to think. It probably would have been a good idea to pause and really go inward, as they say, but I wanted to date again. What had worked for my mother, marrying young, had not been the answer for me. I wasn't interested in committing to one man when there was a sampler platter of possibilities. After years of feeling that imposing "I should," I wanted to see what "I could" experience, so I decided to free myself of expectations and went out with a wider variety of men.

I dated men who, like me, were not interested in signing up for a long-term commitment, so there weren't contrary feelings. It was interesting and a relief not to have to work on maintaining a relationship. Chemistry really is a player in the dating game. There were guys that I wanted to get to know better and a few that I couldn't wait to discontinue. After experiencing the feeling of a rising revulsion when one date leaned in to kiss me, I learned to end mismatched dates quickly with a courteous handshake and a determined solo stride to the front door of my apartment.

I dated a magician, and my Brazilian dance instructor, and a memorable French video artist named Pier (pronounced Pierre). He was exploring his Jewish roots through Orthodox practices. Whenever we would meet up on Saturdays, I, being the Gentile in his life, could turn on the lights in keeping with the Sabbath traditions in his Hollywood apartment, a studio-sized space built on top of a garage. We saw each other for a few months during which he introduced me to a method of therapy called co-counseling. It wasn't connected to any religion or specific practice. I was given a list of people who wanted to practice this form of therapy, although we were mostly all strangers to one another.

We would connect with one other person by phone and then meet up at a specific time at their place or at mine. The entire therapeutic format was to sit across from each other, hold hands between us, and then each person would have a decided amount of time, say, fifteen minutes, to talk nonstop about their issue or a problem in their lives. The other person was not to give suggestions or ask questions, only to listen in agreement with the speaker. I found it to be incredibly effective, because it made me understand that for most issues or problems, we have the answers within ourselves and this method of therapy was great for uncovering the answer. Going from only thinking about a problem to verbalizing it with someone listening in agreement gave it a chance to be shaken out and given air. By the fifteen-minute mark, I would have a new level of clarity. It was both eye-opening and a happy discovery for me that I could figure things out on my own. No money was paid; no advice was given or received.

Without continuous acting jobs to show up for every

week, I went to an art supply store and bought some new canvases and a set of acrylic paints and brushes. It was great to live in a building where all of the other residents saw any type of artistic expression as a worthy cause. Art and design had always been a fascination for me, but as a child it wasn't particularly encouraged by my parents. I was doing a paint-by-number set when I was about seven or eight, and when I got frustrated trying to follow the color grid with the little paint pots, my mother took it away from me, saying that I was "too young to do it correctly."

When I was about nine, there was an ad for Art Instruction Schools that you could do through the mail. You had to draw one of the characters in the ad: Tippy the Turtle, a pirate, a fawn, a mouse in a birthday hat, and a dog's head. It was pitched as a contest with prizes. I drew the dog and sent it in. I probably got a stamp from my dad, without telling him what I was doing. About a month later, a representative salesperson from the school wanted to set up an appointment for my parents to pay for me to take home instruction, as they saw talent in my drawing. My father wasn't unhappy with me, but it definitely didn't go forward. As he explained to me, "It's a gimmick. They just want your money." That was the end of it. I'm sure it seemed too complicated for my parents to balance correspondence art instruction, along with my acting career. I remember feeling disappointed about it, because it was something I had generated on my own that I wanted to do.

On *The Brady Bunch*, Susan Olsen and I would draw cartoons or animals, and Frances Whitfield encouraged me as an artist in our school time, especially during the summer months, when the academics were far less stringent.

Now, with more time to myself, I set myself up to experiment with painting. I would find photos in magazines or books that I liked and attempt to replicate them. I created a lighthearted series of food images from 1950s magazines ads a round layer cake with fluffy frosting on a cake stand, a Ferris wheel of peas and corn, whatever caught my eye.

There was great satisfaction in doing a project that was completely up to me. I didn't have to meet anyone else's expectations or timelines. I was in charge and I could start and finish when I wanted. It was a simple feeling of accomplishment, but one I had not experienced before. I didn't know what it was like to direct my own show, so to speak. I appreciated having the patience to fail and get better through practice and watch my skills and confidence grow over time. Unlike acting, where I had to please a whole group of people, here I found that as long as I was happy enough with what I had painted to put it up on the wall, I wasn't overly concerned with what others thought.

The week my divorce became finalized, I was sitting on my futon couch on a Friday evening, thumbing through my personal phone book. I found the number of a guy I knew during my one year at Cal State Northridge, another time when I felt artistic and free of definitions. I decided to check in with him. Michael was really happy to hear from me and wanted to get together. His enthusiasm made me feel interesting and attractive, and I remembered what a great guy he was. We started going out and got serious pretty quickly. When his apartment building was being sold and he needed to move, we decided to move in together.

The Echo Park house was too far away from everything,

and I had already made a point that I could live there, go to Gorky's late at night on my own if I wanted, and walk around downtown without it being dangerous. I don't know who it was that I needed to prove that to, as it wasn't going to change my parents' mind that there were a million better places to live. I guess it was to myself and my own claim to independence.

Michael and I found a place together in Studio City, and my mother said it was "too soon," when I told my parents we were living together. but I thought it was her sense of 1940s dating life and not pairing-up 1980s Los Angeles. I didn't heed her advice, though it would have been a wise thing to do.

Michael went off to work every day and I spent hours painting and also tried to figure out how to get more auditions. I had never had to promote or advocate for myself before and I wasn't sure how to proceed. I had moved on to a different agency after meeting with a CAA representative for lunch one day to discuss my career. She very honestly told me that the Creative Artists Agency wasn't going to get out there and work for me. They were growing by leaps and bounds and were far more focused on movie actors and directors.

I felt once again that I was well known for my child-actor years, but not thought of as an adult actress. My parents had taken a giant step back from giving me career advice, now that I was in my mid-twenties, so it was up to me to promote myself as an actress. I thought a smaller agency would bring more acting jobs my way, but they were always trying to tread water in an ever-changing industry and attract big-name clients. Most often my acting offers came from producers and directors I had worked with in the past on shows like *The Love Boat* and *Fantasy*

Island and *Wonder Woman*, the shows that wanted well-known guest stars for their episodes.

After spending our first Christmas together, Michael and I took a New Year's road trip to the Bay Area for a long weekend. Driving along the coast, we both fell under the spell of the charming seaside bungalows and village-type atmosphere, very unlike Los Angeles with its endless square miles of development. We had both been born and raised in the San Fernando Valley, so the idea of living somewhere else in California seemed intriguing.

I was standing in the kitchen one evening when Michael returned from work. He had an idea. He suggested that we move to the Bay Area, buy a house near the water, and start a new life. He was sure he could find a different job there, and if I got an audition, I could fly down for the day, no big deal.

Before he even finished speaking, I felt a crushing pressure on my chest. I couldn't take a deep breath. It wasn't a physical issue; it was an emotional reaction. It was the undeniable realization that I would be re-creating the exact same life that I had left behind in Redondo Beach, a life that I was dissatisfied with and that was painful to leave, both for me and for Rick. I didn't want to repeat that scenario. This time, instead of dodging the truth of it, I told Michael directly that I didn't want the life he was suggesting and also no longer wanted to be in a committed relationship with anyone, since I wasn't ready. My mother had been right, though she never did an "I told you so" about it all, at least not to me. It was years later that my sister disclosed that my parents were upset and sad that I divorced Rick, as they really liked him. They never let me know their personal disappointments with my decision, which was generous. I appreciate that they knew I had to make my own choices without them.

Thanks to my mother's good real estate advice—I've always said I have inherited her "real estate genes"—I had bought the house I had rented in Encino during my brief college year, and had been renting it out. The current renters had moved out, so I took the opportunity to move in alone, except for my Dalmatian dog, Topper. I went through a short downturn with feeling directionless and now single, and wishing I had a backup plan. The last time I had lived in this house I had to learn to clean, shop, and cook. This time I needed to plunge in and learn about my own finances. My father had taken care of it all until I married Rick, and then Rick took over. It's embarrassing to think that I let the men in my life handle the finances. Lucky for me, they were two very trustworthy men. Even today my husband, Ken, keeps track of all the bills and the finances. Numbers are natural to Ken, and what takes him an hour would take me a day. Let's call it time conservation.

Through a friend of a friend, I was invited to join in with the 1986 Proposition 65 movement, started by politician Tom Hayden and his then-wife, actress-activist Jane Fonda. The purpose of the proposition was to keep businesses from releasing or dumping toxic chemicals, like dry cleaner solution, into the water supply or ocean and to make consumers aware when products they consume contain toxic chemicals or ingredients. Jane Fonda would hold meetings at her impressive Santa Monica house and the celebrities would fill her living room: Rob Lowe, LeVar Burton, Rosanna Arquette, Kristy McNichol, Michael J. Fox, and others. Actor Ed Begley Jr. was very involved in environmental causes, and also like an encyclopedia of pollutants and chemicals, he knew what they were used for and what damage they did.

Jane Fonda's home was the place I was made aware of plein air paintings, which is an impressionistic style where the artist paints out in nature instead of a studio. Jane had paintings that she inherited from her father, Henry Fonda, and large art books out on the coffee tables. I had always thought that the Southern California landscape was ugly after the late spring when there was no rain and the temperatures rose. The grasses would burn up in the sun and the rolling hills looked brown and dried. However, the plein art paintings changed my perspective on California's beauty. I would have to pull myself away from the artwork to listen to the proposed plan for getting the Proposition 65 message out. Jane Fonda was, and still is, brilliant at getting people to take action in their communities and cities.

We would gather together to travel in the Clean Water Caravan, actually two commissioned Greyhound buses, one for celebrities and the second one for journalists, news anchors, and camera crews who were reporting on our activism work. We rode together all over California to speak to organizations and schools about environmental issues. On one trip our bus was pulled over for speeding. Jane waved us to all pile out of the bus on the side of the road. The police officer looked astounded as Morgan Fairchild, Daphne Zuniga, Rob Lowe, and Michael J. Fox all grouped next to the bus as Jane Fonda chatted with the officer. I don't remember if he actually issued a ticket to the bus driver, but we all gathered together and invited the officer to join us for a group photo. A couple of months later, Jane Fonda sent a large black-and-white photo of the group in an engraved silver frame to every participant that day. Jane was always classy and fun, but also incredibly passionate and persuasive; even Cher, Whoopi Goldberg, Goldie Hawn, and Chevy Chase jumped on the caravan at certain points. The well-known stars drew big audiences at every location. The effort was very effective in getting the proposition passed at the voting booths, but I'm not sure the messages were actually heard over the throngs of screaming fans wanting photos and autographs with Cher, Whoopi, and Michael J. Fox.

Being around so many busy actors and performers left me contemplating my own future in acting. I knew I could paint, but I didn't know how to make a living outside of acting. It was quickly obvious to me that my new agents were busy promoting actors who were in the public eye and already going from job to job. I was no longer in competition with five other fair-haired little girls and I had timed out on being able to get away with playing a teenager. I knew I needed to take some action for myself. Being naturally very shy, I struggled with how to stay current in the acting world. I considered taking some acting classes, which I had never done before, but the more serious acting schools, like Stella Adler's, seemed overwhelming to me as a starting point. I was already feeling vulnerable and the thought of being criticized or pushed into some emotional acting exercise seemed to be too much. There was an acting teacher, Milton Katselas, who had a larger-than-life personality. He taught acting for many professional actors. I was intrigued, but had also heard that he didn't hesitate to goad an actor, sometimes to an on-stage breakdown. There was no doubt in my mind that that type of method would have me running for the Hollywood Hills, never to return.

* * *

I had never attended a show at the Groundlings Theatre on Melrose Avenue in West Hollywood, but I found out that they offered classes in improvisation. I thought comedy would be a different and happier way to expand my world and also meet some new people. I signed up. I didn't know what it would be, but I figured that everyone else would also be a beginner in the first class. From the very first class, in a theater space full of big personalities and extroverts, I knew I would have to push myself to a different level. There are rules to follow with improvisation because when you are on stage, you can't stand back and only observe. You have to be a part of whatever is happening. For someone who had always been handed a script of what to say and do, it was a free fall into improvising, but what was familiar was being able to perform at the word "Go!".

Mindy Sterling, a character actress and Groundlings member, later known for her *Austin Powers* character, Frau Farbissina, was one of my first teachers. We were gently coached into allowing ourselves to be more creatively free on stage. It's a great experience, even for non-actors, as it teaches you almost guaranteed ways to become a good conversationalist. At the end of every six-week class period, the teacher would meet with students individually to recommend if you should move up to Intermediate or repeat a beginning class. I moved up and looked forward to going into classes. I never felt singled out, and if a fellow player on stage tried to point me out as Jan Brady, it would be shut down pretty quickly by the group. I appreciated that, as it gave me the chance to be my current self and not the child actor from the past. The only time I had to draw a line was, because of my small stature, in various enthusiastic moments on stage, male improvisers would pick me up and swing me around or lift me off my feet for some other reason. I had enough years of being physically relocated in one way or another as a child actor, so I would have to tell them, "I know I'm small, but please do not lift me off my feet. I'm not a prop."

One of my fellow students was Adam Carolla, who would become famous for *Loveline* and his radio show. He asked me out on a date and I turned him down because I didn't want the complications of going on a date with someone that I had to be in class with every week. According to him, I came off as "the bitter Brady." I was told he still talked about it on his podcast decades later when Susan Olsen was a guest. Adam and Eve? Come on.

Following the Intermediate classes was the Writing Lab, where you work on developing actual characters that you can use on stage. It was a challenge because I've always been given a character to play. One of the teachers, Cynthia Szigeti, was an incredible influence on me and most of the people who studied with her. She was bombastic and fearless in her teaching style and encouraged the best of what you had to offer. Mostly, she was unapologetic about her opinions and seemed unhindered about others' opinions of her. I was often in awe of the way she walked through life and hoped to absorb some of her boldness for myself the best I could.

Outside of the Groundlings class, Cynthia directed a group of five women who were handpicked to perform together based on an idea from student Stacey Michaels. Stacey had watched *The Kids in the Hall*, a Canadian sketch comedy TV show with a cast of five young male improvisers and comedians. She wanted to create and present a counterpoint of five female improvisers doing sketch comedy. Her plan was to pitch it to studios as a TV show. Cynthia thought the show should be called *Girls Club*, as there were countless boys clubs that excluded girls. Lisa Kudrow, pre–*Friends* fame, was a part of it, as well as Stacey Michaels, Lisa Feinberg, Audrey Rapoport, and myself.

We would go to Cynthia's house to rehearse, which was both interesting and difficult. She was a hoarder, who had almost every available space in her house filled with books or items she had collected over the years. Her brother would step in to try to help her clean it out, but she would end up being upset about letting anything go. Her home had a swimming pool and she offered to dig swimsuits out of her retro collection of bathing suits for whoever wanted to take a dip. I designed the artwork for our logo, a cartoon graphic of a treehouse. We made postcards and flyers for the show and got together to address and stamp them. I helped place phone calls to agents and casting people to have them come to see one of our four showcases at the Groundlings Theatre. A representative from each network did come to see the show, but there were no offers for development.

One afternoon we were summoned to do a private show for Aaron Spelling at his offices. It was a hot summer day and we were ushered into a dark screening room and told to set up whatever we needed to perform. The stage was tiny and not meant for five people and the audience area was so dark, we weren't sure who came in to watch. We performed our sketches in a soundless room and then it was over. For all we know, no one was in the room at all except the person who told us to go ahead and begin. No notes were given or advice from Spelling or anyone. We gathered up our props and costumes and left.

Cynthia started experiencing serious health issues, so any additional shows didn't happen, and we all began to drift apart as members of the group left for other opportunities. In a perhaps not-so-coincidental twist, the idea of an all-female sketch show was bought by ABC in the early 1990s, and was short-lived.

At one point I met another student who was going through the Groundlings program. Kelley Brower introduced herself to me and said, "You and I should write some sketches together." I was game, as when I tried to write alone it was hard for me to percolate ideas. It wasn't the same as painting, where an idea would pop into my mind fully formed. I did better when I could bounce writing ideas off another person. Kelley and I developed a two-person sketch show that could work in comedy clubs and not need a full stage. We called ourselves Feminine HiJinks, and went out to play the open mics available in Los Angeles, usually late nights at The Ice House in Pasadena, or The Improv on Sunset Boulevard. We created character-driven sketches, like pretending to be two of Santa's reindeer in antler head bands. I made hooves out of foam for us to wear on our hands and put tacks in the bottom to fit the *clackity-clack* of reindeer paws when we clapped. All of our sketches had a happy, silly feel to them that made them fun to perform.

When the first set we created got great responses, we wrote more. Kelley suggested that we take the act to New York and do the open mics there, to see what would happen. We packed up our hooves, booked the tickets, and off we went. Before we could do even one open mic, Kelley came down with some horrible respiratory infection and we ended up sitting in a Manhattan emergency room. I felt that she was being ignored by the medical staff for too long and told her that I was going to go find a nurse. She didn't want me to do that and said that she would begin to loudly sing *The Brady Bunch* theme song unless I sat back down. I sat down. By the time she recovered, it was time to fly back to LA.

On the trip home, Kelley said, "You and I should move to New York and really give it a go."

It was another moment of revelation for me. I knew my true aspirations were never in the realm of doing stand-up comedy. I told her that she should move to New York and that's what she did. I'm happy she's still here in New York, where I now live, as we still have a good friendship that survived Feminine HiJinks.

It seemed that someone in the world of casting took notice of me doing improvisation and comedy, because I was cast to play a small role in the movie *I'm Gonna Git You Sucka*. I was only on set for one day, but it was so much fun to play the wife of Clarence Williams III as Kalinga, leader of the People's Revolutionary Army. He and I had briefly met back in the Brady days as *The Mod Squad* filmed on the Paramount lot. When I showed up for hair and makeup that morning, I noticed a wig with many long blond braids laced with beads, baubles, trinkets, and even small toys. I was delighted that it was for me to wear. It was noisy and quite heavy, so I had to stand perfectly still before my entrance. When I walked into the scene, calling Clarence "My great Nubian warrior," they played the title track of *The Brady Bunch* in the background. It was a small part, with only a few lines, but it gave me a chance to play an over-the-top role.

* * *

About a month later, I got a phone call, saying the Brady family was reuniting for a two-hour TV movie, *A Very Brady Christmas*, this time on CBS, the last remaining network without a Brady show. I called Christopher Knight to see if he was going to be in it. He let me know that it looked like it would be a return of all the Brady cast, minus one. This time it was Susan Olsen, who would be getting married and off for her honeymoon exactly when the filming was taking place. For this TV movie, we were all coming home to the Brady house and bringing our problems with us.

Jan was on the brink of divorce. Marcia's husband lost his job. Bobby dropped out of grad school. Peter was dating his boss. I think the only problem Alice had, despite it being 1988, was that our beloved housekeeper still had to wear a blue uniform and white apron, as if frozen in time. Leave it to Carol and Mike, who, in their Mom-and-Dad wisdom, find solutions for all of us. It seems it's going to be a merrier Christmas, until a building Mike has been asked to redesign collapses on him and two construction workers. The other two are saved and somehow Mike is still trapped, until Carol and kids sing carols at the yellow police tape. Following the music, he manages to dig through the debris and gets free. He survives and it's time to celebrate the holidays. Yes, this plotline was completely plausible in the late 1980s.

It was great to be working again and we were all happy that it was the second highest-rated TV movie of the year across all networks. And then the reviews hit the press without a single flattering word, or even a moment of kindly Christmas spirit. One famous New York paper called it "blather for the mindless." It was obvious that we wouldn't need to read the Emmy award nominations that year. Ann B. Davis would hold her status as the only cast member to ever win an Emmy, though Robert Reed had been nominated for other shows, all of it occurring prior to anything Brady. The 1988 Emmy for Outstanding TV Movie went to *The Murder of Mary Phagan,* so maybe the voters weren't in the holiday spirit that year.

CBS seemed to be thrilled with the ratings and Sherwood Schwartz suggested additional two-hour TV movies to play during other holiday seasons. Supposedly, the network asked for a one-hour series, a drama. It's not as if there are countless examples of TV families switching genres from sitcom to drama, and there's good reason for that. We all reunited for *The Bradys* series, except this time it was Maureen McCormick who passed on being involved and she was replaced by Leah Ayres, who did a remarkable job.

In this series Jan is taking over her dad's architectural firm. I appreciated the chance to make Jan more than a middle child or wife, although in one episode the writers felt they had to saddle poor Jan with fertility problems. God forbid she be a professional woman with no intentions of being a mother. The larger issue was, no one wanted to see the Brady family as having serious problems, like Bobby being temporarily paralyzed in a race car accident and Marcia becoming a heavy drinker. The viewers who watched out of nostalgia found the show depressing, instead of fun. The new viewers wanted the light-hearted comedy their parents had told them about. After five episodes CBS canned *The Bradys*.

For the first time, I saw Robert Reed as a man going

through some struggles. The light had dimmed in his eyes and he looked gaunt and exhausted. I was sad, but not surprised, when Florence called me sometime later to tell me that Bob was going through cancer treatments. He did manage to make it to Barry Williams's wedding, to which the entire cast had been invited, and that's the last time I saw him. I sat at a table with Ann B. Davis and we talked as we watched Barry and Diane, his first wife, dance together. During the conversation she said to me, "Funny, people always assume that I'm gay, but I'm not."

Her words came back to me in May 1992. Florence had called me, once again, to tell me that Bob was in the hospital in Pasadena. He had asked Florence to call all the Brady kids and tell us that he wasn't going to survive cancer. He requested that none of us come to see him. After he passed away, it was revealed that he also had complications due to HIV. Bob had AIDS. That was the splashy and controversial headline about his passing—not his varied career, not his years as America's dad, not his years teaching acting in between shows. It was terribly sad to me that Bob was gone, yet even more heartbreaking was that opposite of Ann B.'s experience, people always assumed Bob was straight, but he was gay. He could never risk having a life partner because his career would be over.

Despite his reputation of being argumentative on the set about the script and fighting for more realistic situations and dialogue, it never bothered me. I always saw him as someone who wanted every effort to be the best it could possibly be. He never settled for good enough. He not only cared about how it would reflect on him, he cared about all of us kids, never playing favorites or giving extra attention to one over the others. He took notice of what we liked to do, he talked us up as being talented young professionals, and he doled out great advice. He also gave us memorable experiences at his own personal expense, like the trip on the *QE2*. I had the privilege to learn from and be guided by him in an industry that can be self-centered. Bob was never that. He may have been America's dad to millions, but to me he was my trustworthy and caring second father. All six Brady kids will say the same.

Chapter Thirteen

The look on Neil Simon's face left me crying in my car. In the early 1990s, I got a call to audition for a Neil Simon movie that had been a successful Broadway play, *Lost in Yonkers*. My agent sent me the "sides," the pages of the script they want you to perform. I rehearsed it more than a dozen times at home before the audition. Casting directors, the film director, an assistant, and others were in the room. Neil Simon sat at one of the tables and it was impossible not to notice his demeanor. He looked up briefly and nodded. I know how auditions go, and after the obligatory "nice to meet you" language that takes up the first fifteen seconds, I will jump right in. Everyone is on a schedule and, like my mother before me, I am prompt, organized, and prepared.

My first read of the lines received zero response. No one gave me direction for changes to try, because I think they were all checking Neil's reaction, which was between a frown and boredom. This sent a zing of fight-or-flee adrenaline through my body, like falling down a flight of stairs at a formal event. There is no simple correction, no graceful way to recover. I wanted to flee.

I was dismissed with a noneffusive "thank you," and an expression on Neil's face like a bad smell had wafted under his nose. Two minutes later I found myself sitting in my car in the parking lot with tears spilling out, trying to shake it all off. It wasn't easy to do. My confidence in my abilities was disintegrating with the feeling that I had messed up an opportunity. I had tried to get it right and had failed at my attempt.

Neil Simon came out of the building and walked right in front of my car. I thought, *I hope he sees me crying.* He only continued looking straight ahead, in a seeming hurry to get away as quickly as possible.

One of the most difficult things I had to learn as an adult actor is that most casting decisions have absolutely nothing to do with an individual actor. Talent plays a part, although there are at least ten other elements that determine the outcome of any audition. If you're playing a sibling, as was true with *The Brady Bunch*, we three girls had to look like we had the same mother. It wasn't that I had so much more talent than the brunette girl who could have played Jan, it's that Florence was a blonde and so was I. This is true for every audition. Even if they think you gave a great line reading, any number of things can become a consideration in whether you get the role or not. A casting person might have their favorite actor they want to use, or they may not want to pay actors who live outside of where the movie is being filmed, or the lead actor wants their own daughter cast in the role you're auditioning for and the director wants to keep the lead actor happy. It may be as simple as they already found the person they want for the role and are only auditioning the last three people on the schedule out of courtesy. An actor will rarely know the reason they didn't get a part. It's not personal, and yet it's very hard not to take it personally. For all I know, Neil

Simon dreaded sitting through auditions and I was at the end of a long day of them. Or he was missing a tennis date because the schedule was late. Or maybe he put too many pickled jalapeño peppers on his sandwich and was suffering stomach pain. Who knows!

For the first time in my life, following that day, I began to get the heebie-jeebies about auditioning. I had never had nerves about reading for casting directors before. Perhaps it was because fewer auditions were coming my way. I would feel fine in the waiting room, usually making the check-in assistant laugh, keeping it all friendly. When I would be called into the audition room, I could feel myself shaking. Any attempt to control it only made it seem worse, hopefully not visible to the casting people. I tried thinking about something else or focusing on deep breathing, but still the nerves took over. It became so distracting that I knew I was missing the mark on every audition for almost a full year. I thought, *What do I do? Is there a class I can take on controlling this?*

Then I would overly prepare or try to figure out what they were looking for, instead of going into the audition with what I have to offer. This went on for a couple of years, and what had once been second nature to me, as a child and teenager, now felt like I was an inexperienced beginner. I had no one to talk to about it.

I didn't want to burden my parents, as they had serious concerns of their own. My mother had to undergo cancer treatments for her mouth and neck area after white spots had appeared along her gums. My father was very wrapped up in making sure she got to her appointments and had everything she needed. They had bought a small RV and on weekends they would still drive up to the Los Angeles National Forest and camp. My mother loved her little second house-on-wheels getaway vehicle, her "Minnie Winnie."

I was still attending a Science of Mind church on regular occasions, but more often I was questioning the principles I had been taught. Could we really protect ourselves with correct thinking? Would an affirmation change the outcome? They didn't seem to be working for my audition nerves and they had not prevented my mother's cancer. As I would sit in church, I found myself wondering about the whole approach to life. Positive thoughts and affirmations weren't hurting anyone or anything, but was it really affecting the direction of our lives, or did it only give you a more hopeful outlook? It was difficult not to think of challenges as failures.

After almost a year of not booking a show or commercial, I did get a guest star role on *Lois & Clark: The New Adventures of Superman*. The storyline was that children were being kidnapped by a famous magician, and Superman must step in to rescue them. Penn Jillette played the magician. When I arrived on the set, they were filming a very quiet and dark scene. It was hard to make my way around the set, so I stepped outside of the stage door, into the bright sunlight to have a cigarette. That's where I met Penn, who was loudly regaling someone from the stage crew. He is about six foot seven and I am five foot four, so he towered over me. He was boisterous and very irreverent with sexual innuendo, which he kept in check as best he could. He will say out loud what most of us are probably thinking anyway, so I find most of it pretty funny.

I had been casually dating a man who was a proclaimed atheist and had books on his shelves that were science fiction and more fantastical narratives. He compared organized religion to science fiction, saying that what people thought of as truth was equally implausible. When I met Penn, he handed me his business card, which had *No God* printed on it. I found that to be startling in how blatant it was. It seemed to be such a negative statement that it scared me. Would something bad happen from such a negative statement? But it also helped me to understand that I believed the religion I had been handed and trained in. I had never really made the choice to believe in it. It was part of the package as a child.

I decided to take a step back from it all to figure out what I really believed, what really worked for me, not out of fear or guilt. And that mattered to me on every level of my life. It was one more way I released the expectations of others and also what I had placed on myself. It's now a personal and private choice for me and that has made a big difference in how well I know myself.

After breaking up with Michael because I didn't want a long-term commitment, I went through a string of short-lived dating relationships. I talked to my friends and told them, "Okay, send me your men. I'm not looking to get married. And I already have my own house." A good friend of mine was friends with a pianist who toured with a trio. She thought I should meet her friend Ken Pace, a saxophone player who was single. It seemed like history possibly repeating itself. Was I going to be like Flora June, being introduced to a saxophone player? She told me that "he's a very, very nice guy."

I paused and said, "Okay, but he's not like a sensitive poet type, is he? He's not going to show up in drawstring linen pants and Birkenstocks, right?"

She laughed and said, "No, no. He's great. He also works in information technology as a day job. He does have a goatee, though."

I agreed to meet him in a group situation, and after

some delays, due to his work schedule with Disney, about eight of us went for dinner at Jerry's Deli on Ventura Boulevard. They made room for me to sit at the end of the table, next to Ken.

We started to talk and I asked him why he was interested in working with computers.

He said, "I found I have an affinity for it."

I thought, *Nice. I like a man who can use fancy four-syllable words.*

I did find Ken to be very attractive and I liked his personality right away, but I proceeded with caution. We continued talking, and the next thing I knew, the other six people had left, it was almost midnight, and the wait staff were tapping their toes near the cash register. We paid our bill and stepped out the front door, where Ken suggested we get a cup of coffee across the street. The place was closed, so we said good night and went our separate ways. I knew he had my phone number. The next day he called and asked me out on a real date. I liked that he came with a suggestion in mind.

"I've always wanted to see the Alvin Ailey dance troupe," he said.

"Okay. I haven't," I responded, "but if you want to go, I'm up for it."

Ken got the tickets, and on the day of our date, he arrived at my door, in a suit and a tie, driving a nice car, and off we went. About three dance numbers in, I looked at Ken to see if he had a better grasp on what was going on than I did. The audience seemed to be applauding at various intervals that didn't make sense to me.

At intermission Ken said, "Neither one of us seems very crazy about this show. We can leave if you'd like to go."

It was a relief to know that I wasn't the only one who couldn't connect with what I was watching.

I said, "Let's stay, since you paid for these tickets. Maybe it will all come together for us in the second half."

It didn't. But it was okay. We both could laugh about it. We went out for a late dinner and drinks. He brought me home and I invited him to come in. We've rarely been apart from that day forward.

We dated for a few months and then Ken went to Detroit, where he grew up, to visit with his mother, since his father had passed away months before. He accompanied her on a trip to Scotland for a few weeks. What I thought would be a short stay turned into three weeks and then six. I questioned if he was going to come back, but he promised me that he would. During one of our phone calls, he told me, "You're the one. I know it."

I flew to the East Coast to visit him. We had planned to drive to Canada for the weekend after he picked me up at the airport. When I arrived, he was not there to get me, so I called his house line.

His mother answered and said with a blustery tone, "He left late for the airport."

She didn't seem at all pleased that she was losing her son for three days for him to spend time with me.

I tried not to let it bother me, but I already felt a bit disregarded. For a moment I wondered if I should turn around and fly back to Los Angeles, but I knew that would be extreme, so I waited for him. After our weekend trip, Ken took me to meet his mother, and I had a better idea of her blunt personality. She was also clearly in the early stages of becoming a hoarder.

She walked around the house saying, "I've got to clean up around here."

After I noticed that her bedroom door was blocked from fully opening by a tall stack of old *Prevention* magazines, I suggested that we could help her get rid of them. She looked at me aghast.

"No! I haven't finished reading them!"

Once his mother got to know me, she would make big announcements about who I was wherever we would go. She'd tell anyone who would listen that I was Jan Brady from *The Brady Bunch*. During one visit she insisted that I go across the street and meet some neighbors because they were "big fans." I was suffering from a fever and the flu and told her no. She smacked my arm and said, "You're an actress. You know how to act."

"I'm not going to go. I'm sick," I replied with a gentle smack to her arm.

That worked for one day. Eventually, I did go meet the neighbors.

After Ken returned to LA, we began to take more trips together for fun, and about eight months into our relationship, we went for a weekend to the Grand Canyon and stayed in a cabin. After we arrived, snow began to fall and Ken lit a fire for us to enjoy. At one point he turned to me and pulled a gift box out of his jacket pocket. My heart began racing. *Is this going to be a marriage proposal?*

"Hey, Eve," he said. "I got you that bracelet I saw you admiring at the gift shop earlier today."

My misinterpreting the bracelet box actually made me laugh, a reason I didn't explain it to Ken at that time.

It reminded me of something my mother had told me about my father. She said, "I have to be careful about saying I like something around your father, because he will go back to the store and buy it for me."

In many ways Ken is similar to my father. He's funny, kind, handsome, and intelligent, he's good with tools, he keeps great financial records, and he's a musician.

A couple of years later, I admitted that I thought the

Grand Canyon box was going to be an engagement ring and he explained that he wanted the two of us to be together for a full year before he proposed, which he did on a weekend trip to Laguna Beach at the one-year mark.

We were spending the weekend at one of my favorite motels in Laguna. Ken could not seem to settle down. We would go to the beach and then he would disappear for a while. His good friend Rich was there for a visit and I mentioned that I wasn't sure what was going on with Ken. I think Rich knew what was going on, but he kept mum.

Later we went out to dinner and ran into another friend, Chuck, a Realtor we both knew, who is very effusive and loves to talk. I invited Chuck to stop and get a coffee with us, but Ken pulled me aside and said, "No. We need to go back to the motel."

I still didn't know what was going on, but once we got back to the room, Ken said, "Let's go take a walk."

I was confused by his change of mind, but went along, following him down the zigzag path back to the shoreline. He brought a shopping bag along, which seemed odd, but it had already been that kind of day. There was a small bench at the end of the path and Ken had me sit with him.

From his pocket he pulled a piece of paper on which he had written this Haiku:

Many questions are
asked, and some may be answered
will you marry me?

I read it aloud, then started crying; I tried to answer, but unintelligibly. Ken told me to nod if it was a yes. He proposed to me with a stand-in man's vintage ring he had bought that day at the antique mall in Laguna. He knew he wanted to propose, but wanted me to pick out my own ring, which I did a few months later in the Diamond District of New York City.

From the bag he produced a dozen red roses, a bottle of chilled champagne, and two glasses. We toasted our future together at one of my favorite locations of the past, Laguna Beach.

The first person I told was my mother. She had met Ken a few times. I had asked Ken not to tell my mother his birthday or birth time, as I didn't want her to do his astrological chart and determine that we were not a good match. I already knew we were going to be a great match.

On January 17, 1994, all of Los Angeles was awakened at four-thirty in the morning by the 6.7 Northridge earthquake, which lasted almost ten seconds and shook the entire area through to the coast of Santa Monica. Whatever wasn't bolted down was tossed around in a haphazard way; my parents' home was no exception. My mother's collectibles and dinnerware were shattered, and books and artwork flew off the shelves and the walls. Many homes lost their chimneys, which toppled to the ground, and a few apartment buildings had collapsed roofs. There were relatively few fatalities, although I know people who left Los Angeles permanently the very next week, out of fear of a recurrence.

Following the earthquake, my mother became even more isolated, only going camping with my father on the weekends. She no longer wanted to venture out to a museum or even a restaurant. The tree in front of the house, which my father had a bench built around and where I had posed for the teen magazine photo shoot, became diseased and then had to be removed. It had grown huge over the years and my father often had to cut a new area away from the front deck to accommodate the growing elm. Losing the tree hurt my mother greatly. The tree probably seemed like a family member, since it had been planted by my father when they bought the house.

My spell of unsettled nerves while auditioning was broken when I was called to do a cold audition for *Fudge-a-Mania*, a TV movie based on the popular Judy Blume children's book. I didn't receive the script until I had arrived and only had a few minutes in the waiting room to read over the scene they wanted me to do. Unfamiliar with Judy Blume's book, I had to ask before I went in to audition, "Is Fudge from outer space? An imaginary friend? An actual child?"

"Fudge is a four-year-old boy and you're auditioning as his mom. You also have a son in fourth grade who is the narrator."

I don't know if it was because I had no time to try to get it right, or if my improv training in the Groundlings classes buoyed me through it, but I went into the reading in a great mood and was unconcerned about the results. Right after the audition, my agent called and said the producers offered me the role. They told me that the budget had exactly a specific amount of money for the role and it couldn't be negotiated. In other words: Take it or leave it.

I took it, knowing that two other women were in the waiting room, who would happily take the role at the rate offered.

The best news was that ABC planned to take the show to a series if the TV movie went well, which it did. The TV movie aired in January 1995 and was followed up with twelve episodes. I was thrilled to have another series. And the bonus was being reunited with my Brady mom, Florence Henderson, who would be playing my mother in this series as well. It was great to work with her as an adult and I was reminded about what a positive force Florence was on everyone around her. When she went to work, she left any personal problems or stresses in her dressing room. She never demanded special treatment or acted as if anything was beneath her.

As cute and funny as the book is on the page, there was the challenge that the character Fudge was written as a four-year-old, so the actor needed to be close to that age as well. As precocious as Luke Tarsitano, the child who played Fudge, was, it was still quite a bit of cajoling and pampering, along with occasional meltdowns, sometimes by the kid and once in a while by one of the directors. Childcare doesn't come all that naturally to me and I tend not to be as charmed by little children as most people might be. On this show it actually worked in my favor. Kids can sense when you aren't going to cave in to their moods or demands. For the most part, my scenes with the kids went great. I didn't concern myself beyond that. I know raising a kid is really hard work and trying to coax a four-year-old into paying attention and speaking his lines was something I left to his parents or the professionals.

The older children were good little actors and well behaved, although the stage moms were not like the reserved moms from my childhood acting at all. They were vocal with their opinions and would sometimes send the message that they thought the show was holding their child back from better acting jobs. I never knew what they expected the producers to do about that.

Fudge was filmed in a Van Nuys warehouse building and not on a studio lot. It was close to the airport, so we would constantly have to hold up during a scene to wait for a plane to fly over, as it could be picked up by the microphones.

I had previously dyed my hair red to change up my look and had it cut into a short pageboy style, which was a real departure from my lifelong blond hair. Few people on the street recognized me anymore, which I didn't mind. Before the audition for *Fudge*, I had run into Lisa Kudrow at the Groundlings space and she suggested I try a dark brown color, which I did. I liked the new look; however, it would catch me by surprise when I saw my image in a mirror. I resembled my mother with her dark hair and blue eyes.

My character, Anne, was funny and the writing was clever and I was extremely happy to have an acting job on a series that was doing really well on ABC Saturday mornings. The show ran for two seasons, about twenty-six episodes in total, and then Disney bought ABC and we were all out of work. Disney had their own plans for Saturday mornings.

While I was still on *Fudge*, Ken and I got married. We decided to do a ceremony and a reception with a DJ and dancing. It was quite a bit to plan, and though I know my mother would have liked to help, she really didn't want to go out anymore. I went to Macy's and picked out a dress for her to wear and took it to the house. She had been given a new heart medication and was telling me that it made her feel funny. Despite my encouraging her to see her cardiologist again, she insisted that she didn't want to bother him.

My bridal attendants, Stacey, my friend from Girls Club, and Jann, whom I stayed with in New York, arranged for a lovely teatime shower at a hotel in Pasadena, and my mother, though she probably felt fretful about leaving the house, managed to attend.

As the wedding day approached, she called me to ask if I had invited Aunt Ethel from Oklahoma, she of the mosquito bites comment in Hawaii. I told her that I didn't want her to be on the list as a guest. I know that bothered my mom, but it bothered me that she thought I should have her there. Then my mother suggested that I go to get some Botox to correct the wrinkle line between my eyebrows. I wasn't going to do some last-minute thing to my face when it didn't matter to me. I told her I wasn't going to do that. I was frustrated with her by the time we hung up, as I had a thousand other wedding-day details to keep in order. I don't remember how the conversation ended, but I certainly would have made a different choice about it if I had known it would be the last time I spoke to my mom.

A few days later, a week before my wedding day, my sister called me early one morning. She had to be the messenger of the bad news that our mother had died in her sleep the night before. Our father had gone in to wake her up and found her. I was blown backward, but somehow it seemed like something that could happen. Her life had become so small and reclusive. I'm sure she was dreading having to be around so many people at my wedding.

I didn't know what to do. The wedding venue had been rented, the catering service ordered, and people had responded to the invitations.

My father was in deep grief, and my sister and I were trying to determine what to do. The next day my dad told me, "You must go on with the wedding. It's been planned for months."

We decided to send emails to all of the guests explaining that my mother had passed away, but we wished to continue with the ceremony and reception.

It was awkward to write, but I'm sure it would have been much more uncomfortable for guests to hear the news once they arrived on my wedding day. I asked them to please be happy with and for Ken and me, and that there was no need to extend words of sympathy. In my grief I dropped about five pounds in a week and had to have my wedding dress altered the day before. My father was holding up, but the hardest day was going from the interment of my mother's ashes directly to my wedding rehearsal.

Stacey, Jann, and my sister were all a great support over a couple of days in which I was doing my best just to stay present. My brother and his family, who had come in from Florida upon the death of our mother, stayed on for my wedding.

After the short ceremony and cutting the cake, we all danced the night away. The father-daughter dance was to a recording of "Stardust" that my dad had played saxophone on back in 1940. There was something about the physicality of moving and dancing that shook some of the grief from my system. The cake was completely gone before Ken and I had a chance to have a piece. I didn't care. Unlike wondering what I was doing the first time I walked down the aisle at age twenty-one, this time I knew I had found the love of my life, a strong, stalwart partner in all things. I still feel immense gratitude that I found Ken and he found me.

Ken and I flew off the next morning to a Club Med to relax for a short honeymoon. I ordered spaghetti with a slice of American cheese for lunch. It was comfort food, and it worked. A year later, we ate the cake topper, which had been frozen. It's a tradition to eat it to celebrate the one-year anniversary. We recently celebrated our thirtieth.

A couple of years ago, I found an unsent thank-you note from my mother to me, thanking me for picking out her mother-of-the-bride dress and making it easier for her. That also brought me great comfort, since I always have had a lingering regret about my last conversation with her.

Also in the box with the note were cards that my father had given my mother over the years, proclaiming his unfailing love for her—poetic sentiments that held so much respect and gratitude that she was the love of his life. The petite nineteen-year-old Elk City, Oklahoma, ballerina did really well for herself.

Chapter Fourteen

The most carefree days of my life were always linked to Laguna Beach, starting with long summer weeks, every August, at the seaside as a little girl. I would feel in my element, at home, in Laguna Beach. Long before I understood design or architecture, I noticed and appreciated its seaside bungalows and cottages, Craftsman homes, and mission-style business buildings.

Once *Fudge* had wrapped up its second and final season, Ken and I started to think about where we would like to live. I knew I wanted to stay close enough to LA to come in for auditions and roles, but I definitely wanted to be in a different environment. Laguna Beach was calling my name, and Ken agreed that we could start house hunting there to see what was available.

I've always gravitated towards a good project, something I can improve on, effort applied that makes something look better. We found a house with three small bedrooms that needed quite a bit of restoration, but I was excited to let the drywall dust fly and get involved in a renovation up to my elbows. I especially enjoy being immersed in choosing the new elements for the interior design—the flooring, the tiles, the paint or wallpaper, and the countertops—while at the same time staying in line with the original historic design of the house. We kept a small apartment in Los Angeles, where we could stay if I was cast in a show or had an early audition, or if Ken needed to be in the city for work, but it wasn't often. I didn't work as an actress for about eighteen months. I was so absorbed in my home makeover that I didn't feel the passage of time as acutely.

When our home was almost completed, we were informed that a large apartment building was being proposed for the lots directly across the street from us. No one on our side of the street was at all happy about the prospect. I found out that there was a scheduled public hearing about the project, so we invited our neighbors over to discuss how we could go as a united and organized group to the meeting and let our concerns and objections be known.

We divided up the messages we wanted to get across, since each person is given three minutes to speak, and parsed out who would say what at the meeting. We arrived to listen to the people who were on the Laguna Beach Design Review, regular citizens who had been appointed to hear the pros and cons of every proposed acquisition for the purpose of property changes. I watched closely as the process unfolded and thought, *This is something I could do well.* I understand how design and architectural planning can either improve the look of a place, even a large city, or break up the natural flow in an incongruous way that may ruin sight lines and scenery.

The second issue on the public-hearing schedule that day was about a project that would tear down and replace some 1920s bungalows that lined Pacific Coast Highway. Despite it not being my neighborhood, I got up and spoke about vacationing in Laguna Beach every year as a child and that the bungalows were all part of the charm of the area. I thought allowing modern houses to be built there would detract from the quaintness of the coastline, which is what attracted 5 million tourists every year.

Since I wasn't going into LA often for work or auditions, I applied to be on the Design Review Board, writing in my application about restoring our Laguna Beach house to historic elements. The city council appointed me, and before long I was going to neighborhoods to check on applications that had come in to change a property, add on, build higher, or remove a building, and to speak to the concerned neighbors. Any property changes that were being proposed had to go through the Design Review Board. In certain weeks I was putting in as many hours as a part-time job. My fellow board members tagged me as a "cottage hugger," because my whole aim was to retain the charming inventory of the architecture in a city that I love so much. After a couple of years, I was elected as chairperson and tried to be as fair and respectful as possible. Some applicants would be unhappy with our final decisions, but the board has a crucial responsibility to keep the city livable and unique.

I was on the board for six years total and cycled through being the chairperson twice. Unfortunately I was unable to save the childhood apartment building where I had played on the beach and that held so many wonderful memories. I spoke at the hearing but was in the minority, and the property was demolished and is now a very large modern house.

I did enjoy my time on Design Review, and it was great to learn all about architecture and also the workings of city politics. It gave me some really great friends and confidence in a whole new area of life.

* * *

While one area of my life was opening up, my father's life was shutting down. He had done pretty well on his own since my mother's passing. He was writing an autobiography and going out for his regular mile walk every day, until one afternoon a dog charged up to him and he took a spill on the sidewalk. He wasn't badly injured, but following that incident, he started to lose his confidence about living alone, so my sister and I helped him to move to an assisted-living facility. I didn't tell him that Ken and I had relocated to Laguna Beach, as I knew he might find it concerning that I lived too far away. Ken and I would drive up to visit with him.

On a late Sunday afternoon visit, he seemed very low-key, and instead of chatting with me, he would lay his head back and doze off. Ken and I decided to let him rest and began to tiptoe out of his room. At the last moment, as I turned to look at him from the door, he opened his eyes and lifted his head to tell me, "I love you."

On the drive home, I turned off my phone, as I often did in the car. It was a warm day in early October and I dozed as we drove opposite of all the traffic that was coming back into Los Angeles at the end of the weekend. When Ken and I pulled up in front of our house, I looked at my phone to see that my sister had been trying to call me about four or five times in the past forty minutes. I rang her cell.

"Where have you been?" June asked. "The assisted-living place called me an hour ago to say that Dad had died in his sleep."

It was then that I realized that his "I love you" was also a goodbye. It was the best last words he could have said to me.

Ken and I got back in the car and drove to Los Angeles to be with June and take care of my father's wishes upon his death and arrange the long-haul plans of cleaning out the house I had grown up in, storing what we wanted to keep, and getting the place in a condition to sell.

I struggled through days of deep grief for a few weeks, still well aware of how fortunate I had been to be raised by two people who adored each other and showered me with huge amounts of affection and unconditional love. My little threesome family unit of fun explorations, wise counsel, protection, and security was now truly gone. My father would sometimes end his letters or cards to June and to me by writing, *We adore you.*

I don't think it gets better than that.

I continued to paint almost daily, often as gifts to friends. Laguna Beach is a community that is widely known for supporting the visual arts, with many gallery opportunities. Ken and I went to an outside arts festival one afternoon and I bought a painting. I was surprised when the person hosting the booth said, "I know you. You're Eve Plumb. I've seen some of your paintings. I like your work."

I thanked her and smiled.

She continued, "Listen, my husband and I own a gallery in Laguna and I'd like to show some of your work there."

I was beyond happy about it. To have my paintings displayed in a Pacific Coast Highway gallery was amazing to experience. The owners hosted an art opening for me, my friends arrived in support, and a number of the paintings sold. I was thrilled to think that people would choose my artwork to hang in their homes. That feeling has never left me. The gallery also posted my paintings on the internet, and a gallery owner in Cape Cod called me to say he wanted to represent me and put my work up in his gallery as well.

A young woman I knew happened to be in Cape Cod that week and I asked her if she could see if it was a legitimate gallery. She went in and talked to the owner about me and confirmed that it was all for real.

That summer I flew to Cape Cod after shipping a number of paintings ahead of time, and the gallery owner did an open-house art show of my work. I met a lot of people and other artists. The atmosphere of a Cape Cod summer day in the seaside town of Chatham is hard to beat. As you walk the historic downtown street, it's hard not to fall in love with it all, with almost every home garden hosting bursting plants full of blue, purple, and pink hydrangeas.

The Cape Cod show led to interest from other galleries around the country, in Florida, Arizona, and North Carolina, that were eager to show my work. The momentum was incredibly motivating for me to keep creating original paintings and gave me the confidence to do two series. The first is film noir, a favorite genre of mine from the Turner Classic Movies channel. I would have those movies on while I painted my still-lifes, and then started noticing the cinematic compositions of the scenes. I took still photographs from the television (learned that one from my dad) to paint in black and white. I named the series *Here Comes Trouble*. Each painting has a three-word title—*Now That's Done*, for instance—that I print out and paste to the canvas to look like the typical ransom note—messy and rough. The other series, of Western-themed paintings, came to me one day as I was driving. I knew each painting should have a blue sky and a horse, and be painted in vertical strokes using a limited color palette from 1950s and '60s Western movies. I didn't know how the series would turn out but I gave it a shot, and I'm really happy with the result. I was able to depict the scenes (again from the television) in vertical strokes, despite not feeling confident about the whole horse business. These, along with various still-life paintings, continue to be represented in galleries in Florida, Arizona, and Manhattan, where we live.

I had always felt a pull to New York City, especially when I was flown in from Los Angeles to play a recurring role on *All My Children*. It was great fun to play a bold investigative reporter for three episodes and to do all of my scenes with Susan Lucci. Acting on a soap opera was very different, and a challenge in that the information the characters give is usually repeated in almost every scene so that any viewer can still follow the action if they came in late. The lines needed to be memorized completely without flaw. The pace is incredibly quick and the set is always very, very quiet, as there is no time or room to do multiple takes due to noise interference.

Susan was phenomenal to watch in her quick expressions and sharp delivery of her lines. She certainly knew how to make the camera love her as much as the viewing audience did. She was kind and gracious to me, and since I played her antagonist for three episodes, she would blow me a kiss when the scene was over and jokingly say, "Hate you!" I'd play along and say, "Hate you more!" Susan was an absolute professional.

One day, following a brief bathroom break, Susan, fearing she was late, ran down the hall and to the set in her four-inch heels and designer suit. I remember thinking, *You're the star of the show! You don't need to run!* Yet I know that the true lasting stars know exactly how to last. It's that respect they have for the crew, fellow cast members, and the viewers.

In February 2010 I was invited to perform in the fifth

annual Broadway Backwards, a live fundraiser show, which was held at Lincoln Center. It's a lively and well-attended event to raise money for Broadway Cares/Equity Fights AIDS, in which Broadway show tunes are done through an LGBTQ frame, where often women sing typical men's songs and vice versa. It started out small in 2006 and grew every year, to go from making about eight thousand dollars to now over a million annually. Florence Henderson was asked to host this particular show and the audience adored her. She would turn it up 150 percent, yet she was always humble, humorous, and complimentary about others. When I did my few phrases in the number, she said loudly, "Oh, Evie! I had no idea you could sing like that."

After the show Florence and her assistant, Kayla, Ken, and I decided to go have a cocktail and catch up. It was a Monday night in New York, and at eleven-thirty, many places were already closed. Since it was pouring rain, we went to the hotel where the producers had rented rooms for Florence, Ken, and me to stay that night. There was a bar off the lobby that appeared to be open. The lights were on, but no one was behind the bar. We sat down and waited for about fifteen minutes and finally Florence's assistant got up and went behind the bar to get two bottles of wine from the countertop. She opened them and brought over four glasses, saying that we could pay for it when the bartender came back.

As we started to talk and relax, a large presence cast a shadow over our small table area. We looked up at a hulk-sized uniformed security guard who began asking questions in an intimidating manner about the wine bottles. Ken attempted to say that we were all hotel guests and intended to pay, but before he could speak, Florence looked up at the guard and said, "Do you know who I am? Do you have any idea who you're talking to?"

I leaned back in my chair as the guard came one step closer, obviously indifferent to the identity of the haughty, petite blonde. I thought, *Well, this will be interesting. Imagine if Carol Brady and daughter Jan get arrested on a rainy Monday at midnight in New York.*

The night manager from the front desk came over to help defuse the situation. Florence's assistant produced a credit card quickly to pay for the wine and everyone calmed down. I had to laugh about it later, thinking how you could be a big hit, receiving a standing ovation on the Lincoln Center stage in one hour, and the very next hour be seen as a foursome of grifters, trying to pilfer a couple of thirty-four-dollar bottles of wine.

On the plane, heading back to California, I began to think about moving again. I didn't want to live out my days in a breezy, low-key beach town, without exploring other places I might want to try, at least for a while.

A few months later, the company that Ken was working for had an offer to do business in Switzerland. They wanted Ken to go with the company, and that would require a relocation to Geneva. We talked it over for hours on end. My acting work was so sparse, I decided that there was no reason not to go for a full-out adventure. I wasn't exactly looking forward to life in Geneva, but it is a European hub and I thought it would be exciting that I could take day trips into Paris. I would fly back to the United States for art shows, whenever needed.

We began to plan the move in earnest, figuring out what paperwork was necessary to take our little terrier, Maggie, with us. One afternoon we were shopping for cold-weather clothes, trying on winter coats, when Ken's cell phone rang. He was saying things like "I understand" and "Thanks for the update," so I could tell that the Switzerland deal had fallen through. We wouldn't be moving there. Ken still needed to fly there and stay for two weeks to work with a firm, and returned home grateful that we didn't make the move. He found the city very industrial and corporate, with very little neighborhood charm. I count myself spared, though I'm sure we would have found a good lifestyle there with a bit of effort.

Because we had been planning the move for a month, we continued to think about where else we would like to live. Ken's job was becoming more flexible and he could often work remotely. I had such good memories about the times I spent in New York and the art, performance, and theater scene there that I brought up an East Coast move. It is an international city with cultural influences from around the world, but we wouldn't have to learn a new language. I also thought it would benefit my career to have a New York agent and perhaps more jobs would come my way on the East Coast. It had become patently clear to me that if I intended to continue to be an actress, I would have to advocate for myself in a bolder way than I ever had before.

Since Ken's job relocation had dissipated, we knew if we wanted to live somewhere else in the United States, we would have to make the choice to do it. Ken stayed in California and I went off to New York on the premise that if I got an agent and a subsequent acting job, we would get an apartment and move to New York. After a week of staying with a friend of a friend who lived way up on the east side of Manhattan, I stayed at my friend John Bolton's apartment in Hell's Kitchen for about a month as he was going out on a Broadway tour.

John, known as "Broadway's John Bolton," has worked continuously on the stage in plays and musicals, both in New York and out on tour. I met him in 1991 at the Bucks County Playhouse in Pennsylvania when I was doing a summer stock show, playing Ensign Nellie Forbush in *South Pacific*. John was coming in with the next show on the bill, *Into the Woods*. The cast knocked on my dressing-room door that evening to say hello, and John and I struck up a conversation. I had a feeling that we would become good friends, as, like me, he had a passion for antiques shopping and also loved L. Frank Baum's original Oz books. We connected on that day and have been friends ever since. Because the casting director knew we were friends, he joined one of the episodes I did of *All My Children*, playing a crew member in my character's scene. John went on to have a recurring role on the series as the DA of Pine Valley. He is like the mayor of Hell's Kitchen and I've never walked anywhere in New York with him where we didn't have at least three or four people stop to chat him up.

Within a month, through various recommendations and introductions by other acting friends, I was able to meet some managers and a few agents and was signed to one for theater and on-camera work and another for voiceover and commercials. Before he left town, John and I had breakfast, and a theater producer and writer, Ken Davenport, stopped by our table to greet John. John introduced me and told Ken that he should have me come in and audition for a new play that Ken had co-written and was producing called *Miss Abigail's Guide to Dating, Mating, and Marriage*.

It was my very first New York audition. I did a cold reading, as the script was brand-new and not yet in print. Most likely they described the character to me over the phone. Miss Abigail is a stylish relationship guru who doles out relationship advice in a funny "one fits all" way from vintage books. The audition was in a large, empty rehearsal room. Ken and his co-writer, Sarah Saltzberg, and a few other people sat behind a folding table at one end of the room and they had a script reader at the other end. I'm sure, because it's a play, they need to know that the people they cast can be heard and look good on stage. I felt confident and no previous nerves were present.

I called my husband that night and told him, "Okay. I've got two agents and am playing the lead role in a new play, off-Broadway, small house, but it's an Equity show. So what do you think?" He said, "It looks like we need to move to New York."

The show was staged in a basement club of an Italian restaurant, Sofia's on West 46th Street, near Times Square. The stage was about a foot off the floor and with a very small set, only a couple of chairs and a bookcase. There was a bar in the back of the audience area and also red leather booths along the walls.

It was a two-person show, me and my delightful assistant, played by the very funny Manuel Herrera. The play has certain sections of audience participation, where a chosen audience member joins us on stage to read passages from a book, and so every show was different, and yet not improvised. One evening I called a gentleman on stage for the book-reading portion, and after the show, he stayed to say hello. I wasn't sure why, but it turned out to be someone who was in my high school graduating class. I didn't recognize him at all while we were on stage and explained it as having to stay focused. I was embarrassed, but he didn't seem to mind. We performed eight times per week and were only heckled by drunk theater attendees once or twice.

The show opened in October 2010, the reviews were really good, and almost every show would sell out. I remained in it until May 29, 2011, and I was very happy to be a working actress again. I found an apartment and furnished it with the basics. That Christmas Eve my husband, Ken, and Dennis, my brother-in-law, arrived with Maggie in tow, after driving across the entire country. I couldn't wait to see my cute little Maggie dog hop out of the car onto a Manhattan sidewalk. I'm pretty sure she kissed me all over my face before Ken did. I'm not sure which one I had missed more.

In September 2011, John Bolton and I were offered to star in a production of *Same Time, Next Year* at the Surflight Theatre in Beach Haven, New Jersey. Because we were friends, we agreed to share the Craftsman-style cast house provided by the theater. It's a two-person show, so we'd go back to the house after rehearsing together all day and say "How was your day? Do anything interesting?" We continued to get along swimmingly despite all the hours spent together, enjoying the fact that we were able to have our dogs with us, Maggie for me and John's wonderful Rottweiler mix, Roz. One day we were pulled out of rehearsal, with the only explanation being that we had to go back to the house immediately. I was half certain that we were going to be told the show wasn't selling and we should pack up and drive back to New York City. It turned out to be a little more frightening. Maggie had pushed through the screen of the second-floor bedroom window I had left open, and had been prancing around on the sloped roof, going in and out and enjoying the crowd she drew that feared she would fall or jump. I went upstairs and was able to convince her to come back in as I closed the window for good. The show was great fun and performing together will always be a favorite memory of ours.

In October of that year, I went to audition for the rotating cast of *Love, Loss, and What I Wore*, an off-Broadway production written by Nora Ephron and Delia Ephron. It's a versatile, easily staged show with five female cast members, mostly in monologue, talking about events in their lives that had a strong effect on them and how their clothing fit into the experience. After my audition I was told that the co-writers were there, watching from the audience seating. I'm glad I hadn't known beforehand—I would have been nervous, as I was familiar with the films they both had written and directed. A new cast is brought in every four weeks, and I was part of the November cast. On the first day of rehearsals, the director said, "This show will change your life." I suspected she said that to every incoming cast, but to my surprise, the feeling of "sorority" among cast members, both past and present, does feel like something I had never experienced before. I made good friends on the show and we have stayed within each other's inner circle. I was asked to return the following January to replace an actress who had a prior commitment, and then went out with the cast for some national performances in Texas and Virginia, which widened the sorority circle for me.

Ken had cleaned up our Laguna Beach house and found renters to lease it. We kept the car he had driven across the country and used it for getaways on my day off and also to go see his family. Ken is really close to his siblings and every year a house is rented off the coast of Massachusetts on Plum Island, which only rhymes with my name. We all meet up there every summer for a week of vacation. In the summer of 2013, my agent called to see if I wanted to audition for a low-budget movie titled *Blue Ruin*. I read the script and was ready to turn it down, as I don't like horror movies or to do bloody gunplay scenes. I can't watch them, either. My manager, Jodi Schoenbrun Carter, called and said, "You know, I think you should do this. It would be good footage for your reel if nothing else."

It was no small feat to get off the island and take a series of trains back into New York, but I decided to commit to taking a role, if it was offered. They had asked me to read for the part of one of the police officers, and then, after that audition, they wanted to cast me as the gun-wielding cousin who ends up in a pool of blood on the floor behind a recliner chair.

I took a train down from Penn Station to Virginia, where they were filming my scenes in the director's uncle's home out in the country. We worked overnight, as my scenes took place late in the evening, and there were only so many hours to film before dawn intruded through the windows.

In my scene I was to leap to my La-Z-Boy recliner and pull the lever to raise the footrest, under which I had an automatic rifle hidden, which is . . . of course . . . where one keeps a weapon. Then I was to jump up and fire off a number of rounds. I knew they were only blanks in the modified barrel, but I was still very nervous about it. For several of the takes, the gun jammed and wouldn't fire at all, and in one take, the gun made my hand jump out of control and blasted a hole in the paper lantern being used to mute the lighting. I was relieved when the number of takes needed for the scene was over.

I didn't take up time to explain to the crew that I had briefly known Jon-Erik Hexum, a handsome young actor who was my age, when we did a scene together, I think for a commercial. Years later, in 1984, Jon-Erik was on a set when he held a prop gun up to his head and pulled the trigger. The force of the blank fractured his skull, causing his death. So I knew that even blanks could cause considerable damage.

I rode the train back up, exhausted by twenty hours of work and slept almost the entire way. I had no idea what the overall movie would look like or how it would be received, which is part of acting. You can only give it your all, and the rest is up to many, many other people who will have their hands on it before it makes it to the screen.

I had met Seth Rudetsky, an actor and versatile musician who also created a popular Sirius radio show about Broadway shows, and his husband, James Wesley, an actor, singer, and playwright, through doing Broadway Backwards. James had written a new semiautobiographical play, *Unbroken Circle*, and Seth called to ask if I would take the role of June, the alcoholic aunt. It was in development for a number of months and then eventually previewed at St. Luke's Theatre, near the famous Joe Allen restaurant. I appreciated that my character had the dry zinger lines in the play. The laughter from the audience was great to hear and the *New York Times* gave me a great mention in their review. The play previewed and then opened in June 2013. It was an invigorating time of my life. I was happy that we had made the choice to move to New York and felt that my career was being revived in an all new way. Then it tumbled down, in an unexpected way, for a full year.

One night my husband discovered that I had a sizable lump on the underside of my breast. Oddly, I had not noticed it at all, though it was about the size of a walnut, a rather shocking statement about my level of self-care.

My stomach dropped when I thought about the most-feared cause of the lump. I had a zoom out–zoom in feeling of adrenaline and "what do I do now?" I knew the options of fleeing or freezing in the face of this oncoming bear were not the right choices. I'd have to have it checked and then wait for results and, hopefully, not have to fight for my life.

I went to a gynecologist, who signed me up for an outpatient biopsy at a hospital. I knew they weren't going to put me under or cut my skin, but I was unprepared for the test, as it was like a spring-loaded needle that shot with incredible force through the lump. The shock of it piercing through so quickly was both physically and emotionally painful. It was over within a few seconds and the doctor and nurse left me to change back into my street clothes.

Once I was alone, tears spilled from my eyes. The nurse came back into the room and asked, "What's wrong?" I managed to make her laugh and myself, too, when I replied, "You just shot my breast with a gun!"

Two days later I had finished performing at the matinee of the show and went to a local grocery to get something to eat before the evening performance when my phone rang. With a casualness of voice, as if I was being informed that a prescription had expired, I was told that I had cancer. As it often happens for people receiving that kind of news, my mind went into a state of otherworldly, blurred reality. I stumbled out of the store and onto the sidewalk. I called Ken next, though I don't remember how I made it back to the theater and through the evening performance, but I did. The angry and crying scenes came very easily to me that night.

The next day I met up with my manager, Jodi. We went for a walk together and I told her I had to begin treatments for breast cancer. I knew I wouldn't be able to continue doing the stage show and needed her advice and help to end my contract without them knowing that I had breast cancer. I didn't want it to leak to the press and I felt that might happen unintentionally. Jodi was sympathetic to my feelings and wisely said nothing to add to my anticipation about it, only expressing that she would handle it. I felt bad about leaving the show early, and I never found out what she told James or Seth, but I was released and replaced.

I decided to tell only a select few people, whose sense of privacy I could trust and who would only listen and encourage and not give me more concerns. Often people will tell you stories of others who went through treatment, successful or not. I know that's how people feel that they can empathize, but I knew I couldn't hear about other women and I saved myself from reading statistics or survival rates. I was better off not knowing.

I called the oncologist nurse the next morning to ask about what to do next. Though she was rather brusque in tone, she told me, "This is the worst part of it all, is to be in the days between diagnosis and a treatment plan." She was right and that was helpful.

Once I visited the oncologist and received my treatment plan, it looked like I would need to focus my energy on getting through the treatments and surgery over the next year. First there would be chemo infusions, then radiation and surgery. I was told that it was up to me where I preferred to have the chemo treatments.

I called my friend Jenny Allen, from the *Love, Loss* cast, who had been through cancer treatments herself. She has a funny, blunt personality, and I had to laugh when she said, "Oh, Eve. Who *doesn't* have breast cancer? You'll get through this."

She gave me her advice about where to go for treatment and I checked out about three places on my own. One place featured recliner chairs in a circle with only a light curtain on a pipe between patients. Another hospital seemed gray and noisy, with harsh lighting. The one I chose, that Jenny had dubbed "the chemo spa" had small private suites, with a recliner chair and a door that could be closed. Ken would come with me and sit in a chair next to mine, getting work done on his laptop. He was working in New York, but his job took him to Texas every other week. It was rough, but his company's insurance was what was making my treatment possible. This was the most comfortable option, but it did have a backfire element to it when every week, in a full waiting room, a nurse would call my name out loud when my chemo suite was ready. "Eve Plumb! Eve Plumb! You're next." So much for staying under the radar.

About a week later, Ken was at work in his Texas office when he received a call from the *National Enquirer*, wanting to confirm that I was getting cancer treatments. He managed to respond in a composed manner that he didn't know what they were talking about. That was the closest we came to it leaking out.

As I watched my hair begin to shed within two weeks, I thought about the hundreds of times as a child that I dreaded having my long blond hair brushed by my mother and how I couldn't wait to cut it off once I reached my twenties. Now all I could do was watch it swirl around the shower drain, clump by clump. I knew that I either had to start wearing a hat constantly or make a different choice. My friends John Bolton and Sean McKnight met me at a place in midtown Manhattan called Bitz-n-Pieces, where they specialize in wigs and extensions. They sat through the try-on process and helped me to pick out a wig called "The Scene Stealer," which looked like a recent hairstyle I had pre-cancer. We decided that would be a better choice than the black curly-haired one, despite the hilarity factor. Then another dear friend of mine and I went back later to have my hair cut close to my head. I don't think I understood how quickly I would go bald, but by Halloween I was thinking that I could paint my head silver and go to the New York City Village Halloween Parade as an alien.

As soon as I acclimated to losing my head hair, I went to put on mascara one morning and realized that my eyelashes and eyebrows were all gone as well. I had been wondering why my sense of smell had become so acute and then concluded that my nose hairs must have fallen out, too.

As the colder months approached, I bought a knit hat with some blond hair sewn into the band to make it look like a hat on a full head of hair. This is what I would pull on to take Maggie out for a walk if Ken was in Texas for work. One afternoon I was crossing the street and a well-known television actress was walking toward me. I thought about how different my life had become within a matter of months. I went through cycles of it all seeming unreal, as if I were acting in a TV movie that wouldn't wrap up.

A few months later, there was a talk show that was celebrating Florence Henderson and all of the Brady kids were to reunite to surprise her. I was right in the middle of treatments and couldn't fly to LA. I didn't tell the producers why, but I offered to send in a videotape with my wishes, which I did, wearing my Scene Stealer wig. The other five cast members attended. After the show I called Florence to explain the reason I couldn't be there. Before I had a chance to say another word, Florence promptly turned to the other cast members and said, "Eve didn't come because she's going through chemo for breast cancer." It was another instance where I appreciated that we Brady kids have, for the most part, had a code of privacy about our personal lives when talking to fans or to the press. Despite Florence spilling the news, my Brady family never spread the word and I continued treatments without any press about it.

I thought I would use this treatment time as personal time and paint more, read more, learn a language, and other interests. Little did I know that the chemo would turn time into a hazy numbness, where the most I could do was watch a TV show or two in between naps. I would have little energy and even less appetite. Just as I was beginning to feel better, it would be time to go in for another chemo infusion and the whole process would begin again. It all came with an exhaustion that I had never experienced before. Most of my treatment time became one long vague and relentless year, except for one week in Park City, Utah.

The director of *Blue Ruin* had called me to say that the movie was selected for screenings at Sundance. He wanted the cast to be there and do the press lineup for the movie. I really didn't want to miss the chance to go to the film festival. I weighed less than I ever had in my adult life, so I had to shop for some clothes. I wore the excellent wig I had bought. I decided to don my glasses and had to pencil on some eyebrows and put dark eyeliner around my eyes, hoping no one would notice that I had no eyelashes or brows. My manager, Jodi, went with Ken and me, and it ended up being a perfectly timed distraction from the tedium of treatments. We had a great time. I returned home exhausted, but it was worth it.

Following the surgery and radiation treatments, I was pronounced "cured." My hair began to sprout from my scalp in little duckling feathers and my energy began to return slowly. In the middle of the treatments, Ken proposed that a strong motivation for getting through it all would be to take a vacation to Sweden for a couple of weeks, once I had come out the other side. We called it the "I didn't die" trip. It was like being set free and viewing it all with a fresh perspective.

For the first couple of years that followed, the mammogram would highlight the scar tissue from the surgery and they would require a second mammogram. At first, it gave me that stomach-dropping feeling, like the cancer was back, but then the doctors confirmed that it was only scar tissue as they compared the tests. As of now, I'm more than ten years "cured," which I will take as the best news.

Ken and I have traveled many, many more times during that decade, and we have no plans to stop.

Chapter Fifteen

"Grease is the word." It was the word my agent was calling me about, which began with a question: "Would you like to audition for *Grease: Live!*—a remake of the 1978 musical film, being shot at the Warner Brothers Studios and being broadcast live on Fox network seconds later?" I was told that I could audition in New York, though it was being categorized as an "LA hire." If I was cast, I would have to figure out and pay for my own transportation from New York, accommodations, meals, rental car, all of it.

After auditioning for the very charming director, Thomas Kail, the director of the hit musical *Hamilton,* I was cast as Mrs. Murdock, the auto shop teacher. I was thrilled to be a part of it all. I loved jumping into the role and was costumed by Broadway costume designer William Ivey Long, who created the amazing fast-change outfits for the show. Wearing coveralls and a fun Vivian Vance from *I Love Lucy*–style wig, I was fine with the fact that playing Mrs. Murdock didn't hold an ounce of potential for showing my dramatic chops, and there would be no solo number to sing, and, for the most part, the cast members danced very impressively *near* me and not *with* me. I still liked the whole idea of it. I was back to feeling healthy and with that came my eagerness to perform. I wanted to do shows and this was the fun stuff.

The principal actors had already been rehearsing for a few weeks by the time all of the supporting cast arrived. We rehearsed for a week in a dance studio room in Van Nuys, where they had taped the floors in the configuration of the set. After that, we had full production rehearsals with the entire cast, crew, and musicians. It was astonishing to hear all those fabulous Broadway voices singing songs we all recognize from *Grease*. Tommy Kail was incredibly respectful, never yelling, not even once, though he was under incredible pressure to have the whole thing come together with no second chance for the live broadcast. He always made us feel appreciated and valued with his inspiring end of day notes. For some reason I kept blowing my lines during rehearsal and was holding my panic at bay that I might do that in the live show. But, lucky for me, the fairy of good memory bonked me on the noggin with her wand and the lines came out flawlessly for the actual performance. All in all, it was a challenging and rewarding experience and a great callback to the days of early television, when shows like the actual first broadcast of the musical *Peter Pan* went live on the NBC network.

When Thanksgiving Day, 2016, rolled around, I had a vast appreciation for being fully recovered from cancer and also having my energy level return, as well as the possible acting opportunities that might be ahead. We celebrated the holiday with friends and were at our neighbor's apartment having a nightcap when my cell phone rang. It was one of the organizers of Broadway Cares calling. He wanted me to know that Florence Henderson had been admitted to the hospital with heart issues and it wasn't looking like she would make it. I'm not sure when she actually passed away, but it was in the news the following morning. I added Florence to my growing list of gratitude. What a privilege it was for me to have known her and worked with her on and off for forty-seven years of my life. She continued to perform until her final days and had performed on *Dancing with the Stars*, telling me it was the hardest job she'd ever had. When Maureen was on the show, Florence was in the audience to cheer her on. She always called us "family." She set the tone for how we continue to treat and respect each other as individuals.

Sadly, a month or so later, my sister June called from Los Angeles to tell me that she had been diagnosed with esophageal cancer. Though she had done occasional guest star roles on shows like *The District* and *Mad Men*, my sister spent most of her time as a teacher at Los Angeles County High School for the Arts near downtown LA, helping many teenagers appreciate the works of Shakespeare and other playwrights. Instead of continuing to audition for television or film, she had also changed professional lanes into audiobook narration as she got older. She and her husband, Richard, built a soundproof recording booth in their home and June had narrated a number of book projects before the cancer treatments and radiation made it impossible to continue. Her husband was her full-time caretaker during her treatments, so one week I flew to Los Angeles to be with her and give him a break. We rented funny movies, went to the famous Patrick's Roadhouse restaurant along the coast, and I found her a place for a massage.

Before I left to go back to New York, June told me,

"I've got this big book to narrate. The author said they wanted to wait for me to finish my treatments, instead of using someone else for the audiobook."

I liked knowing that she had something to look forward to doing as motivation to stay strong. She was very unwell, and as my plane crossed the country, I decided that I would go back more often to be with my sister and see her through her treatments. I never got to do that. A few days after I returned to New York, her husband called me to say that the radiation had weakened her aorta and caused massive bleeding. She was gone. She was seventy-three.

For weeks I would cry at my distinct memories about my childhood with this phenomenally beautiful, graceful, and smart older sister, and how, as a young child, I would visit her in her old 1920s canyon cottage and we would make decoupage bracelets and string beads for necklaces. She would grind her own coffee beans by hand and eat yogurt before the rest of the United States had probably ever heard of it. She loved the stage and the classic playwrights and taught me about following your own interests. If she would have been unable to use her talents and her voice in the same way, perhaps her quick passing was the best for her, but somehow I feel like I'll always be that little suntanned kid, standing at the beach house kitchen window, waiting in happy anticipation for my sister, June, to arrive.

Forty-three years after the final original episode of *The Brady Bunch* aired, when the very first generation of viewers were now hosting baby showers for their latest grandchild, HGTV came up with the idea to buy the Brady house, featured in the opening moments of every show, and renovate the interior to match the original set from the Paramount lot. I had always known where the actual house was in North Hollywood, chosen for the exterior shot, as did thousands of fans who drove down that street every year to be photographed in front of *The Brady Bunch* house.

The goal of the proposed HGTV show, *A Very Brady Renovation*, was to reunite all six remaining Brady cast members to roll up our sleeves and re-create, to the smallest detail, the way the set looked into the actual house interior. It was a challenge, considering that the house was a one-story home and a whole second floor would have to be added on for the bedrooms and the famous staircase to be real. It took the construction crew a long time to build it up, as it was a very rainy winter season in Los Angeles. As they worked on that, the producers and the cast put out a call to find replicas of all the original furnishings and décor. The horse statue in the living room was re-created by 3D printer, and fabrics and wallpaper were made to match the originals. It was quite a process. We were to work with other HGTV stars, like the Property Brothers and Jasmine Roth from *Hidden Potential* I had a couple of lively and interesting days shopping for house props with host Lara Spencer from *Flea Market Flip* and *Good Morning America*. We went antiquing in Connecticut for pieces for the house. She's a lot of fun and a naturally curious person, the best type of companion for diving into antique shopping.

One day I was appointed to the job of making the little art projects that the Brady kids had that were setting around here and there, like a handmade clay rope knickknack called a coil pot, which held small objects. Brother-sister designers Steve and Leanne Ford, from the HGTV show *Restored by the Fords,* were doing a demonstration of how to make the snake-shaped rope of clay. As we crafted the clay, Leanne asked Steve, "What are you going to call your little snake?" I devilishly quipped, "Oh, I think he has a name for his little snake." They both turned bright red while laughing. Surprisingly, HGTV edited out that moment.

The production team would have to fly me in from New York for my segments of the show, so I really did not spend much time with my castmates until we went out and did press when the show aired. We fell right back into being who we always are together: a family who shared their childhoods. As living proof of the power of *The Brady Bunch* being appreciated by multigenerations, the four episodes of the show, which ran in 2019, were a smash hit for HGTV, garnering 22 million viewers. We were all thrilled and looked forward to opportunities that might have sprung from its tremendous ratings. But, as worldwide fate would have it, the pandemic struck, and, along with every languishing business, Hollywood shut down.

During the pandemic, HGTV came up with a clever way to create a design show with social distancing. It was called *Design at Your Door,* and I was asked to film an episode from our apartment in New York. They sent GoPro cameras and audio equipment and trained Ken via Zoom on how to use them. Then a family was chosen to receive a one-room makeover long distance and by delivery of décor items and lots of instruction by me over live computer video consultation. It was a good distraction from a difficult time to be able to do some design work for an imaginative show.

Also during that time, we original Bradys were invited to be on an episode of RuPaul's *Dragging the Classics*. The COVID restrictions were firm and the entire episode was filmed with only green screens behind us, on which the set would be projected in postproduction in a very realistic manner. Mike, Barry, Chris, Susan, and I participated and had a good time. The *Drag Race* audience seemed to love this special.

Barry played Mike Brady, Chris and Mike each played themselves, and Susan played Margie, a birthday party attendee. I didn't want to play Jan, so I played the Pam Ferdin role in the original "Will the Real Jan Brady Please Stand Up?" episode that is so often referenced, and I thought that *Drag Race* star Kylie Sonique Love pulled off the Jan Brady attitude and the black wig in an unmatchable way.

While working on the HGTV show, I realized that I still had an unexplored dream to design products for my own gift store. I had always admired Martha Stewart's versatile and extensive company. The name for my store, PlumbGoods, came to me first. We met with some professionals who help to create brands. I was 100 percent into learning the hows and whys of branding a product line. One of the questions they asked me to answer was a fill in the blank: "PlumbGoods exists to . . . ?" Spontaneously, I answered, "Put a smile on your face."

We narrowed down the message to "PlumbGoods . . . Happiness Included," the idea that we wanted our customers to receive when they viewed and used our products. We came up with ideas and began to catalogue what we thought best represented our message.

We set up an online store, beginning with our custom-scented candles in glass jars. Then we decided to start creating our own designs to go on a wider variety of PlumbGoods. I looked at the fun that could be had with a daisy design, with a throwback to the mod-1970s color and six petals to represent the six Brady kids. Ken helped to design and upload the artwork to be printed out individually with the orders. The product line is varied: mugs, key chains, coasters, water bottles. It has grown to include tote bags and pet products.

Ken next came up with the idea to start a coffee company: Happiness Included Coffee. We both walk around with a thermos of coffee most days and feel a deep affection for the idea of coffee as our first date, and many of our travel experiences included sitting for a good cup of coffee and talking. But we are both very particular about it being really good coffee. For our own line, we sampled the product from many coffee bean providers before we landed on one we thought was perfect.

I've always loved the art deco imagery of terriers, like our dog, Maggie. The logo on our coffee packaging is a silhouette of a leaping terrier named Perky, and the tagline: *Happiness Included Coffee—When you need a little wag in your walk.* Each unique blend of whole bean or ground coffee is named for a terrier breed and a puppy-type activity like "sniffing the breeze" or "chasing squirrels."

We keep adding new designs because we keep becoming inspired. The original daisy pattern comes in the original as well as many different styles—Halloween, Christmas, Fourth of July. There is a multicolor Perky design for totes and phone cases, and a design of sailboats and nautical motifs. Ken and I really enjoy coming up with new ideas, and seeing them appear in real life on our products is very fufilling.

Along with the isolation of the pandemic years came the thought of using my voice as the actor. As I've aged, I've added a lot of character to my voice. I called my agents and said, "Send me for voice-overs! I'll audition for anything you have, but especially would like to be considered for animation. I'll play the old witch, the school principal, or the sad cow." It's so much fun to choose a voice to use.

Most often I get called to do voice-overs for a prescription ad, where the voice has to be engaging and authentic. It can't sound preachy or like an announcement in any way. Those are often a challenge because it's a great quantity of information they need said in thirty seconds.

The most delightful audition was for the creators of the animated series *Praise Petey*, a spoof on cult life. We were on Zoom and they asked me to read the character of Big Judy. I decided to let loose and have fun and gave it my animated all. Their delight in the audition was very confidence building and they hired me to do the voice for the episodes. They appreciated any off-the-cuff variety I brought to the lines vocally, so they could choose the reading they liked most. It was a very fun and original concept show to be a part of and I wish it had been given more of a chance to find an audience.

When the six original Bradys were invited to make an appearance at the 2022 Emmy Awards honoring classic TV theme songs, we all decided to go, except for Maureen. It was a very hot and humid September afternoon in Los Angeles. The representative of Barry, Susan, and Mike thought we should all make an appearance out of an arriving limo at the curbside of the red-carpet entrance. Chris Knight and I, being like the no-frills middle children we played for five years, thought otherwise. To avoid sitting in a limo in traffic, we walked over to the Microsoft Theater in downtown LA from the hotel across the street. Despite the heat and humidity being not at all conducive to doing long interviews, and at one point feeling like I could faint, Chris and I made our way through the press line, doing about fourteen interviews. When Barry, Susan, and Mike finally arrived, we went back to take red-carpet photos with them. The opener of the show was a dance performance done to the theme music; at the end of *The Brady Bunch*'s theme song, the announcer had us stand at our table to be acknowledged as the original cast members.

I looked around the room at all the many actors and actresses, directors and producers, who have been in shows or produced creative projects that provided television shows to over 300 million Americans and countless people worldwide and felt honored to be among them. *The Brady Bunch* may not have been a standout in the world of production, storylines, editing, or performance, but it holds its own in cultural history and it continues, for over five decades now, to do what television was created to do: to bring entertainment into people's homes.

My career has been a lifetime of sticking with it and saying yes to opportunity, which has served me well over the years. I'm glad I've stayed with it through the ups and downs, because it has offered me experiences I have enjoyed that not many get to have. The good thing about it is that it doesn't have to end until I do, and I'm looking forward to the next adventure in showbiz.

Acknowledgments

Marcia Wilkie—thank you for guiding me every step of the way for this book.

Stacey, Jann, and Kelley—thanks for helping me to remember and clarify.

John Talbot—thank you for the good advice.

John Scognamiglio—thank you for shepherding the project.

Jodi Schoenbrun Carter, my manager—thank you for always being on my side.

My husband, Ken—I love you so much, and for thirty years you have helped me and us navigate the world.

And my parents—I wish I could thank you in person for making me the person I am.